For Sara Kusser with best wishes & gratitude.

Amjad Hussain

2/18/10

Treading a Fine Line

A Collection of Op-ed Columns with Readers' Comments

By Dr. S. Amjad Hussain

The Long Riders' Guild Press

www.classictravelbooks.com
www.horsetravelbooks.com

ISBN: 1-59048-194-1

Cover: Oil painting by the late John Newman of Ann Arbor, Michigan showing a few of the author's favorite books:
1. The Qura'n
2. The Edwin Smith Surgical Papyrus
3. A collection of Urdu poetry by the 19th century Indian poet Asadullah Khan Ghalib.
4. Surgical Papers by Arthur Tracy Cabot (1899)

Publisher's note: Letters to the author have been reproduced here exactly as they were received.

Also by Amjad Hussain

A Brief History of the Frontier Town of Peshawar 1993, 1994, 1998, 2000 and 2004

Yuk Shehere Arzoo (Urdu) Winner of Abasin Literary Award 1995

Of Home and Country: Journey of a Native Son 1998

Aalam Mein Intikhab: Peshawar. (Urdu) 1999, 2003

Mati Ka Qarz (Urdu) 2000

The Taliban and Beyond. 2001

Citra(N) Wala Katora (Urdu) 2003

Dar-e-Maktab (Urdu) 2006

Collaborative works

First 150 Years: A History of Academy of Medicine of Toledo 2001
With Barbara Floyd and Vicki Croll

Riding the Fence Lines 2001
With Bernie Keating et al

APPNA Qissa: A History of the Association of Pakistani Physicians of North America 2004
With Barbara Floyd

From bouquets to brickbats to outright ugly

A spectrum of responses to one column

Why is U.S. foreign policy hostage to Israel?

May you continue to be a voice of conscience and justice
Nadeem Z

You raised a very good point as to why U.S. foreign policy is being held hostage by Israel. I'm not pro-Israel or pro-Palestinian, just an American citizen who is appalled at what Israel did in the Gaza strip recently. It was nothing short of genocide. I love my country but I don't understand our blind loyalty to Israel either.
Tom

One can only give credence to your arguments if one gives moral equivalence to the Palestinians. Civilized people protect their women and children. They do not use them as human shields and they do not glorify them as suicide bombers. Wild animals in the forest have more respect for their young and protect them better than the Palestinians……………..
Sheldon.

I just read your column and I just wanted to let you know that you are a supreme FAGGOT. Have fun being fucked in the ass by 72 demons in hell, you fucking loser…(and)…..you muslim cocksucker.
Rob

Dedicated to
John Robinson Block
an uncommon friend
and
publisher of Toledo *Blade* and Pittsburg *Post Gazette*

Introduction
Khalid Hasan

Dr Amjad Hussain is the only Pakistani-American whose regular column has appeared in a mainstream American newspaper for the last 15 years. A citizen of two worlds, whose sympathies are universal, he has sensitized hundreds of thousands of readers who wait for his fortnightly column in the *Blade*, to the history, culture and aspirations of what to most of them would have remained the other end of the earth, unknown and unknowable. Over the years, he has built many bridges, small and big, and in a world that is increasingly jittery and where trust in others is disappearing, Amjad Hussain's sane and soft voice of reason and understanding one hopes will be joined by voices like his.

Amjad Hussain writes with compassion and honesty. He is never afraid to express his opinion but he is never confrontational. Even when responding to harsh and unfair criticism, he retains the softness of his voice. His writes with the conviction that it is important for people to understand different, even alien points of view. Most prejudices, if analyzed, stem from ignorance. What people don't know, they often misunderstand. Amjad Hussain has done more than any columnist writing in the American press to bring about understanding between different cultures.

He writes clearly and simply. In 2004 in a column on the Iraq war, he wrote: "Unattended grievances always breed militancy and fanaticism and each slight or insult adds to the layers of resentment in those affected by our policies." Of a summer storm he writes, "A summer storm is nature's way of making us understand that there are powerful forces that cannot be controlled at the flick of a switch or the push of a button." In a column on the Arab-Israeli conflict and the silence of the Arabs settled in America, he writes: "And where are the self-appointed and self-anointed custodians of the Islamic faith who, while good at preaching to the choir and browbeating others to their restrictive religious viewpoints, are less than honest in their public discourse?" In a 2006 column on the rise of what has come to be called jihadist Islam, he wrote: "The Muslim majority should make it clear that they have nothing in common with the bloodthirsty jihadists and declare them beyond the pale of Islam."

When the teaching of evolution was banned by the Kansas School board, he wrote: "Poor Charles Darwin. He got lynched again, this time in Kansas." When the Danish cartoons were printed, sending shockwaves across the Muslim world, he wrote" Freedom of the press is a sacred privilege, but it comes with some responsibility. The press in Western countries does exercise restraint in general, but when it comes to Islam, these restraints go out of the window." Of those who pick out isolated verses from the Quran to justify extremist conduct, he writes: "Most of the revelations came in response to a particular need of the nascent Muslim community, first in Mecca and then in Madina. While certain passages are eternal, others are topical or dated. The latter were revealed to address a certain situation and their presence is only of historic significance and thus cannot be applied to current times." This is what the poet philosopher Muhammad Iqbal meant when the urged Muslims to practise *ijithad* so that they could live in harmony with contemporary times.

Khalid Hasan
Washington, D.C.

January 2009.

A journalist and writer par excellence, Mr. Khalid Hasan had served as press secretary to Zulfikar Ali Bhutto, the Prime Minister of Pakistan in the 1970's and later in the ministry of foreign affairs of that country. Of late he was the Washington correspondent for the Daily Times and Friday Times of Pakistan. He wrote this introduction a few weeks before his death on February 6, 2009.

Preface
John Robinson Block

So much could be written about my polymath friend of more than two decades, Amjad Hussain.

In a remarkable lifetime reflecting the zeitgeist of 70 years of world history, Dr. Hussain has been many things and seen many things.

He was born a colonial subject in British India, in Peshawar, now in Pakistan's North-West Frontier Province, an area currently the focus of much international concern.

As a child he lived through the partition of the British Indian Empire, witnessing first-hand how hatred and intolerance corrode the human soul.

Reaching Toledo in the early 1960s after finishing medical studies in his homeland, Dr. Hussain began a four-decade surgical career, treating thousands of patients and (in his inimitable style) copiously making friends.

But there is so much more to say about him:

He has been a broad-minded, liberally educated man – an internationalist, a bridge between two worlds. He has been a researcher and teacher in medicine; he has been a published writer (in at least two languages) for many years; he has been a poet and a painter; he has been an explorer and adventurer; he has been (in a sense) an unofficial diplomat and public relations executive on behalf of Pakistan, and he has been an immigrant.

He is beautifully American, a wonderful example how our country strengthens itself by opening its doors and offering opportunity.

Dr. Hussain has selected for this latest volume some memorable columns that first appeared in The (Toledo) *Blade*. Rereading them is similar to encountering old friends one has recently missed. I hope new readers of Dr. Hussain' columns might sense what inveterate readers have long admired, his remarkable curiosity, energy and irrepressibility.

I predict he will continue to write, study, learn, and explore as long as he lives. And he never misses an editorial deadline.

John Robinson Block
Pittsburgh
January 15, 2009

Foreword
Mohsin Ali OBE

Dr. Amjad Hussain's collection of evocative essays are like a rainbow bridge that connects the prose in us with the passion.

The eminent Toledo surgeon and scholar from the old Indian subcontinent is one of a growing band of writers like Salman Rushdie and Arundhati Roy who in recent decades have taken command of the elegant English language with short and simple Anglo-Saxon words.

To the readers of the venerable newspaper, *The Toledo Blade*, he just gives hard facts in proper historical perspective.

E. M. Forster, the author of the classic novel *A Passage to India* called for Two Cheers for Democracy: "one because it admits variety and two because it permits criticism. Two cheers are quite enough: there is no occasion to give three. Only Love the Beloved Republic deserves that." How true this is of Dr. Hussain's newspaper columns in this some 300-page symposium. *Treading a Fine Line of Opinion* covers the Politics, People and Places. It ranges from his birthplace of Peshawar near the famous Khyber Pass, through which Alexander the Great crossed from Afghanistan to India, to his present home of Toledo.

Dr. Hussain, Professor Emeritus of Thoracic and Cardiovascular Surgery at the College of Medicine of the University of Toledo, follows Schopenhauer's principle of Objectivity: "Unhinge the self until you feel no fear or hate."

Like a good physician he tries so hard to be fair and balanced that he seems to follow the wise Zen advice: There is no need to seek truth, only stop having views.

A Man for All Seasons, he is modest, moderate and always courteous.

He best explains his own feelings by saying that it is a privilege to be a columnist. As of this writing he has written close to 500 columns and essays for the *Blade* and a few other publications and he adds: "Privilege brings in its wake a responsibility to be honest and fair. One has to recognize and tread the fine line between issues and personalities, between faith and the faithful, and between genuine patriotism and misplaced nationalism that sometimes borders on jingoism." Dr. Hussain, an author of several books in Urdu and English, is also a calligrapher, photographer and explorer.

The guiding insight of the soft-spoken Dr. Hussain's work is synthesizing the perspectives of the Pakistani and American ways of life.

In "A Fine Line of Opinion Columns," he draws a compelling social and political history against the background of our current age of economic globalization and fast high tech' communications.

Mohsin Ali, O.B.E.
A former Reuters Diplomatic Editor in London. He now lives in
Pinehurst, N. C.

Author's Foreword

In the marketplace of ideas opinions are important. They generate the debate that is essential for a free democratic society. At times such debate is noisy and boisterous but a high decibel noisy debate is much better than a tranquil and mute silence.

My journey from an Urdu playwright and short story writer to a mainstream English language print columnist was arduous and difficult but it was very exciting. There were two hurdles that I had to cross. One was to adapt to English that was my fourth language and my knowledge of English was limited to school books, radio broadcasts and an occasional novel. And this was the formal, flowery and archaic language with abundant echoes of a long past Victorian age. How could I think and dream in Hindko (my mother tongue), Pashto and Urdu – thee three languages I grew up with – and translate my thoughts into easy to understand colloquial English? Languages, because of their own vocabulary, nuanced metaphors and cultural hues, do not mix easily.

The other, probably more difficult, hurdle was to switch from fiction to opinion columns. Some cynics would say that most columnists live in a world of fiction anyway. But in reality while writing fiction one lets the imagination run wild and weaves a yarn from multi-colored fragments that are believable if only by the force of narrative. The freedom from restraints in fiction writing is however liberating.

On the other hand writing an opinion column is both liberating and confining. Liberating because it gives one the privilege to voice one's opinion, no matter how outrageous or controversial. But that privilege also confines one to be responsible; to be honest, factual and respectful. This is the bedrock of credibility that most journalists and opinion writers strive for.

What I have enjoyed the most is the way my readers have responded to my opinions. Not all responses were in accord with my arguments. Except for a few notable exceptions almost all of them were polite and civil and educational. It has taught me to understand and in due course appreciate the vitality of differences of opinion.

Surely there were a handful whose sole purpose was to insult, to malign and to enter into a contest that is best suited to the exuberant activity of teenage boys out by the wood shed.

It is strange, but my journey of discovery through words started early in my life when I was growing up in the dusty small frontier town of Peshawar in northwest Pakistan. From crafting crude posters with famous quotations or poems in grade school to a hand-written biweekly poster newspaper in high school to editing literary magazines in undergraduate college and later in medical college, this journey also took me to radio and stage along the way. All those experiences and observations were an integral part of my thinking when I started writing 24 years ago for my English-speaking audience. I believe roots give us a special perspective and do matter in life.

To cull hundreds of opinion columns into a group of 51 was a difficult task that I was not prepared for. I am grateful to Elizabeth Irwin, a freelance editor and writer, who did a marvelous job of selecting pieces included in this book and editing them. She was much more objective than I would have been. There are a few columns in this collection without readers' feedback. Ms. Irwin decided to include them as human-interest pieces and I concurred with her.

I am most grateful and indebted to my friend John Robinson Block, Publisher of Toledo *Blade* and Pittsburgh *Post Gazette* for taking a chance in offering me a regular spot on the op-ed pages of the *Blade*. While it was a leap of faith for him it was a frightening proposition for me. I am sure he had to contend with muted and silent protests by some of his people at the *Blade* who, pardon the bluntness, believe as an article of faith that only professional journalists ought to be given space in the paper. Thank you John for giving me this unprecedented opportunity.

I will be remiss if I do not acknowledge a number of op-ed editors at the Blade who used their editing skills to make my columns presentable to the public. Thank you Tom Walton, (the late) Tom Wellman, Anne Aboud, David Shutt, Ken Downes and Rose Russell.

I must also in closing thank another person who I hold in great esteem. Mr. Mohsin Ali OBE, retired diplomatic editor of Reuters, has been a friend and a mentor. I can't thank him enough for his counsel and advise over the years.

S. Amjad Hussain

Toledo, Ohio
February 2009

Contents

POLITICS

PEOPLE

PLURALISM

PLACES

PASSAGES

POLITICS

Treading a fine line of opinion
February 16, 2003

Every two weeks I stand on my little soapbox and talk about issues and events that I consider important.

This is my 200th appearance on this page. I beg your indulgence as I look back at the distance this column has traveled these past eight years. In a way, the changing nature of subjects in this column reflect the changes I, too, have undergone as a person and a writer.

I am often asked the inevitable question as to how I landed on the op-ed pages of *The Blade*. Beginning in 1976, I was a frequent contributor to *The Blade's Toledo Magazine*, and occasionally to the *Behind the News* section. When the magazine's format changed in the early 1990s I had written in excess of 40 pieces, including 14 cover stories. But I had lost my favorite perch.

Soon thereafter, in 1994, John Robinson Block, the publisher of *The Blade*, offered me an alternate spot on this page. The transition from a slow and laid back pace of a newspaper magazine to under-the-microscope scrutiny of an opinion column was not easy, but thanks to the support of the late Tom Wellman, then editor of this page, and Tom Walton, editor of *The Blade*, it was made painless. To them I remain grateful for their guidance and for smoothing out the rough edges of some of my pieces.

I took the plunge on December 11, 1994, with a piece on Bosnia. Since then this column has addressed as varied subjects as geopolitical issues, religion, science, and occasionally the mundane and ordinary. I have received my due share of criticism and condemnation as well as some praise from my readers. Over the years, I have earned the wrath of just about every interest group.

I have been labeled anti-Hindu for condemning the wanton killings of Muslims by Hindu fascists in Gujarat, India; anti-India for pleading the cause of Kashmiris; anti-Pakistan for condemning the rise of militant Islamic fundamentalism and brutal killings of Christians in Pakistan; anti-Semitic for supporting Palestinians rights; and anti-American for pointing out the fallacy of our flawed and failed foreign policy in the Third World.

The most interesting "anti" label, however, came from some ultra-orthodox Muslims who thought I had betrayed my religion when in the wake of the 9/11 attacks I pleaded for *ijtehad*, or interpretation of the Muslim sacred texts according to present times. They called me a disgrace to my religion. It is hard to rationalize with people who insist on living in the fossilized world of 7th century Arabia.

Then there are some who with blatant disregard for history try to re-invent it. Many contemporary issues of the world have deep roots in historic events. Unless we are willing to look at the continuum, we are liable to be carried away by a single snapshot. A snippet reveals only one part of the whole. One can apply this to any of the outstanding and intractable problems facing the world today, including Palestine and Kashmir.

To appear on this page is a privilege, and privilege brings in its wake a responsibility to be honest and fair. One has to recognize and tread the fine line between issues and personalities, between faith and the faithful, and between genuine patriotism and misplaced nationalism that sometimes borders on jingoism. I try my best to act responsibly while enjoying the privilege. On occasions I have faltered.

I am grateful to many of my readers who take the time to write. Their comments, critical as well as complimentary, help me set the tone of this column. And as always, I am indebted to my editors for their support and understanding.

Via e-mail, February 16, 2003:

Dr. Hussain,

Congratulations on your 200th article published in the Blade's *opinion page.*

I'd like to share, with you, some of my feelings about today's Blade *articles.*

The front page story "Millions worldwide on march for peace" gave me some comfort in seeing so many individuals question the current direction towards war with Iraq. I have conflicting feelings about our country's position and I saw the photos accompanying this article as others having similar concerns. To me the strength of the photos was that these are real people, just regular citizens (the photos show no "uniforms" or obvious "groups").

The third time through reading your article in today's Blade, *I took the time to get out my dictionary and look up "jingoism." Hopefully some of our leaders will also take the time to consider the meaning of this word.*

I liked article #200, I like your writing style and I hope the Blade *continues to support your efforts.*

Sincerely,

Steve

Via e-mail, February 16, 2003:

Yours is not one of the columns I read in order to seek agreement nor disagreement. Your column is one I read in order to become more educated. I don't always agree with you. I don't always understand the perspective you present. But I am often challenged. You have a knack for making me rethink my oppositions, and realize some of my shortcomings.

Don't get down on yourself. There are too many idiots out here ready to condemn you. There are, hopefully, more idiots out here who appreciate the different perspective you bring to some old beliefs. Many times I don't agree with a different opinion expressed in one column or another, and come away from it agitated and angered. I come away from your columns without an antagonism toward you, but rather a respect for your opinion that makes me reflect on the correctness of my opinion. I think that's what this is all about.

Carry on! And thanks.

James

With a free press comes responsibility
February 13, 2006

The publication of a number of cartoons caricaturing Prophet Mohammed by a Danish newspaper has inflamed the Muslim world. To add fuel to an already raging fire, newspapers in many European countries, including France, Spain, and Norway, have reprinted the offensive cartoons. And all this in the name of so-called freedom of speech!

There is absolutely no justification for the violence carried out in the name of Islam. Neither the Qur'an, the sacred book, nor the traditions of Prophet Mohammed, allow that. Instead the religion, selective and out-of-context quotes aside, advocates compassion, mercy, and forgiveness when someone trespasses against a Muslim. The Prophet himself forgave those who had heaped verbal and physical abuse on him during his lifetime. He would be aghast at the magnitude of violence being done in his name.

To a great majority of Muslims the cartoons are offensive. These are the people who do not take to the streets to protest and to destroy. But they are offended just as deeply as the screaming masses on the streets of Jakarta, Cairo, Dhaka, or Baghdad. In a simplistic deduction bordering on stupidity, the media lump all Muslims together and, using the red-hot iron of freedom of speech, brand them as backward and intolerant.

A case in point is the February 4 cartoon published in *The Blade*. It showed a Muslim complaining to God that the cartoons are offensive. God answers that He is offended by radical Muslims condoning suicide bombings in His name. Perhaps in the mind of Kirk Walters there is an equivalence between the two statements. For the majority of Muslims, including this columnist, there is none. It would be like blaming all Christians for the killings of innocent men, women, and children in Northern Ireland, blaming all Jews for random acts of violence against the Palestinians by a handful of Jewish settlers, or blaming the Hindu majority for the atrocities committed against the minority Muslims in Gujarat, India.

Muslims have the same reverence and love for Mohammed as Christians hold for Jesus, even though Mohammed is not divine. Every child growing up in a Muslim family learns to love, respect, and to follow Mohammed's teachings. This relationship remains intact even for those Muslims who do not follow the religion strictly. So when Mohammed is insulted it affects all Muslims to their very inner core.

Now let us consider the hypocrisy in selective application of freedom of speech. A few years ago the same Danish newspaper now in the center of the controversy had turned down a number of offensive cartoons about Jesus. The reason? It would be insulting to Christians.

Like the Danish newspaper, the press here in America does exercise restraint over what it publishes. They do not publish anything that could be offensive, even remotely, to African-Americans. You will be hard-pressed to find a frank criticism of Jews or the state of Israel. The former will earn a well-meaning journalist the title of bigotry and insensitivity and the latter the all-encompassing label of anti-Semite. How many times have editors and broadcasters yanked something out because it was just "too sensitive?" Call it self-censorship due to intimidation and political pressure, but the result is the same. In democratic France it is a crime to question the Holocaust. When democratic countries start making laws to silence dissenting voices, no matter how distasteful or offensive, they forfeit their right to sit in judgment of others.

Freedom of the press is a sacred privilege, but it comes with some responsibility. The press in western countries does exercise restraint in general, but when it comes to Islam those restraints go out of the window. Some people just cannot get out of the dark ages of their own making.

Via mail, February 13, 2006:
Dear Mr. Hussain,
Which is worse, publishing cartoons that are offensive to Muslims or slamming airplanes into buildings and killing thousands of people? Who is scarier, cartoonists making fun of the Prophet or suicide bombers killing Muslims and others and doing it in the name of their God? The point of Kirk Walters' Feb. 4 cartoon was that while Muslims may justifiably find the cartoons offensive, they are not morally equivalent to the murdering of innocents.

If, as you wrote, the media are unfairly viewing all Muslims "as backward and intolerant," who has contributed to that view? Could it be Osama bin Laden and the suicide bombers in the U.S., England, Spain, Israel, Saudi Arabia, Egypt, Iraq, Pakistan, Indonesia, Malaysia, etc? Like it or not, these political/religious fanatics are becoming the defining public face of Islam.

Perhaps Muslim rage and demonstrations should be directed against those people rather than against newspapers and the countries that publish offensive cartoons.

Bob
Sylvania, Ohio

Via e-mail, February 14, 2006:
Dear Dr. Hussain,

I read your article in today's Blade, *and I found it to be an interesting read. However, when you stated that the American press exercises restraint over what could be considered offensive, you may have forgotten what was printed a few years ago as news from the art world.*

The New York Times *refused to reprint the "Mohammed" cartoons, yet the Blessed Virgin Mary made from elephant dung was fair game, as was Andres Serrano's "Piss Christ" and Athen Grey's "Stripping Jesus" in other national newspapers. This was offensive to Catholics, yet I do not recall even a single Catholic burning a car, a building or a flag. Even when a Catholic priest while praying was recently murdered by a gunshot to his back at the hand of a 16 year old Muslim youth, I did not hear of a single Catholic setting fire, protesting or calling for a fatwa or the beheading of said youth. Most Catholics were mourning his passing and were comforted by our strong belief that this good priest became a martyr because of his faith.*

The differences between Catholics and Muslims are many . . . however, it is an undeniable fact and indisputable statistic that when a Catholic becomes a martyr, he or she, on an individual basis, dies for his or her faith. When a Muslim becomes a martyr for his or her faith, he or she takes out 3,000 (WTC) bystanders as well.

In the same way the Neo-Nazi visit to Toledo was made worse by people who were looking for an excuse to cause trouble, I believe we all have a choice in life as to how we respond to matters that offend us. If people would just ignore the media in general, then we wouldn't have to worry about the power of the press . . . they wouldn't have any power, much less the power to offend people.

I give you a great deal of credit for publicly distancing yourself from the radical factions causing trouble in the world. When the priest sex abuse scandal came to light, the victims were staunchly defended by everyday Catholics who were ashamed of these events and who called for the ouster of the bishops who aided and abetted the priests in question. Perhaps if more persons in your position would publicly denounce the violence, the Western world would not cast such a wary eye on persons from Muslim dominated countries.

I hope you do not take offense at this discussion of your editorial . . .I wish you well. By the way, we are in great need of vascular surgeons especially with Dr. Hageman cutting back on his time in the OR... know anyone?

Take care in this crazy world!

Charmaine

P. S. I'm not trying to be a smart-aleck, but seriously, could you answer two questions for me? Why is the number "72" as in "72 Virgins" significant? In Catholicism the number "3" is important, as is "9" and "40", but what about 72? And when a woman dies as a martyr, what does she get when she gets to heaven? That question has come up time and time again in discussions with people, and I don't know who else to ask to get a truthful answer. Thanks.

Hello, Charmaine:

Please rest assured I do not take offense. On the contrary, I welcome such debate. I agree with the thrust of your letter. When you emphasize how brutal some Muslims are, you are trying to lump them along with people who do not condone/approve/support such actions. Unless there is public recognition of moderate elements in Islam, the militants would continue to think they represent the majority.

I disagree with your comments about the child molestation scandal. The Church has not been forthcoming and has blocked the investigation at every step. I do not think the majority of Catholics have publicly opposed the Church for its stand.

Incidentally there is no religious basis for the reward of 72 virgins. It is not in the Qur'an and the only reference is found in a secondary

literature of Hadith (sayings of Prophet Muhammad). That, too, is not
accepted as authentic by most Muslims.

Please say hello to John. I miss seeing you guys.

Regards,

SAH

Via e-mail, February 15, 2006:

Dear Dr. Hussain,

*I certainly understand that you, and millions of other Muslims, have
been offended by the publication of cartoons depicting a violent
Mohammed. I also understand that responsibility comes with free
speech. However, nobody in the Muslim world seems to care very much
about the responsibility individuals must take not to destroy other's
property or murder others just because they are offended by something.
If all of us took that course of action each time we were offended this
would be one hell of a place to live. Yes, your column says the violence
is unjustified, but you don't condemn the violence nearly as much as
you do the cartoon. Why not? One has to ask the question as to why
supposed civilized men take to violence against people who had
nothing to do with the cartoon's publication. You talk about how
Muslims are all lumped together when being judged, but you say
nothing about the vast majority of Western news outlets who have
chosen no to republish the cartoons out of deference to Islamic
sensitivities. And, if Islam is so tolerant, why did Middle Eastern
Interior Ministers meet in Tunis with one prayer leader urging
beheading as a punishment to the journalist who published the cartoons. Beheading! Now, to me, that is the ultimate disrespect toward
another individual. And the action is real, not just pen and ink on
paper or one person's opinion. . .*

*. . . Sinead O'Connor ripped up a picture of the Pope on Saturday
Night Live a few years back. It outraged many Catholics, but did you
seem them destroy buildings or kill people over it. Do you see
Christians beheading people? Do you see Jews walking around with
suicide bombs? Do you see Western people gathering by the thousands
shouting death to Iran? No. The only group of people doing this are
Muslims. I'm sorry if Muslims were offended by the cartoon, but to me,
Muslims as a group have many more serious problems starting with
their own behavior and disrespect for half of the world. It's not the*

disrespect that bothers me, it's the fact they are trying to kill me that bothers me. My wife doesn't think I should send this email for fear that you will have my car blown up. Trust me, that is a much more real problem to Muslims than a thousand offensive cartoons. It is very discouraging to me that you don't seem to realize it.

    Rick
    Toledo, OH

    Via e-mail, March 1, 2006:
    Dear Mr. Hussain,
    Since I've written a letter to the editor of The Blade *about your recent column, I thought it only fair to send you a copy first. Here it is:*
    "In a recent column, S. Amjad Hussain wrote that one should not 'confus[e] freedom of speech with a license to demean a faith and thus insult Muslims everywhere in the world.' Unfortunately, it is Mr. Hussain who is confused about freedom of speech. What is free speech if not a license to say things with which others may disagree or may not like?"
    Now for some other comments, just for you. I confess to being curious – have you actually seen the cartoons that are at issue here? (If you haven't, I'd be glad to send them to you.) And if so, can you explain how they insult Muslims everywhere in the world? What is the nature of this supposed insult?
    The cartoons to me seem to be fair, non-racist commentary about various things, including:
    – the way some Muslims treat women and attempt to provide a religious justification for that treatment;
    – the way some Muslims interpret the Koranic concept of jihad;
    – the way some Muslims claim a religious basis for their censorious impulses.
    Are you claiming that these topics must be off-limits to writers and cartoonists? Are you arguing that these topics are examples of "profanity"?
    You write for a newspaper – you practice freedom of speech. I find it disappointing that you seem to be arguing for a kind of self-censorship. I wish you had come out foursquare in favor of the right to criticize people, religions, beliefs and practices. I hope you will reconsider your position.

Very truly yours,
James

Dear James:

At least one of us is definitely confused. Yes, I have seen the cartoons and they are repugnant to me the same way the movie *The Last Temptation of Christ* and the painting of Mary done in elephant dung were repugnant. I will not put curbs on individual rights to free speech but I will ask that the people of conscience would condemn such blatant attacks on another faith.

The points you make towards the end of your e-mail, treatment of women, jihad etc., are rather silly. Those are minority views and to tar every Muslim with a broad brush will be like condemning all Christians for the ranting of a handful of Christian fundamentalist preachers on the extreme right.

Regarding making certain topics off-limits I have addressed the question in my column yesterday. Perhaps you will consider writing letters to the media urging them to demand repealing laws against free speech in Europe.

I am grateful that you took the time to write.

Regards,

Amjad Hussain

Iraqis deserve unqualified apology
May 10, 2004

The ever-expanding scandal of torture and humiliation of Iraqi prisoners has been making headlines around the world. Those horrific and graphic pictures took everyone by surprise. The most bizarre response, however, was that of the army brass and their civilian bosses in Washington. They had known about the systematic torture and abuse of prisoners under their control but had looked the other way. Their mock surprise, disgust and indignation are sickening.

The pattern of abuse started soon after the invasion of Afghanistan three years ago. At that time, Afghan and Al Qaeda prisoners were tortured during interrogation at the Bagram Air Base in Kabul and later on the tiny atoll of Diego Garcia in the Indian Ocean. Upon arrival at Guantanamo Bay in Cuba, they were placed in outdoor cages. It was only after worldwide protests that the prisoners were removed from cages to sheltered accommodation. At the time Donald Rumsfeld had said that clean fresh air is good for them. Three years later, the bulk of those prisoners remain in that Caribbean purgatory without being charged of any crime.

Amnesty International and Human Rights Watch brought the torture and abuse of Iraqis to the attention of Bush Administration more than a year ago. The U.S. Army launched an investigation and confirmed those allegations. The report has been gathering dust for the past few months and despite the explosive nature of the conclusions no one in authority, including Donald Rumsfeld, had read it. Now everyone, including the President, has gone in overdrive to contain the fall-out. They are more concerned about the tarnished image of this country than the actual abuse heaped on prisoners. If they were concerned about the prisoners, they could have stopped the practice long before CBS broke the story.

Who are these prisoners?

Most of them are ordinary Iraqis. Whenever U.S. soldiers come under fire, the army sweeps the area and arrests everyone around. Most of them have nothing to do with acts of sabotage. During interrogation, they are forced to come up with names of possible culprits. To save their hides, they name names and that leads to more arrests and interrogations. Thus the cycle continues. According to experts, one cannot glean meaningful information by torture.

Most of our soldiers still think that the invasion of Iraq was retaliation for 9/11. This myth has been willfully perpetuated by the Bush administration. There has also been what the *Washington Post* called "a pattern of arrogant disregard for international conventions that dictate the treatment of prisoners." This include not only humane treatment but due consideration for their beliefs and traditions. Our soldiers have shown total disregard for the cultural traditions of Iraqis.

Nudity, male and female, is an affront to Arabs. Forcing men to take their clothes off in front of other men and in the presence of female soldiers and then forcing them to indulge in real or simulated sex is worse than putting a bullet through their heads. What is really appalling is the way our soldiers gleefully posed with the naked trophies at their feet. The image of a female soldier, a cigarette dangling from her lips, posing triumphantly by her 'kill' and in another picture holding a leashed naked Iraqi is not the way to bring American values of decency and compassion to the Iraqis. The damage done by our soldiers would last many generations.

President Bush's hurriedly arranged interviews with two Arab television networks did not change any minds in the Middle East and for that matter anywhere else in the world. Instead of tendering an unqualified apology he promised to bring the culprits to full justice. He was right in saying that these acts do not represent American values. But his words do not carry any credibility with a common man on the Arab street.

Throughout recorded history mankind has struggled to bring some dignity and decency to the ugly nature of war by laying down codes of conduct. Most armed forces, ours included, have written codes of conduct. Then there are the Geneva Conventions addressing the same issue. And still such things continue to happen.

For us as a country the only honorable way is to own up to our mistake and tender an unqualified apology to the Iraqis. And Donald Rumsfeld should be asked to resign for dereliction of his duty to the president and to the American people.

Via e-mail, May 10, 2004:

Dear Dr. Hussain,

I have read many of your articles in the Blade *& feel that you are an intelligent individual & I hope a great surgeon especially if I ever need your services. Your profession, however, does not make you a "expert" in ANYTHING else so I am not sure how you can have all the answers even though your ethnic background gives you some insight to the Iraqi thinking!*

I especially take exception to the paragraph that starts out "Most of them are ordinary Iraqis." How do you know the contents of this paragraph for sure, as you appear to be comfortable living here in Toledo?

You want "an apology" as your headline says! I want one from all the Arab leaders in the middle east from Israel, Egypt, Saudi Arabia to Iran including Iraq who have been actively encouraging their people to "kill the infidels" for years with inducements of $$$, or Virgins upon death, and the latest idea from al-Sadr that any female prisoners can be "sex slaves" for their captors. How about asking for "an apology" for some of these statements and actions that follow!

It is well known and documented that many of the worst torture over the centuries has been by "your people" and usually upon your own or factions within. That, to me, is even more troubling.

Looking forward to your next article on "dissecting a frog."

Sincerely,

Don

Dear Don:

I do not think I could dissect a frog anymore but I would like to respond to your letter.

1. The arrests in Iraq have not been selective but general. This has been reported in the press for the past 6 months. If we consider each and every one to be a criminal then we ought to be able to arrest almost all Iraqis for the resistance to occupation is wide spread.

2. I am an American (have been for over 30 years) and I do not profess loyalty to anyone but the country I adopted. I hope you do make a difference between criticizing the policies of the government and criticizing the country. If you start using a litmus test for patriotism then more than half of our countrymen would fail because more than

half of Americans do not agree with the foreign policy of our government.

3. I agree that we demand an apology from all the countries you mentioned in your letter. If they encourage terrorism against this country we should deal with it. No disagreement there.

4. You are right in a way that my profession does not make me an expert on international affairs. But I have been a student of international politics and international relations. What I am trying to do is to bring a perspective to the discussion. This perspective – religious, ethnic, cultural – is something that is important while discussing international problems. I assure you that had our soldiers known about the cultural sensitivities of the people they interrogated they would have been more understanding and much less sadistic.

What we see in those pictures is not the expression of American values. I know that. I have been part of this society since 1963 and have always found Americans to be fair, honest and generous.

I am grateful that you took the time to write.

Sincerely,

Amjad Hussain

Via e-mail, May 12, 2004:
I KNEW YOU WOULD HAVE A LOT TO SAY ABOUT THE DISGUSTING, ABUSIVE ACTS THAT SOME OF OUR SOLDIERS HAVE COMMITTED. YOU ARE RIGHT TO COMPLAIN AS ALL OF US ARE AND THE IRAQIS DESERVE AN APOLOGY. THEY HAVE BEEN RECEIVING ONE FOR THE LAST WEEK FROM EVERYONE FROM PRESIDENT BUSH ON DOWN! NO MATTER WHAT THEY SAY, YOU CALL IT " SICKENING". HOWEVER I DID NOT SEE YOU GIVE ANY MENTION TO THE OPEN HEARINGS OR THE OPEN TRIALS THAT WILL BEGIN. SOMETHING NO OTHER COUNTRY WOULD DO!! THIS IS IN VERY STARK CONTRAST TO THE TREATMENT YOUR PEOPLE HAVE GIVEN ANY IRAQI OR AMERICANS YOU CAPTURE. YOU, THE MUSLIM LEADERS AND YOUR CLERICS ONLY CALL FOR MORE TORTURE AND KILLINGS OF THE VERY PEOPLE THAT ARE TRYING TO HELP THEM HAVE FREEDOM AND A BETTER LIFE.
YOU SAY THERE WAS A "TOTAL DISREGARD FOR THE PRISONERS CULTURAL BELIEFS AND TRADITIONS" BY NUDITY.

I WOULD GLADLY GIVE THAT UP IN PLACE OF STREET DRAGGING OR BRIDGE HANGING AND NOW BEHEADING. AS I HAVE ASKED YOU BEFORE – WHERE IS YOUR OBJECTION TO ALL OF YOUR TORTURE!!!
   GEORGE

Via e-mail, May 21, 2004:
Dear Dr. Hussain,
   I was honored to play the violin with my string quartet for your family wedding last month. I couldn't seem to find the right opportunity to speak with you. I've had your most recent column on my desk for quite some time. I simply want to let you know how much I appreciate your intelligent interpretation of events overseas for the Blade. *I was deeply opposed to the war to the point of standing on street corners with signs. Your perspective offers so much more than what the average American could offer. I thank you.*
   Sincerely,
   Cecilia

Airline profiling aimed at those from Mid-East
November 23, 1997

It was eighteen months ago when TWA flight 800 plunged in the Atlantic Ocean off the coast of New York's Long Island. After a thorough and exhaustive search the FBI has concluded that it was not an act of terrorism. This leaves mechanical failure as the cause of that tragedy.

In the wake of the TWA tragedy, the FAA alerted airlines to be more vigilant in screening their passengers for possible terrorists. Since terrorists do not walk around with an ID badge pinned to their chests identifying them as such, the government has generated a computer profile to identify them. Terrorists are not the bumbling idiots portrayed by Hollywood in a string of movies that sprouted after the rash of hijacking in the seventies. Just look at the Irish Republican Army in Northern Ireland or their Protestant counterparts or for that matter the masterminds of the Oklahoma City tragedy. Who would have thought that such clean-cut men as Timothy McVeigh and Terry Nichols could be terrorists?

Under the new guidelines the airlines are supposed to check the names of passengers, their flying habits and any sudden change in their travel plans. They are also to note if the ticket was paid for with cash or credit card. This would be wonderful except for a small problem. This profiling system singles out people of Middle Eastern background. A most recent example and one close to home is that of Hussein Shousher, a long time Toledo Arab-American businessman who while traveling back from Lebanon, was interrogated in Frankfurt and was subjected to humiliating body and baggage search in full view of other passengers.

I admire the State of Israel for meting out equal treatment to those entering or leaving the country. Before departure every foreigner, irrespective of the country of origin, must undergo a polite but lengthy interview – sometimes as long as 30 minutes. For security conscious Israelis every passenger is a potential terrorist. On a visit to that country last April, I did not mind being treated equally with others from diverse backgrounds. I was, however, amused at the indignation of so many European and American passengers at being subjected to such scrutiny. As Professor David Harris of the College of Law, University of Toledo noted in one of his recent letters to the *Blade*, in the Israeli system the burden is shared by everyone instead a few people who happen to have one kind of last name or destination. And the system is much more reliable than a computer profile.

In the proverbial American melting pot, faces and traditions do melt in time but names do not, unless one is willing to break with the past and change one's name. One would hope that after a generation or two the names would also cease to carry an ethnic negative connotation and would become part of the mosaic we call America. For Arabs it has not happened. How long will it take, one wonders, to establish one's bona fides in the mold of other ethnic or religious groups like Italians, Irish, Polish or Jewish Americans?

It always takes me much longer to clear U.S. immigration on returning home than others. I am asked questions that the agents never ask other Americans. One time it took inordinately long time to clear immigration at Kennedy airport. After the agent checked and rechecked his computer, he excused himself and consulted his superior. Finally when they were satisfied he handed me the passport and nodded me to proceed.

My wife, a frequent witness to such happenings, asked the agent if my name was the problem. "Yes, ma'am," the agent said.

"I swear," my wife assured the dour agent, " I will never marry him again."

The agent could have said that she should have not married a foreigner to begin with.

Spare us the condolences of self-righteous bigots
November 22, 1998

Recently a priest wrote to the *Blade* expressing his sorrow on the shooting death of Dr. Barnett Slepian, the Buffalo gynecologist. The priest's condolence was closely followed by the all too familiar party line. Even when they distance themselves from wanton bombings and killings on abortion issues, they punctuate their sorrow with a qualifier but or yet. We feel sorry for the killing, they say, but don't forget the man was guilty of bigger crimes. Their sorrow is as phony as a three-dollar bill.

Granted, the religious right has not openly advocated violence against abortion doctors or against those who dare to have a different opinion or a different life style. But it does not absolve them when their anti-abortion and anti-gay rhetoric ignite passions in those who, in total disregard to the laws of the country, want to carry out the "Will of God" as preached by some of their clergy. The message coming out of some of the pulpits has the same lethal potential as that coming out of the barrel of a loaded gun. Such rhetoric and violence, in the so-called age of enlightenment, must make the framers of our constitution turn in their graves.

When 21-year-old Mathew Shepard was tortured and strung on a deer fence in Wyoming because he had different sexual orientation, the outrage from religious groups was muted and accented with their usual buts and yets. To add insult to injury some of the self-righteous bigots appeared at the funeral of the young man with signs condemning him to hellfire. The arrogance of piety has no limits.

To the frustration of Pro Life activists, the abortion issue has not been center stage of late. The past two general elections were a far cry from the heady days of 1992 when the Christian Right dominated the political agenda, dictated Republican platform and doomed George Bush's chances of a second term. The result was fragmentation and splintering of the movement.

One such splinter group is the American Coalition of Life Activists, which openly preaches the gospel of violence to attain their narrow objectives. They distribute WANTED posters that list names and addresses of doctors who provide abortions. They also publicize on the Internet a list of such doctors – called the Nuremberg Files – and cross off a name when the person has been eliminated as it was done with Dr. Slepian's name. Their head honcho, the Reverend Donald Spitz of Pro-Life Virginia, is stridently anti-choice and anti-gay and never misses an opportunity to spew his hatred of these groups. His recent letter to *Time* magazine reflects his self-righteous mindset.

The public is getting tired of all this violence. Even the mainstream of the Pro Life movement has had it. A majority, 86%, in a recent *Newsweek* poll, disapproved of the tactics the movement has adopted. Seventy percent want the government to pursue and identify those who commit violence against the clinics and doctors. But an elaborate network of sympathizers, a religious Mafia of sort, helps and protects these criminals. In Buffalo the police are pursuing leads that the killer of Dr. Slepian was aided by some pro-lifers in that area.

There have always been people and groups who look at the world through the prism of their own beliefs. They consider it their God-given right to impose their beliefs on others. In their wisdom any one who dares to be different is dispensable.

It is time these Christian Taliban understand that the laws of this country are supreme and that their Bible thumping and hellfire rhetoric aside, they are subject to these laws.

Via e-mail, November 27, 1998:
Dear Doctor:
Thank you for your wonderful column, "Spare Us the Condolences of Self-Righteous Bigots" in the Blade *... I think folks are finally beginning to see through all this b/s that the so-called Christians are flinging at our society. Articles like yours really help along those lines.*
Richard
Atascadero, CA

Via e-mail, November 30, 1998:
I enjoyed your column on the modern day Talibans, and keep up the good work. I am sure you are getting roasted for it so I thought I would send a little thank you. Keep it up.
Tim

Healthcare crisis evident in flood of hospital bills
February 26, 2007

We often hear that health care in our country is in crisis. It usually refers to either the escalating cost of health care and the increasing rolls of uninsured people, about 50 million, who have no health coverage. Lost in this debate however is another important facet of health care: rude and callous attempts by the hospitals to chase and harass patients for paying hospital bills. Never mind the insurance carriers end up paying most of them anyway. The avalanche of bills after a hospitalization is enough to drive a sane person to the fringes of insanity.

When I was still a surgeon, it was not unusual for some of my elderly, and sometimes not too elderly patients, to come to my office with a stack of bills, threatening letters and occasionally a quasi-legal notice of non-payment that they had received after hospitalization. My staff would plow through the confusing and insulting mess, refer to the insurance company manuals and then make phone calls to straighten out the muddle.

I always thought these things happened to people who are not tuned in to medical profession and hence they are not savvy enough to understand billing procedures. I also thought that the hospitals work with patients to deal with insurance carriers.

I was sadly mistaken.

The rude awakening came just a day after my wife's death. A call came for her from the hospital where she had been a patient two days earlier. When informed of her death the caller asked who would be responsible for her bills. A complaint to the hospital CEO about this unprofessional and rude behavior did elicit an apology. I have no way of knowing if the apology was made to placate an irate member of the medical profession or there was a sincere effort made to change such practice.

I am at a loss to understand the dichotomy between pleasing the patients when they are in the hospital and then unleashing their pit bulls when patients leave the hospital. Ordinarily no one without the proof of insurance is admitted to a hospital. So why this urgency to pin the patient down as soon as the cash register is closed and the patient is wheeled out of the front door? Some hospitals do not even wait for the patient to leave. The billing people come to patient's room to talk about the bill and co-payment while the treatment is still in progress.

Toledo is not unique. This attitude plagues the whole health care industry. I have received bills from some of the prestigious centers in the country where they do not wait for the insurance companies to pay the bills and start billing the patient. I have been receiving bills from MD Anderson Cancer Center in Houston, Mayo Clinic in Rochester, Minnesota and the Cleveland Clinic for months after the our visit to those institutions. Eventually they were all paid by the insurance.

Now here is another contradiction. These centers accept a referral only after they have cleared it with the insurance carrier. So wouldn't it make sense if they would spend a few extra moments perusing the bill with the insurance company rather than harassing the patient?

There have been many efforts in the past to have a comprehensive Patient Bill of Rights. One such measure, McCain-Edwards-Kennedy Bill in 2002, did not pass. The American Hospital Association has its own version that in part promises to make a patient's bill clear, concise, correct and patient-friendly. Unfortunately that laudable goal has not been achieved. Anyone receiving contradictory and overlapping bills can testify to that.

The diagnosis and treatment of a simple hernia generates a plethora of bills. There is a bill from the family physician and a bill from surgery consultant. Add to that a bill each from lab and radiology. After the operation a bill comes from the surgeon, the anesthesiologist and the pathologist. And then there is the hospital bill for the use of operating room, facilities and pharmacy charges.

It would be refreshing if the patients could receive only one bill for their illness and that the bill is written in clear and simple language and that it clearly indicates what the total charges were and how much the insurance has paid.

Is it too much to ask?

Via mail, March 3, 2007:
Dear Dr. Hussain,
I am writing to you in reference to your article in the Blade *concerning the patient billing cost in local hospitals and other health care places. I extend my condolences to you in the loss of your wife.*

*I am sure many people would like to be able to consult with some-
one when receiving the billing for a recent overnight stay at a local
hospital.*

*My concern happened shortly after the new St. Anne Mercy Hospital
opened. Upon entering the assigned bed, an attendant came in with a
large clear plastic mask, which my whole face fit into. In objecting to
this, his answer was, "This was assigned to you and I already opened
the package." I openly refused using it and he became very objective.
I answered that I did not order this. I only use a small nebulizer which
he also had with him in a package.*

*The following day, in preparing to leave, the nurse was present
while gathering my clothes. I mentioned I was not allowed to bring in
my own medication. As an asthmatic person I was not allowed to bring
my own nebulizer. Her quick answer to me about my objections was,
"You must realize this is a business."*

*. . In taking the billing home and reviewing the charges and
accessories, I decided I wanted to talk to someone concerning wording
I had no knowledge of the meaning. I was advised to go to the old
Mercy Hospital where the billing was done. In approaching the desk
inside the entrance, I was told to go to an upper floor. In doing so, I
was told to go back to the main floor, near the entrance. In doing so,
there was only a very small room, one computer and one person who in
turn knew nothing about billing and had no idea where to send me. I
could have saved time and gas in going there.*

*In reviewing the bill at home, I noticed charges which were higher
than at the local pharmacy.*

Yes, Dr. Hussain, I can agree with your explanation in the Blade.
*Many people like me can't afford the cost of an attorney. To me,
Medicare does not POLICE the hospitals properly.*

Thank you,
Larry
Toledo, OH

Via e-mail, February 27, 2007:
Dear Amjad,
*Peggy and I both related to your article today. There must be a
better way! There are many concerns about how health care is*

provided in this country and the longer we wait the more difficult it will be to correct.
Benjamin, CIC

Via e-mail, February 27, 2007:
Good column this morning, Dr. Hussain!
And I can relate to the topic. I was "rushed" to the hospital a few weeks ago (a very life-threatening situation). I moved quickly into surgery, and woke up in a recovery room where I remained until the next morning. I was in and out of the hospital in 24 hours. The recovery room was an expanded closet with a curtain for a door. And aside from having my blood pressure taken every 2 hours during the night (which damn near broke my arm), I received no attention until I was dismissed the next morning by a technician. Never saw a doctor after the surgery (yet is was described as very life threatening).
I received a bill for $32,243. I was charged $2,500 for the room itself. I'm not going to put a dollars and cents value on my life (the doctor really did save my butt) so if this were his bill, I'd be hard put to complain. The bulk of all this charge, however, was the hospitals. I viewed it as criminal. They even sent me a balance due of $360 (and they wanted it paid within 4 days of receiving the bill). Who is responsible for this kind stuff . . . lawyers? Insurance companies?? Who? Thirty-two thousand dollars is year's tuition in some Ohio school, or it's as much or more than many/maybe most people make in a year. And they made it in one day!!!!!!!
S.A.M.

Via e-mail, February 27, 2007:
Enjoyed your column, I am 100 % positive that the apology you received was because you are in medical profession, no CEO would stoop so low as to apologize to a consumer, oops! Patient. It is no surprise that people are going to Thailand for medical treatment, NPR did a very good story this morning on outsourcing of medical care. I have printed a copy of your column for Saeed.
Hope to see you soon.
Rasheeda

Via e-mail, February 27, 2007:
Dr. Hussain,
Bravo on your article in the Blade*! I recently had a stay at Flower Hospital and ended up with my bill being turned in to a collection agency. I had been paying on my bill monthly. When I spoke with the billing department at Flower I was told unless I set up a prior payment plan with Flower, their policy was to turn over any bills not paid in full to the collection agency. I will now have a mark on my credit report!*
Thanks for coming out with this info.
Sincerely,
Becky

Via e-mail, February 28, 2007:
Dr. Hussain,
I always read your columns. My thoughts are with you along with my sympathy to you on the death of your wife. My husband, Frank, died on June 25, 2005 and I am still dealing with my loss. I too experienced a flood of bills and it hasn't stopped yet. Shortly after he died the bills began to roll in from all the different departments and from all the doctors involved, for services rendered that I had to question but paid anyway to get them out of my hair.

What is and was irritating was not one bill but many came from same people, departments etc., why not wait until all the insurances have kicked in and make out one bill? I pay what is billed then here comes another. Then I get a few dollars back; I overpaid. Last week a check made out to Frank came, I endorsed it, went to bank, and cashier asked why he hadn't endorsed it, she looked dumb and mumbled "I'm sorry" when I said why he didn't.

It's not just the bills but having to remind the doctors he has died, getting mail addressed to him for all sorts, calls reminding him he's due for his next check up. I assumed they all were notified of his death but called them anyway. I still got snippy notes about how it is overdue when it's first notice.

We have good insurance; after I pay a bill I get notice how much they paid and wait for refund which takes some time. This could scare the daylights out of the elderly and younger, no wonder they bring their bills wondering. I had gotten used to all the bills coming in the past 11 years since he had the "botched" prostate cancer surgery that totally ruined his health leading to his death, and I had learned how to deal with them all.

I complied with his wishes of donating his body to MUO without any qualms. My son's widow went through the same thing when my son died ten years ago. I was dealing with bills for months after my mother's death three years ago since I was in charge of her estate.

I agree, one bill, in full, with explanation in plain common words anyone can understand but everyone is afraid they won't get every last dime and dollar.

Just letting you know you are not alone . . . .

Doris

Hospital industry's focus on bottom line fuels resentment
March 26, 2007

My February 26 column on hospital billing practices elicited a flood of mail from near and far. Readers wrote to complain about the escalating cost of medical care, confusing bills, and high-handed tactics of hospitals to recover payment. Some of them also cast doubt on the honesty and integrity of the hospitals for hidden charges.

In any business there are always going to be dissatisfied and irate customers. The situation here, however, is different. There is a groundswell of resentment against hospitals for the way they treat patients once the patients leave the hospital. Unfortunately, the driving force in the hospital industry has become the bottom line, and that does not leave any room for compassion in dealing with its clients, the patients.

Illness brings a measure of vulnerability to all of us. To hit people when they are at their most vulnerable, either due to recent illness or the death of a loved one, is beyond the pale of civilized behavior and contradicts all norms of human decency.

What follows is a small sampling of responses I have received.

H.H. of Toledo: "I would like to see not only the complete bill but also the details of the services provided. I have found frequent errors in bills and at times [there were] charges for services I did not receive."

D.B. of Bluffton, Ohio: "My hospital care was splendid. Recently I received a bill saying the insurance company (Medicare and supplemental insurance) did not pay. Why should I be penalized when insurance companies drag their feet in paying?"

D.G. of Toledo: "I pay my bills promptly and wait for the refund, which always takes time. Since the death of my husband two years ago the flood of bills has not stopped. I would like to see ONE bill, in full, with an explanation in plain common words . . .

B.B. of Toledo: "After a recent hospitalization, the bill was turned over to the collection [agency] even though I have been paying on my bill monthly."

R.B. of Kansas: "What the hell ever happened to the PATIENT in PATIENT CARE?"

The cost of medical care was also on the minds of many readers:

N.P., a professor at the University of Toledo Health Science Campus, wrote: "I had to pay $15,000 for an angiogram (for an uninsured relative) after having been told ahead of the procedure that it would cost $5,000. The hospital demanded full payment of the billed charges for hospitalization even though no insurance company pays more than 60 percent of the billed charges. Why should the uninsured be penalized?"

This sentiment was expressed by many others as well.

S.A.M. of Toledo: "I spent one day in the hospital where I was rushed for a 'life threatening' condition. The bill for a one-night stay was $32,243. I never saw a doctor after the initial contact. I was charged $2,500 for the room. The insurance paid all but $360, which the hospital demanded I pay within four days. Thirty-two thousand dollars is a year's tuition in some Ohio schools. It is much more than most people make in one year."

S.H. of Toledo: "There is no mercy in the health care industry. Our legislators are oblivious to our plight because they get lifetime first-rate care (at our expense). When we complain, we get generic responses sent by their minions. I have seen 'managed care' turn into 'mangled care.'"

Some readers also complained about the hidden charges.

T.S. of Toledo wondered about some of the charges in his bill. They appeared in the too-convenient catchall category of "other services." A box of tissues was billed as a "mucus retrieval system" according to M.S. of Toledo. One has to wonder if the health-care industry has borrowed a page from defense contractors.

In my previous column, I had suggested that hospitals should send a unified bill written in simple language detailing the nature of charges.

To that L.R.E. of Toledo responded with one eloquent word, "Amen."

And to that let us all say a loud "Amen" also.

"Experts" ignore root cause of terrorism
April 9, 2007

Last week, I participated in a seminar on terrorism at Case University School of Law in Cleveland. What attracted me was the catchy and provocative title of the seminar: *Sacred Violence: Religion and Terrorism.*

Now, I did not think the seminar would be discussing terrorism waged by any other people but Muslims. After all in the past few years Islam, Muslims and terrorism have become interchangeable words. Perhaps a group of experts while discussing approaches to terrorism would also discuss its root causes and try to separate the good guys from the bad ones. My confidence was misplaced.

I was struck by the inability or unwillingness of the so-called experts in the field of security and terrorism to point out that out of 1.2 billion Muslims worldwide there is a small number who commit such acts. To give those acts a religious cover – note the title *Sacred Violence* – has the unintended consequence of throwing away the baby with the bath water. And some of the speakers did throw away the baby.

They had somehow assumed, in a tacit and un-declarative way, that Islam is violent and that source of this violence is Qur'an, the sacred text of Muslims. This self-serving and convenient premise is not unlike the cute and tricky question: when did you stop beating your wife?

There were in all eleven speakers from as disparate disciplines as law, political science, philosophy, psychology and religion. The two Muslims on the program were Pervez Ahmad, a professor of finance from Florida and chairman Council on American Islamic Relations, and myself.

The speakers read their papers from their own professional perspectives but most of them did not address the root cause of terrorism. Instead, the thrust of their argument was to tackle terrorism using legal, financial and law enforcement tools. They just were not interested in discussing political reasons behind the violence.

The most provocative speaker was Louis Rene Beres, professor of International Relations and International Law at Purdue University and an advisor on nuclear issues to the Prime Minister of Israel. In a convoluted logic reminiscent of a Rube Goldberg Machine, he advocates a preemptive Israeli attack on Iran's nuclear facilities. He justifies the loss of Iranian lives on moral and legal grounds in order to protect Israeli lives in case of a potential Iranian attack on Israel. During his talk he conveniently sidestepped the crucial question of why Iranians feel so negative about the U.S. and Israel.

Like Professor Beres, a few other speakers also emphasized tackling terrorism but none of them connected the dots between terrorism and the causes that lead people to commit such horrendous acts. They were less inclined to explain the phenomenon of terrorism than to suggest forceful remedies.

These experts are more prone to drawing their conclusions from a few snap shots rather than connecting the dots between cause and effect. A group of blind people cannot describe an elephant when they feel only a small part of it. I felt a veiled hostility towards Islam that was conveniently covered with a flimsy fig leaf of self-serving laws and innovatively crafted definitions. The questions and answers by the audience supported that observation.

In all fairness there were also some speakers who discussed terrorism in philosophical, psychological and religious terms. Their discourses were enlightening.

A few weeks ago a one-time CIA analyst who had worked in the White House and is currently a teacher of security studies at Tiffin University gave a public lecture at the Islamic Center in Perrysburg on security issues. In his 40-minute talk he painstakingly discussed the way the Bush administration goes through sifting through an avalanche security reports to assess potential terrorist attacks. The thrust of his message? The government works very hard to protect you Muslims.

For a security expert to talk down to his mostly Muslim audience in a patronizing way was rather insulting. He appeared to be somewhat uninformed about the history of jihadist culture and asserted that most people around the world approve of American foreign policy.

As a responsible (and hopefully an enlightened) citizen I do not take the menace of terrorism lightly. I have been critical of those Muslims who hide behind euphemisms and clichés about their religion and are not willing to condemn terrorism being waged in their name. But I also point an accusing finger at the hypocrisy of the so-called terrorist experts who cannot see a forest for the trees.

Or may be they just don't want to.

Via e-mail, April 9, 2007:

Hi, Dr. Hussain,

It was a great pleasure meeting you at the conference. Sadly, most of us did not realize that the focus of the event would be how to know, and thereby hunt down our enemies. The notion of a preemptive nuclear strike is too horrific to even consider. When one of my students asked why I gave a paper on suicide bombing, I answered: "The purpose is twofold, to understand the fantasies and motives of certain people, and to understand how forcing people into abjection violently will ensure that death becomes a sacred form of transcendence."

My objective was to show with irony how injustice guarantees that retaliation will become sacred. I was dismayed that they either ignored it or merely saw this as a way to hunt people down. My friend Sheldon's talk was similarly misunderstood – for the implication is, to what degree is talking about terrorists, and the discourse of hunting them down, a reaction to our own fear of death and paranoid need to accuse enemies?

Thank you for the column.

In friendship,

J.P., Case Western Reserve University

Department of Philosophy

The pleasure was mine as well. I was very impressed by your discourse and Dr. Solomon's presentation. These were the real "jewels" of the program. I hope our paths cross again. Could you kindly pass on my column to Dr. Solomon?

Regards,

Amjad H.

Via e-mail, April 10, 2007

You did not explicate what you think is the root cause of terrorism.

Until you can articulate what you think the cause is, you cannot criticize nor comment.

The root cause of terrorism is a spiritual issue. This spiritual issue is man's willful rebellion against the authority of the God of Abraham,

Isaac and Jacob. This rebellion leads to the evil that surrounds our daily lives: both the imaginable and the unimaginable.

There are only two positions to choose from: either we are for the God of Abraham, Isaac and Jacob or we are against the God of Abraham, Isaac and Jacob. There is none other. When we choose to be for the God of Abraham, Isaac and Jacob, we choose life. When we choose to be against the God of Abraham, Isaac and Jacob, we choose death. When we choose to be for the God of Abraham, Isaac and Jacob, we choose to "bless" the seed of Abraham through Isaac and Jacob. When we choose to be against the God of Abraham, Isaac and Jacob, we choose to "curse" the seed of Abraham through Isaac and Jacob.

The fool chooses to willfully rebel against the authority of the God of Abraham, Isaac and Jacob over his life. Thus, the fool chooses and reaps: death, destruction, despair, hopelessness, hatred, violence and evil, along with curses such as oppression, famine, injustice, pestilence, and poverty.

Be wise. Choose to be for the God of Abraham, Isaac and Jacob. Choose Life. Choose Blessing.

Moll

Via e-mail, April 9, 2007
DEAR DR. HUSSAIN,
RATHER THAN BEING INSULTED BY THE PANEL ON TERRORISM, WHY DONT YOU TRY TO EXPLAIN WHAT WE SHOULD DO NOW TO STOP IT? THE CREATION OF ISRAEL CAN'T BE UNDONE, NOW, THE FREEING OF IRAQ OF SADDAM'S BUTCHERY SHOULD BE APPLAUDED, THE MUSLIMS IN AMERICA SHOULD SPEAK OUT MUCH MORE STRONGLY AND STOP SUPPORTING TERRORISTS, ETC.

PERHAPS YOU CAN EXPLAIN WHY THE CULTURE OF THE WAHABES (SPELLING?) RESTRICTS SO MUCH FREEDOM AND SUPPORTS THE KILLING OF "INFIDELS".

HOW DOES THE WORLD GET THE GENIE BACK IN THE BOTTLE, NOW??

THE CRAZIES IN IRAN AND OTHER MUSLIM COUNTRIES, NOT JUST AL QAEDA HAVE SWORN TO WIPE OUT ISRAEL AND

*KILL US WHILE TRYING TO WRECK OUR ECONOMY. WHAT ARE
RESPONSIBLE MUSLIMS DOING ABOUT IT?*

*I THINK THAT IF A NUCLEAR WEAPON IS USED AGAINST
THE U.S. OR OUR ALLIES, THE RETALIATION WILL WIPE OUT
MOST OF THE MUSLIM CIVILIZATION, AND IT WILL TAKE
CENTURIES TO REPAIR WHAT THE MISGUIDED ZEALOTS HAVE
BROUGHT ON THE CULTURE THAT PERMITS OR ENCOURAGES
TERROISM.*

*I RESPECT YOUR SENSITIVIES BUT YOU HAVE A LOT OF
EXPLAINING TO DO TO CONVINCE THE WORLD THAT OUR
FOREIGN POLICIES ARE THE CAUSE, WHEN THIS GREAT AND
GENEROUS COUNTRY ONLY SEEKS PEACE AND SECURITY.
WHAT ARE THE MUSLIMS DOING FOR THE SAME??*

*I'M AN OLD MAN NOW AND WHAT EVER HAPPENDS IS LESS
IMPORTANT TO ME PERSONALLY BUT I HAVE CHILDREN AND
GRAND CHILDREN WHO I CARE DEEPLY ABOUT........
PLEASE TELL US HOW TO SOLVE THE PROBLEM, NOT JUSTIFY
IT!!*

F.N.H. MAUMEE AND NAPLES, FL

Thank you for your note.

People have committed atrocities in the name of religion throughout
history. It is our job to differentiate militants from the moderates. When
I read an e-mail from an intelligent person like you I am left speechless.

Please do know (if you do not already) that Iraq was attacked on
false pretext. Saddam was a cruel man but the U.S. Constitution does
not allow us to topple a government just because it is ruled by a tyrant.
If that were true, then we should be attacking China and removing most
of the rulers in the Middle East and Africa.

Palestinians have been dealt an injustice that only the U.S. can help
correct. Our Congress in the clutches of the Israeli lobby and the
Administration supporting Israel at the expense of the Palestinians
would help continue the cycle of violence. It is up to people like you,
Mr. Harris, to raise your voice in support of the victims rather then
identify with the oppressors.

I also have grandchildren and I also worry about them. This puts
more responsibility on you and me to stand up for what is right and
what is wrong.

I am grateful that you took the time to write.

Regards,

Amjad Hussain

Via e-mail, April 10, 2007:

Dear Dr. Hussain,

Thank you for your civil reply, but the question remains "what should we do now?"

We can flog the past decisions and the basis for the forever and it won't solve anything. Indeed it will just harden the hatred that exists.

Help with a plan if you can. More rhetoric and lament of past decisions will not be useful. The exposure of Muslims in our country helping terrorists and the fact that cheering by the same in Dearborn at the 9/11 event will endanger good Muslims.

There is only one side to the search for sanity . . . . . . stop the killing and the religious justification for it.

You could help by not taking sides and suggesting it's all our fault. Sorry for some typing and spelling errors old shaky hands are the blame, perhaps due to past decisions.

Please help to set a new course of action.

Kind regards.

F.N.H.

I have for over 15 years pointed my finger both at Muslims and non-Muslims who violate the limits of tolerance and civility. Consequently, I take the brunt from both sides and that is just fine with me.

Please do read the last paragraph of my column.

Regards,

Amjad Hussain

Via mail, April 14, 2007:

Dear Dr. Hussain,

I always read your articles and appreciate them. Thank you for being "another voice." Your last article on 4/9 talked about supposed experts not talking about or dealing with the root causes of terrorism. I wish you would write an article about what you perceive to be those causes. I certainly struggle to try and understand. Maybe they were perplexed also.

The causes I would list would be: hatred of Israel and hatred of the USA for supporting Israel; poverty and lack of opportunities in the Arab world; Western values, they perceive, are corrupting theirs; US presence in Iraq. From what I read about the Koran, or parts of it, it says to kill all those who are not Muslim. That will be a lot of people but they seem to be on their way, and killing fellow Muslims also. As you can see, I am very confused. Please write the article to help me understand!

Sincerely,
Marilyn
Perrysburg

When will Americans' patience run out?
July 4, 2005

Last week, President Bush delivered a major policy speech at Fort Bragg on the war in Iraq. While full of rhetorical flourishes the speech was awfully short on substance. He repeated his oft-repeated mantra that despite the difficulties the peace in Iraq is winnable and that much progress has been made. In the end it was the familiar "trust me" attitude that has accented his Iraq policy for the past two years. The American people in the meantime are unhappy and losing patience with his handling of the war in Iraq. A recent *Washington Post*-ABC poll shows that most Americans do not believe progress is being made in Iraq but they are willing to support military presence in Iraq for an extended period. This reservoir of understanding however is not inexhaustible.

During his speech Mr. Bush again connected the dots between 9/11 and Saddam Hussein and tried to give the impression that somehow invasion of Iraq was the consequence of terrorists attacks on 9/11. While no one with a bit of intelligence believes that fiction, the president continues to perpetuate the myth by connecting those imaginary dots. Iraq was on the radar screen of neo-conservatives long before bin Laden, huddled in some remote camp in Afghanistan, planned the attacks on American soil. Recently released documents from Great Britain prove beyond any doubt that Mr. Bush was determined to attack Iraq and the invention of the Weapons of Mass Destruction and his U.N. diplomacy was a smoke screen and a charade.

Now let us connect the dots from the invasion of Iraq two years ago to the present and see how within this period we have come to an impasse. The cheering crowds that welcomed the American forces have vanished and have now been replaced by an increasingly bloody and debilitating insurgency. So who are these insurgents?

Mr. Bush would lead us to believe that Islamic militants from outside Iraq are behind the insurgency. There are, to be sure, foreign terrorists in Iraq who have come to Iraq to fight the U.S. occupation. The majority of the insurgents however are Iraqis who are waging a fierce resistance against the U.S. occupation. No insurgency can ever gather so much steam without a wide indigenous support.

The insurgency has taken its toll in lives and morale. Since the invasion of Iraq 1750 American soldiers and more than 100,000 Iraqis have died in the conflict. The frequency and viciousness of attacks have also increased with time and has put the administration in disarray. Vice President Dick Cheney says the insurgency is in its last throes whereas Secretary of Defense Donald Rumsfeld says it cannot be won militarily and it is going to take long time to control it. We have a tiger by the tail and really do not know how to tame it.

Mr. Bush has understandably (I would say wisely) refused the demands by the Democrats and some Republicans to set a timetable for quitting Iraq. Such a timetable would be disastrous for Iraq and would not serve any useful purpose except to embolden the insurgents. What he should have done is to point out some tangible benchmarks of progress tied to incremental withdrawal of troops. This would have given the American people a little more than the usual Staying the Course rhetoric. The American people have the right to know that the current Iraq policy has not worked and that in order to achieve the overall objective of a peaceful and independent Iraq Mr. Bush is willing to make necessary changes. We broke the pottery barn, to paraphrase Mr. Colin Powell, and two years on it is still broken.

Mr. Bush and his extreme right-wing Christian supporters still believe they are the righteous ones and they alone have the God-given right to set the world right. In this self-righteousness they fail to understand the link between America's tarnished image abroad and the heavy-handed policies of this administration. A recent Pew Global Attitudes Project found persistent negative attitude towards America around the world including Europe. When asked as to what would be their country of choice for migration, America was not the favored destination by people of the world with the sole exception of those living in India.

There is a lot to ponder on this 4th of July.

Via e-mail, July 4, 2005:
Dr. Hussain,
You start out your poorly rationalized editorial stating, "While full of rhetorical flourishes the speech was awfully short on substance." Your editorial fit this description to a tee. You make statements without

any factual backing like, "Recently released documents from Great Britain prove beyond any doubt that Mr. Bush was planning to attack Iraq" which the documents show a belief, not a statement of fact!

Also, you state "Mr. Bush would lead us to believe that Islamic militants from outside Iraq are behind the insurgency. There are, to be sure foreign terrorists in Iraq who have come to Iraq to fight the U.S. occupation. The majority of insurgents, however, are Iraqis. No insurgency can ever gather so much steam without wide indigenous support." This statement has no solid support, not even in logic. History has shown that an insurgency can continue without widespread support if fear and intimidation are in play, which has been stated to be the case by people in Iraq. Also, you glaze over that the leader of the insurgency is not Iraqi, but a Jordanian terrorist! What is your basis for saying over 100,000 Iraqis have died in this conflict when even most anti-U.S. groups do not state that number, or did you get that all from the anti-war nay-sayers who predicted 250,000 to 1,000,000 dead prior to the war. Or are you including the Iraqi soldiers who died in the war, which means you are attempting to mislead the people in Toledo to think that the 100,000 were innocent civilians and did not include any combatants?

. . . You also paint with a broad brush all of Mr. Bush's supporters as "his extreme right-wing Christian supporters," which only belies a true anti-Christian attitude or why state it at all? You have extreme Islamic-fundamentalist supporters amongst your readers, I am sure, but I will not accuse them of all being so nor of your being so. You need to realize your arrogance and how your beliefs affect your view of the world. In fact, I am not a practicing Christian so do not paint me in that manner as an excuse for your poor writing.

I think that Toledo does need diverse attitudes the bring to bear other views of the world, but those that show the good and the bad and do not look to immediately condemn any actions taken by one specific party in the U.S., nor defend the actions of the rest of the world as if they are to say they are perfect. Sometimes doing the right thing is not popular. Remember, there was a great deal of anti-U.S. sentiment around the world, and not just in the Islamic world, when the U.S. invaded Afghanistan, which was undoubtedly the right thing to do. Also, remember that France and its ilk have long followed a policy of not upsetting the status quo…is that the right thing to do?

Sincerely,
T.B.

Via mail, July 7, 2005:
Gentlemen:
On the fourth of July, the best my old friend Amjad Hussain could do was repeat his tired glass-is-half-full mantra that Bush lied, we're losing the peace in Iraq, and it's the fault of Christian supporters. And only India has a population that would favor America for migration. What nonsense!

Saddam Hussein was responsible for the deaths of millions of Muslims. He's gone. This is progress. Especially since they are killing each other over there and not here. In past wars, America lost more in single battles preserving freedom than we've lost in our years freeing Afghanistan and Iraq. Have we now lost our sense of proportion? And yes, Christians would welcome more Muslim support especially from those who have chosen to make America there homes as they either fled the dictator in their homeland or merely wished to improve their lot.

For such a generally cheerful and favored adopted American, I can only suggest that he change whatever he's been smoking.
Joe
(hand-written footnote on same letter)
Amjad –
Life is tough when you have to take this from your friends. Hope Dottie is doing well.
Best regards,
Joe

Via e-mail, July 4, 2005:
What a way to start the morning on this our American Independence Day reading your "words of wisdom." You really caused me to see fireworks, and the celebrations haven't even started yet this morning.

Your slanderous remarks against our president and our nation are disgusting indeed. For you to imply that all Bush supporters are "extreme right wing Christians" is ludicrous! Talk about extreme . . . . I would suggest, sir, that YOU are extreme in your radical left-wing liberal thinking:

1 . . . .America is always wrong.

2 . . . .America is the bad country.

3 . . . . Everyone hates America.

4 . . . .Everything is always America's fault (especially when Republicans are in power)

In light of all this, one can only wonder why you continue to live here????? Wouldn't you be far more happier returning to your country of origin??? After all, it must be terribly embarrassing for you to call America home, in light of the fact that the whole world hates us.

You appear to be giving the Democrats talking points, and you see where that gets you . . . even more losing elections!!!!! I guess we should just encourage you to talk more, so that '06 and '08 will bring even more victories!!! Your statements are so misguided and untruthful on many counts.

Counterpoints:

Count # 1 . . . . Iraq is making progress and there are positive things happening there, if only the liberal press (you included) would only choose to show it. But that wouldn't fit into your liberal agenda.

Count # 2 . . . . The world and the region are far better off without the ruthless dictator at the helm. Unless of course one believes that gassing, torturing, murdering one's own countrymen is preferable. Weapons of destruction, mass graves, and yes . . even terrorists indeed have been found in Iraq.

Count #3 . . . . Freedom, stability, and change do not just happen overnight. It takes time. (Perhaps you should check our history, and world history for references)

Count # 4 . . . . President Bush doesn't repeat MANTA. He repeats his belief!! Belief that Iraq and the region will benefit from freedom. And somehow, I believe that maybe . . . . just maybe . . . . . President Bush has more information and facts at his disposal that you do. (But don't ever let the facts get in the way when a liberal is speaking!)

Count # 5 . . Recently released documents???? What a joke!!! We all are well aware of "documents" and how factual they are. Nice try.

Counts # 6 . . . .Finally, as for no one in the world wanting to come to this evil place called America . . . . . why then are there thousands (millions) trying to get in???????

You sir, seem to side with the part of Europe that is most liberal and anti-American. Have at it. Europe is more that just France, Germany, etc. And believe it or not, some European countries that are less to the far left, actually do support America! So, again I say . . . . you and all your "Bush Bashers" on the left . . . .Keep up the good work!!!!   We Republicans benefit every time you liberals open your mouth.   So, perhaps I should say Thank You .and yes . . . . we DO have a lot to ponder on this Fourth of July!   God bless America . . .. and all the world.

C.T.

I appreciate your comments about my July 4 column in the Blade. However your incoherent rambling left me bewildered. In a civil discourse one can disagree without being disagreeable.

I am amused at your suggestion that I should go back to where I came from. I wonder if you have the same advice for those Americans who have been here for generations but disagree with this right wing fundamentalist government of Mr. Bush. If that comes to pass 54% of Americans would have to leave.

My comments about recently released documents pertain to a Downing Street Memo which I thought a person of your insight would have known and understood. This memo clearly proves that Mr. Bush was determined to invade Iraq irrespective of the facts.

Like you I am a registered Republican but I do not blindly follow the party line. I am grateful that you took the time to write.

Regards,
Amjad Hussain

Via e-mail, July 4, 2005:
Excellent article with good insight. Thank you.
Jack

Via e-mail, July 4, 2005:
Hi!
With world oil production peaking round about now and about 35 years supply left, 50 years at the most, before it runs out completely, and with Iraq sitting on the world's second biggest reserves, the chances of America "exiting" from Iraq are just about zero. American forces are already well advanced in building futuristic self-contained forts which they optimistically call "enduring" bases.

Virtually all wars, in the remaining time we have left, will be fought about who gets what's left of less and less gas and oil. Even if the insurgency in Iraq is successful in sabotaging oil production (which it largely is), as long as America is in occupation, no one else gets it.

People who complained, and still do, of America having no "exit strategy" are merely demonstrating their ignorance as to why Bush and the oil barons ordered the invasion of Iraq in the first place.

Good luck,

B.E.

UK

P.S. For once in his life Bush tells it how it is (but it wasn't in a big speech on TV): "We're hooked on oil from the Middle East, which is a national security problem and an economic security problem." - 30th June '05

Via e-mail, July 5, 2005:

Dear Mr. Hussain,

Happy 4th of July. I can't imagine how you would celebrate it but enjoy. After reading your extreme left wing religious intolerant opinions in your recent column "When will Americans patience run out," I would like to point out a few things. I currently have 3 family members and 1 friend fighting against these ANTI-JESUS CHRIST and ANTI-Israel extremists so you can spew your all-knowing how-America-feels rhetoric. I suppose if you graduated from college with left wing professors and believe the extreme left wing media that currently controls the airwaves, you would be brainwashed into the mindset in which you now have.

Another contributing factor would be an extreme left wing religious faith. Islam, regardless how much the media portrays it as a religion of peace, and for that matter Catholicism, has never been and never will be a religion of peace or tolerance. Funny the left wing media and political parties all preach we are the tolerant ones. I beg to differ. They are tolerant as long as you agree with them...example Howard Dean, The Reverend Jessie Jackson, John Kerry. If you don't agree with them then you are hateful and religious bigots. Islam is not a religion of peace as your media friends would like us to believe, never has been and never will be. You tell me where it has brought peace anywhere. There is always bloodshed and intolerance. If you think I am wrong then you tell me how long I would last standing on the streets of any Middle Eastern country with Bible in hand quoting scripture.

Another thing I would like to point out – Everyone thinks they are right when they voice opinion. Would you write the articles you write if you thought you were wrong? You are attacking what you call the extreme right wing Christian supporters of George Bush saying they believe they are the righteous ones and they alone have the God given right to set the world straight. I can assume that you are an extreme left wing anti-Christian non-supporter of George Bush that believes you are the righteous ones and you alone have the little-g-god given right to set the world straight. You, sir, fail to recognize how America came about. There is a reason why America has been blessed over the years. It is because of religious tolerance. Many spilled their blood in this country over that very thing so you can spew your Anti-Christian hatred. America has been blessed in the past because of a fear of GOD and a belief in Gods Holy book THE BIBLE which I assume you reject and believe only the parts that fit your left wing viewpoints. America is blessed because of our support of Gods chosen people THE JEWS, "Which I take it you hate. I will bless them that bless thee and curse them that curse thee" Genesis 12:3....

Regards,
G.G.

Thank you for your comments on my 7/4/05 column in the *Blade*. It is hard to carry on a civil conversation when you are so angry and up-set. Here are short answers to the questions you raised.

Yes, I do celebrate Independence Day just as you do. My view of this greatest country in the world is perhaps different than yours. I love the country, its people and what it offers not in material things but a freedom to think and differ. This is what I have learned in the past 40 plus years that I have lived here.

Your comments about Islam and Catholic religion indicate your deeply rooted hostility towards those faiths. I consider all religions noble and worthy of respect. And that includes your religion too.

You assumed that my comments about the extreme Christian right make me anti-Semitic. Only an uninformed person would make that deduction.

I am very grateful that you took the time to send me your comments.

Regards,

Amjad Hussain

Via e-mail, July 6, 2005:

Dear Dr. Hussain,

When will America's patience run out? When it comes to the war in Iraq, I hope never. Personally, I think the war in Iraq was a huge mistake. However, I think a bigger mistake would be to pull out of country without making sure the present government can guarantee a peaceful existence for its citizens.

It is one hell of a mess, but let's not put all the blame on George Bush, neo-conservatives, and right-wing supporters. Maybe they are one and the same in your mind. I am not Christian, Jewish, or Muslim. I am not conservative or liberal. What I am is an American. And damn proud of it even if the rest of the world has a tarnished image of us.

You didn't say in your column where America ranked on the list of favored destinations by people of the world, but I bet it was pretty darn high. And, where do the Muslim nations of the world fit into that survey? Do you really think the insurgency in Iraq would end if America pulled out our troops? Do you really think the Sunnis, and their allies, are going to stop blowing up people until they are in power again? I don't have much respect for right-wing Christians, but what little respect I have is much higher than the respect that I have for fundamental Muslims who think blowing up innocent people is justified to effect social change. At least the Christians use the power of the ballot box. Whether you agree with them or not is what American is all about.

Regardless of our tarnished image, our country did not deserve 9/11. Don't try connecting those dots. I think the world knows that Iraq did not have direct hand in the carnage, but I'll bet there was a lot of cheering in Iraq when it happened. In this country, supporting a crime makes you just as guilty as the one who actually committed it. The world knows that it is the vow of fundamental Muslims fanatics to kill as many Americans as possible. Heck, they are on record as saying they want to bring down our whole economic system. But, I never read any negative comments toward them from you. In your mind, it's only the U.S. that is responsible for the mess in the world and there are no self-righteous Muslim people. Give me a break! How much more self-righteous can you get when you blow up people for political gain?

Your bias in this matter is understandable. However, I think you should know that there are plenty of ordinary American people, without political or religious agendas, who want something positive to be accomplished in Iraq. Many of us do not want to see our sons and daughters slaughtered, beheaded, tortured, and abused in vain. What is taking place in Iraq that is despicable is not the occupation of American troops trying to help the government rebuild a country, but the day-to-day slaughter of innocent people by others who will not participate in a government run by rule of law.

Personally, if I had the power, I would undo everything that has been done by American in Iraq. I regret our involvement in the Middle East. I regret every life that has been lost and every dollar that has been spent to help Muslim populations. Obviously, it has not helped our tarnished image. What I do care about is the spread of intolerant Islamic beliefs and the sincere threats by Jihad Muslim fundamentalists who vow to take our country down. You know, I don't care if you don't like American attitudes. But please, don't kill us just because you think your way is better.

R .J.

Toledo, OH

I guess we look at things differently.

I also agree that at this juncture for America to pull out would be a disaster. However, the president could establish some bench marks and make a gradual (incremental) withdrawal linked to those bench marks.

Yes, I agree Iraq was a mistake. I think it is unfair for you to equate my opposition to our policies in the Middle East (and occasionally elsewhere in the world) as synonymous with supporting Islamic fundamentalism and terrorism. I am against all kind of fundamentalism, whether religious, political or nationalistic. If we agree with this premise then all those Americans who oppose the war in Iraq would automatically be labeled as anti-American and therefore pro-terrorism. You and I both know it is not true.

I have lived in this country since 1963 and what this great country has taught me is to be forthright and speak my mind. It is the love of this country that prompts me to at times be critical of our policies.

Even though we disagree on many issues, I am grateful that you take the time to write and give me the opportunity engage in a civil conversation.

Regards,

Amjad Hussain

Narrow viewpoints serve no one well
June 19, 2006

In the 12 years that I have appeared in this space, a number of *Blade* readers have felt obliged to comment about what I write. They have expressed their views either in the Readers' Forum or have written to me directly. While many of them wrote in support of my opinions, many others took exception and told me so in no unclear words.

These interactions were conducted with the civility and decorum that is the hallmark of a civil society. And, yes, on occasion I have had to eat my words.

There have been notable exceptions though. There are some die-hards who cannot or will not entertain any point of view other than their own deeply prejudiced one. They do not write to have a discussion; they write to condemn, to malign, and to dismiss.

There is this one gentleman from the Indian subcontinent who, no matter the subject or context, would always find reasons to broadside Pakistan. My recent essay on the crossing of the India-Pakistan border at Wahgah gave him yet another reason to condemn Pakistan for the Kashmir issue. The irony is that the essay was not about Kashmir or other contentious issues between the two countries. In that piece I suggested Muslims, Hindus, and Sikhs from the subcontinent should accept their responsibility for slaughtering each other during the fight for independence from the British in 1947.

Regarding Kashmir, he would be better informed if he met with the dozen or so Indian Kashmiri families who live in this area. They all have relatives living in the valley of Kashmir and they visit them often. Unfortunately, his outbursts have been a source of embarrassment to both Pakistanis and Indians in this town.

There is another gentleman from the subcontinent who apparently has not met a Muslim he did not dislike. His sole purpose in life, it seems, is to cruise the Web to find the most insulting and derogatory article about Islam, Muslims, and Pakistan, which he then dutifully forwards to me and others. It would be more appealing if he would write something himself and publish it under his own name rather than hide behind other people's writings.

Another detractor has a particular distaste for words like Palestine, Palestinians, Palestinian state, Middle East Road Map, and Occupied

Land. In his view of the Middle East the Palestinians have no right to their own land and they all should be evicted and pushed across the Jordan River. He sends frequent bulletins containing anti-Palestinian, anti-Arab, and anti-Muslim articles written by Israeli apologists. In his eyes, Israel can do no wrong.

Armed with the bucket of tar and a broad brush he does not hesitate to paint all those who question Israeli policies in the occupied Palestinian areas as anti-Semitic.

A number of years ago I received a picture of an Ashura procession from Lebanon. In that picture Shia children with headbands were breast-beating to commemorate the martyrdom of Imam Hussayn in 680 in the desert of Karbala in Iraq. For Shias, the Ashura processions are part passion play, part spiritual fulfillment, and part catharsis. They mourn the watershed incident in their history with sadness and intro-spection. And what did the sender say about the picture? This is how they train their children to be terrorists.

Fortunately most people are not that extreme in their views. It's important to remember that when you insult, minimize, dehumanize, or reduce other people, cultures, or religions, you are in fact doing the same to yourself.

Via e-mail, June 19, 2006:

I can't pretend to understand other cultures. I can't say I agree with everything you say. However, your column is always interesting and informative. As for being critical, I'd find that difficult to do. In the mid-90's, you operated on my father, who had lung cancer. That surgery gave him an additional 8 years of life . . a life cancer free. He died of a heart attack following surgery to repair a broken leg.

Because you gave him those extra 8 years, I could never be critical of you. I can only say thanks and keep up your interesting and informative column.

Sincerely,
M.E.D.

So kind of you to write.

In fact it was your father's resilience and the love he received from his family that kept him alive long after his lung surgery. I wish I could take the credit but, knowing that we are but very small part of God's design on this earth, I cannot.

Regarding criticism of what I write, I am always pleased to receive critical comments as long as they are civil and pertinent.

Warmest regards,

Amjad Hussain

Via e-mail, June 21, 2006:

Dear friend, Amjad Hussain,

Tasleemat:

When I was a student in Forman Christian College, Lahore, our Prof. Abdul Majid Khan once uttered these words in the class room, "If there is a God and if we are all His children then His teachings have to be the same for every one." These words changed my life completely and I bought translated versions of the Holy Books - the Qur'an, the Bible, the Vedas, the Gita, the Grunth Saheb and started studying them. I noticed that I was a different person. After reading the books a couplet came to my mind and I wrote:

> *"Tu Allif mein tu hai Laam mein tu hi Meem mein tu hi Aum mein*
>
> *Tu Saleeb mein tu Granth mein tu hai her eik Mazhab - o- Qaum mein"**

Even now I have placed all these books in my prayer room and read them whenever I am in tension and need peace of mind.

I fully agree with your suggestion that Hindus, Muslims and Sikhs should bow down their heads in shame and condemn the happenings in 1947. At the same time I also feel that all of us, unitedly, must condemn the ruthless, fiery and instigating speeches delivered by the political and religious leaders of both sides at that time. Unfortunately the people of this subcontinent are hero worshipers and follow their leaders blindly and these happenings were the result of the same. I was a young boy at that time but I could not understand as to why this was happening. Today I believe that if the political leaders and the governments of both sides had taken proper and stern action and honestly helped the people to move from one side to other safely, this bloodshed

---

* You are in the beginning, in the middle and in the end and in the word peace You are in the Cross, in Granth Sahib and you are part of every religion and nation.

could have been avoided. However today that is only history and we can only condemn the atrocities committed on both sides.

What we must do today is to try and bring the people of Pakistan and India closer together. The Governments should make the crossing of the border easier - preferably on the lines as it is in Europe where it takes just five minutes to move from one country to the other. After my recent visit to Pakistan I am fully convinced that people from both sides are the same as they were before. Some even asked us "why don't you come back and live here?" We were certainly moved by their sentiments.

With warm personal regards,
R.R.C.
Bohpal, India

Via e-mail, July 12, 2006:
To me it appears that in any nation with a sizeable Muslim population, terrorism is a fact of life. Muslim Terrorism does not seem to be limited anywhere. More and more I am hearing in these diverse nations, the nucleus of the Terrorist Movement is the Mosque.

Rather than whine about the intolerance of a few local people who simply disagree with you, you ought to examine Islam to determine the philosophical basis that provides Muslims with Satanically like executioner status over non-Muslims. It must be there; otherwise Muslim terrorism would not be so widespread. It may be subliminal.
R.L.

While I am always grateful to receive your comments, this hateful e-mail does not need any comment. Somehow your real colors come through.

Cordially,
Amjad Hussain

Sorry for not explaining myself better.
My statements were based on the following facts:
(1) Muslim Terror Groups are active in nearly all parts of the world. They are at war against people of other religions; therefore ordinary citizens of those countries are fair targets. This type of warfare is advocated in Islamic schools and Mosques.

(2) Al'Qaeda, Hammas and Hezbollah are three examples of which I am familiar. All have broad support among Muslims and are well financed by Islamic institutions

I am sure you have heard the old saying, "Bad things happen when good people do nothing." Currently, Islam is being hijacked by terrorists because good Muslims, like you, are not doing nearly enough to prevent it.

As a columnist, you can do a lot of good.
R.L.

If you expect for me to condemn my faith you are barking up the wrong tree.

If you expect me to condemn terrorism and those Muslims who terrorize, I have done that *ad nauseam*. Perhaps a person with his mind already made cannot see what others have done or are doing.

I invite you to go through the archives of *Blade* to see what side I have been on.

Regards,
Amjad Hussain

Via e-mail, July 16, 2006:
Dear Amjad,
Would it help if I told him that you have seldom tried to kill me?
Jack (Lessenberry, ombudsman for The Blade*)*

Embassy in Pakistan gives girl a sad view of American ways.
September 3, 2000

Earlier this summer, my family in Pakistan was refused visas to come to the US for our long awaited family reunion. Maryam, our ten-year-old grand niece, was devastated. After receiving rather rude and shabby treatment at the hands of the visa officers at the American embassy, she thought all Americans were rude and insensitive. This is my lame effort to console her.

Dear Maryam:

I was shocked that the American Embassy in Islamabad has refused to grant you visa to come to America for our family reunion. I am personally embarrassed because I am the one who had persuaded your parents to visit us during summer vacations. After all it has been ten years since we all got together for our daughter Tasha's wedding here in Toledo. Much has happened in the past ten years; there have been marriages, new babies have come along and many of our elders have passed on. Family reunions are important because they keep us connected and help us put things in perspective.

I can only imagine the hardship you had to endure in getting to the capital for the mandatory interview for which you had to stand in line for better part of the day in 110 degrees under a blazing sun. Your Baaba (father) told me that the officer made his decision in less than a minute. The officer was suspicious that the family will end up in America for good. It did not matter that your Baaba has a flourishing family business. It also did not matter that I had also sent affidavits of support. Those visa officers consider every one to be a crook unless proven otherwise. They do not consider the proof of innocence either.

Why didn't I complain to the President of America, you asked. You see, Maryam, the President and his staff, with the weight of the whole world on their shoulders, can't possibly be interested in the disappointment of a little Pakistani girl. In the great scheme of things it is not important.

I did, however, ask our Congresswoman, a really nice and neat lady, for help. Even though she is very busy with myriad problems that members of the Congress have to deal with, she did send a letter on our behalf. The head honcho in charge of issuing visas – his official title is consul general – probably tossed that letter in a wastebasket. According to him, he receives thousands of such letters every year and does not pay much attention to them. So why do our lawmakers write toothless letters without a vigorous follow up? Because politicians never say no to their constituents. They go through the motions of writing letters that have little or no effect. It is like the story of Henry and Liza and a bucket with a big hole.

No, Maryam, the American people are not rude or condescending. The real Americans are the most generous, courteous and friendly people around. The Americans you saw at the embassy are a bunch of small people with big authority over hapless visa seekers whom they treat as cattle. The pity is you have to get through those arrogant snobs to meet the real folks.

I don't want you to get disheartened. We will try again because we must. I am still looking forward to a big backyard picnic with all of us together. And I still want you to see our beautiful zoo, ride on the tallest and fastest roller coaster at Cedar Point and stop at the neighborhood Dairy Queen for an extra large ice cream cone. Your five-year-old cousin Hannah is anxiously waiting to join you.

Your auntie sends her love and kisses.

With all my love,

Gagul

Via e-mail, September 3, 2000:

Dear Dr. Hussain,

I was born and raised in Toledo so I have been reading the Blade *on the Internet and I just read your letter to Maryam and it really touched my heart. I sincerely hope that it won't be long before she and her family will be allowed to come over for a visit. You are very gracious despite the way our embassy has treated your loved ones. I just wanted you to know that your letter has been seen and read down here in Titusville, Florida and I will be praying that God will make a way for Maryam and her family to come and see you.*

Sincerely,

S.H.

Via e-mail, September 4, 2000:

Dr. Hussain,

You may remember that I wrote you two or three months ago, telling you that I'd lived in Lahore for three years and that I enjoyed reading your column.

I was sorry to read of the U.S. Embassy's failure to grant visas to your family. This incident is an example of the bureaucratic "power trips" we endure all over the world. The fact that an individual, even a congressman or congresswoman, has no influence over the "system" whatever it represents or wherever it's located is disheartening.

As a cancer patient I work hard on my own behalf to research and explore all treatment possibilities. My biggest roadblocks are the clerical staff who refuse to allow me access to the people or documents which could help me.

We have had our passports seized (once, in Africa, at gunpoint), been fined on trumped up charges, and generally been denied access to the person who could help us or give us the information that we seek on so many occasions, not only abroad but so often here in the U.S.

I realize that everyone has a job to do; how unfortunate for many that the "job" stands in the way of reason or humane treatment. I hope that you do try again and that you and your family can be reunited. I'd like to say that I know someone in the Embassy that could help, but . . . .

L.H.

Findlay

Via e-mail, September 7, 2000:

Dear Dr. Hussain:

On a trip north to visit relatives, I read your column about the problems your family has with the U.S. Embassy in Pakistan. As I'm sure you're aware, this problem of INS and embassy high-handedness is not unique to the U.S. offices in your family's country.

My wife is Colombian, and the process one must go through to obtain a simple tourist visa to visit the United States is remarkable for its callousness and lack of efficiency. All visas must be applied for in person at the embassy in Bogotá, regardless of where the person resides. The applicant must bring extensive documentation to prove that he or she is a solid citizen with resources in Colombia and the wherewithal to support himself/herself in the U.S. The applicant is interviewed at length by embassy staff regarding his/her intentions. For many people, particularly the elderly, this is terribly difficult. Though they often only want to visit relatives, they are forced to stand in line, regardless of the weather (the climate in Bogotá is cold and rainy) waiting for their appointments, and then waiting to collect the visa. If a visa is denied, there is little option for appeal.

I might add that the problem's roots are in Congress – and our legislators unfortunately reflect the biases, fears and ignorance of our citizens. I hope and pray for change and thank you for your efforts to educate people and show how we appear to the rest of the world.

Yours truly,

D.K.

Why is US foreign policy hostage to Israel?
January 12, 2009

The ongoing carnage in Gaza raises some disturbing and sobering questions for the people of conscious everywhere and that includes Toledo, Ohio. As of this time close to 700 Palestinian men, women, and children had died and three times as many had been injured.

The pivotal question is why Hamas, the ruling Palestinian faction in Gaza, resumed firing rockets into Israel after six months of relative calm following a cease-fire put in place in June 2008?

A ceasefire requires lack of hostilities between the parties. On November 4, Israel, in clear violation of the cease-fire, went into Gaza and killed six Palestinians who Israel declared were terrorists. That incident and an ongoing siege and blockade of Gaza were enough reasons for Hamas to resume hostilities against Israel. It was retaliation plain and simple. Israel has been preparing for this onslaught for the past six months and chose this time while George Bush is still president.

Ever since the withdrawal of Israeli forces and dismantling of illegal Jewish settlements from Gaza in September, 2005, the area has been under siege. A total blockade has turned the narrow coastal strip into a virtual prison where 1.5 million inhabitants depend on a trickle of humanitarian aid allowed by Israel. Mary Robinson, the former United Nations high commissioner for Human Rights called the ongoing situation in Gaza the destruction of a civilization. Her comments were made during the cease-fire.

In January 2006 Hamas won elections in Gaza in a fair and impartial vote. The US had, on the behest of Israel, declared Hamas a terrorist organization. As such they were denied their legitimate right to govern and to have the cooperation of the international community. If fighting for one's dignity, one's land and one's freedom is terrorism then most countries that became independent in the post-colonial era got there through terrorism. Even Israel's establishment as a sovereign state was based on many acts of terrorism against the British and the native Palestinian population. There is an extremely thin line between a terrorist and a freedom fighter. All one has to do is to look at the life of Menachem Begin, a terrorist turned prime minister of Israel.

It is no surprise that most Arab governments have sold their soul at the altar of the United States and Israel. Every time there is an incident like Gaza, and there have been innumerable in the past decades, they get together to make phony noises of solidarity that result in nothing. At a recent press conference at the United Nations, the Arab ambassadors went through the usual hand wringing, expression of frustration, their inability to effect change. Missing in the whole macabre spectacle was a conscientious Arab journalist with a sturdy pair of shoes.

Why is American foreign policy hostage to Israeli whims? It is for historians and writers such as John Mearsheimer and Stephen Walt, former Congressman Paul Findlay, former president Jimmy Carter, writer Norman Finkelstein etc. to analyze the phenomenon, which they have done at their peril. The question, however, begs for an answer. Why does an Israeli cause become an American cause? And why does a Congress elected by the people of this country become beholden to the interests of a foreign country?

Israel is the most powerful country in the Middle East whose survival is not threatened by rag tag bands of so-called terrorists. At the heart of Israeli actions is the determination to hang on to the occupied lands. All peace initiatives on a two state solution are bound to fail because of the dominant role Israeli right and the militant settlers play in Israeli politics. They are loath to give any land back to the Palestinians.

In the end Israel would rather see a fragmentation of Palestinian society, reminiscent of Apartheid South Africa, and allow them a measure of watered down and wholly dependent self-rule.

Surprisingly a great majority of the world has endorsed a two-state solution along 1967 borders in the form of the UN General Assembly resolutions. All Arab countries have endorsed it. Even Hamas has expressed its willingness to accept that broad solution. The only countries voting against the resolution are the United States, Israel, Australia and an atoll of small island nations in the pacific.

And finally where are the moderate voices of American Jewry? While there is a vigorous debate inside Israel about occupied lands, there is hardly any dissent in this country. Given the history of last 60-years, there must have been a few occasions when the people of conscious should have spoken out against the policies of Israel. Instead they always found reasons to blame the victims or remain silent.

One of my Jewish readers put it more succinctly by saying, in private of course, that if he ever raises a voice against Israel policies he will be crucified.

Via email, January 12, 2009
Dear Amjad,
As I read today's article, some of my grief over Gaza melted. Please continue with your astute writing, which destroys the myths, e.g, the 2 letters to the editor that I could not finish reading.
We are so grateful for your many contributions to the cause of peace.
Tom and Anne

Via email, January 12, 2009
I'll bet you made a fairly good living operating on infidels too stupid to know better all the while living the good life in a country you so obviously despise.
R.L.

Thank you for your comments. I am not judgmental of other people's faith. I believe every religion is deserving of our utmost respect. I conducted myself accordingly when I was practicing.
I wish you peace and tolerance.
Regards,
Amjad Hussain

Via email, January 12, 2009
Very strong and effective op-ed you wrote for today's blade, Amjad.
You are an important spokesperson for fair-minded Americans. Thank you.
Roland

Via email, November 11, 2008
Thank you for writing this column. it's past time for us to ask why our Congress is beholden to AIPAC and all things zionist. the rest of the world knows the USA bias towards Israel is criminal.

It is only when people would start talking and asking pertinent questions as you have raised in your e-mail.

Thanks for writing.

Amjad Hussain

Via email, January 12, 2009
Mr. Hussain,

In your column of today, Monday, Jan. 15, there is a glaring error, most likely the fault of the typesetter. I respectfully point out the words "people of conscious" should be "people of conscience." I wonder how many people will note it, or care. Thank you for your time, and expertise. I was glad to see the correct word, "effect" used later in the story, and the correct word "conscientious," as well. With the use of email, correct spelling is falling by the wayside, in my elderly opinion.

D.M.R.
North Baltimore, Ohio

Thank you for your correction and comments. I appreciate your insightfulness.

Regards,
Amjad Hussain

Via email, January 12, 2009
Dr. Hussain,

You are welcome, sir, and I thank you for your courtesy in replying. I think the teaching of English and Spelling is not being taught as thoroughly as it was in my youth. I am 80 and read avidly. I admire your accomplishments and wish you good luck in this New Year. – also good health. Good day.

DM.R.

Via email, January 12, 2009
Hi Amjad,

Sorry to hear you were not feeling well. Glad you're home and on the mend. I missed seeing you at the meeting. We had fun after the meeting watching the Marlon awards. They were quite entertaining, and it was good to be with the whole staff.

I read your article this morning in The Blade and appreciated your thoughts. I have been disturbed also that Jimmy Carter met with such resistance when he tried to remind us of the truth in his recent book. I'll be interested to hear what kind of feedback you receive from this community.

Stay well and hope to see you next time.
Debbie

Thank you Debbie for your note. I am sorry I missed the meeting. I heard it was a blast.

Regarding Gaza and broader Middle eastern issue, we need to keep talking about it. Unfortunately Americans have been duped by the slick propaganda. I have received an overwhelming number of e-mails supporting my views.

Regards,
Amjad

Via email, January 12, 2009
Dear Mr. Hussain,

I want to thank you for one more lucid article by you. It is so frustrating that our government is held hostage by Israel in our whole approach to problems in the Middle East and especially sad when it continues to cost the lives of so many in Gaza.

Do you know if Marcy Kaptur supported the resolution passed in the House of Representatives last week? I missed the news at the time and only know that Dennis Kucinich and 4 others did not support it. Marcy's office only would say they will send me information.

Sincerely,
L.J.

I have heard she supported the resolution. She is, like most of our lawmakers, between the hard and the rock. It still does not justify her appeasement of Jewish lobby.

I am grateful for your words of appreciation.

Please do write to the Blade and express your opinion.

Regards,
Amjad Hussain

Via email, January 12, 2009
I always enjoy reading your column in the Blade. The subjects you write about, their variety, and you point of view, not to mention the quality of you writing, are always very interesting and informative. Having said all this, I do believe that today's column is below your normal standards of fairness and objectivity.

I would not trouble you to go into a debate on your rhetoric on the issue, but in short it is much more complex than you seem to be saying, and there is plenty of blame for all the parties. The stew of Arab State interests (which are not all the same); Israeli interests; Palestinian Interests(there are many more than one of them), and those of Iran is one big morass. All this fed by historical racial and cultural interests makes this a real mess. To my way of thinking this makes the Indian and Pakistan dispute to look quite simple.

I pray for a solution to the conflict and hope to have the opportunity to meet you some day.
D.B.
Toledo

Thank you for your comments.

Most complex issues can be broken down in easy to understand parts. What I try to do is to look at issues in historic perspective and then render my opinion. I don't claim, never have, the last word of the issue.

I am grateful you took the time to write.

Regards,

Amjad Hussain

Via email, January 12, 2009
Dear Dr. Hussain:
I can only imagine that this column will receive some nasty blow back. I agree with your general premise that U.S. foreign policy has been hostage to Israel and I've asked the same question many times about our foreign policy with Cuba being hostage to Cuban-Americans.

Make no mistake, I am a supporter of Israel. That is, I support her survival within secure borders and I have tremendous respect for the accomplishments of the Israeli people. I do not support the way Israel treats Palestinians and tries to steal Palestinian lands. I have come to the conclusion, as you apparently have, that the peace process is hostage to extremists on both sides who seem to willfully work together to sabotage any chance at peace.

No where in writings spawned by the current crisis or in prior peace efforts have I seen much mention of two key elements of peace. I believe that until we have peace proposals that offer the Palestinian people both dignity and prosperity, they will have no incentive to stop enduring the privations caused by their miserable leadership. 60 years of privation has accomplished nothing but suffering, and extremism continues to grow. Hamas can not continue to fire rockets at Israel but it remains to be seen if Israel can stop them. You claim Israel is not threatened with its survival. That is the primary thing I must disagree with. I can't even imagine how frightening it must be for Israel to have Hamas firing rockets and to understand clearly that if those rockets could be based on the West Bank, no where in Israel would be safe. I'm quite sure that if Mexico launched rockets at El Paso, our reaction would be swift and violent.

This past week's Newsweek has an extensive article on what peace might look like, but it too fails to clearly offer dignity and prosperity in its solution. I wonder if you could explore how dignity and prosperity could be achieved along side secure and peaceful coexistence with Israel?

As always I look forward to your excellent analysis, even when I don't fully agree,

J.T.

Via email, January 12, 2009
Thank you! The whole situation is so very sad!

Via email, January 12, 2009
Hi,

Thanks for your column. I assume you will get a lot of negative response to it so here is a note of support and appreciation.

There are protests going on all over the U.S. against the Israeli massacre in Gaza, including in Boston where I live (we've been to several protests organized by Jewish and non-Jewish groups) but pro- test and dissent in general (and definitely on this issue) simply do not make it into the U.S. corporate media so you probably have not heard about them. I have many friends who write letters to the editor of the Boston Globe regularly on this issue and they are rarely published. Instead, endless pro-Israel letters are published, skewing perceptions so that the public believes the vast majority of those in the U.S. (including all Jews) support Israel no matter what.

Additionally, 10,000 protestors marched in Tel Aviv the other day (the video is on youtube).

Best,

Aida

Via email, January 12, 2009

Hello,

Well, I certainly hope you are asking questions rhetorically when you wonder why our country is so beholden to Israel. I think it might have a lot to do with the jewish population in the U.S. I always ask this question when people want to scold Israel and make the actions of Hamas somewhat legitimate: why is Hamas bringing a knife to a gunfight?

Hamas is profoundly outgunned, out manuvered, and surrounded. They also are destroying the infastructure of their people by picking a fight with Israel. They are bringing about the total destrustion of their people which is an ironic twist to their charter.

The situation over there is not simple, but Hamas doesn't seem to care that they will not win this and they are giving up their children's future for a stupid tit for tat fight against F-16's. Hamas is a death cult and really doesn't care too much for any prosperous future for their people.

A very good friend of mine said recently about pride, "I'm the first person to shoot themselves in the face to prove a point." Aptly put for this situation.

One of the things I find discouraging about your column is the tendency to cherry pick information to prove a point. You see what you want to see and not everything that is there. Makes for good reading, but I know you're much smarter than that.

What can I say, I'm a wishy-washy artist.

Much love,

Ron

PS I will be in town Jan 22nd and 23rd. If you'll have me, I'd like to stay at your place.

Via email, January 12, 2009
Assalamu Alaikum Dr. Amjad,
Nice piece of writing . . . it should cause a flurry of "feedback" from all fronts - I'll be interested in the follow-up/responses . . .
Insha'Allah, you and yours are in good health and spirits.
Salamat,
Khalid

Via email, January 12, 2009
Superb article doctor sahib! And very bold too. I am sure it will stir up some response in the Blade.
Sajjad

Via email, January 12, 2009
Dr. Hussain,
I am 59 yers old and like to think I am a person of history. I am of German heritage and have no connections at all to either Arab or Israeli points of view.
I write to let you know that I could not have written your article any better myself. It is everything I believe and that I feel. The only thing I would have added, although it probably wasn't the place, is that Isreal was created by driving the Palestinians out of their own lands to start with and that is what created all those terrible refuge camps I grew up hearing about as a youth. I always try to mention that when talking to others who want to take a stance on the problems of the middle east but have no clue on what brought them all about.
Your article was very well written Doctor. Keep up your good work and someday maybe even the united states will understand this portion of the middle easts problems, how it impacts what goes on over there, and what it will take to resolve it.
J.I.

Via email, January 12, 2009
Dear Amjad,

Thank you for your column in today's paper. You, as usual, have dealt with a thorny issue in a fair and insightful manner. There will be some whose noses will get out of joint, but the truth sometimes has that effect on some people. Bless you in all that you do.

On another matter, I am at the point where I am getting together the materials for the book on Arab Americans and I have a question about a reference you made to an editorial The Blade *published about Imam Khattab. I need to get permission from The* Blade *to reprint the editorial as part of your contribution, but I am unable to find any reference to it online. I think there is a typo in the date you cited (November 7, 2008) for the editorial. I would appreciate it if you could double-check and let me know what the correct date is.*

See you Thursday at the search committee meeting.

As ever,

Samir (Abu Absi)

Former Chair, Department of English, University of Toledo.

Via email, January 12, 2009

Dear Sirs; I read your column with great interest, as it is the topic of the day.

I do not get involved in world politic where as we have lots of politics and blood is being shed in our country and in our own city. I am sure you know that Political House in Peshawar is called Pukhtoon Khowa House now. To me that is Gaza .

Your column is very moving. Our Islamic Center organized a protest march in Albuquerque I was in the meeting of board.

There are 2 things come to my mind. No1. the demonstrations are taking place all over Europe, but I with limited excess and knowledge to world news I have not seen any protest marches in our Muslim countries. From Libya to Morocco. from Saudi Arabia to Qatar?

Secondly, we all know that Israel does not want to go on war because her country is always on the path of survival. Ahmidi Nijad wants to eliminate them from the world map. but this not my question. My question is knowingly, that Hamas is weak and unorganized why don't they use science's and do not fire on Israel's territories? They know they will loose, and have been loosing all the time. Who is behind them to do so?

Love
Irshad
Rio Rancho, NM

Via email, January 12, 2009
I have read many of your columns and generally they are good. I take exception with your views on the current battle in Gaza. If the Palestinians would quit bombing Israel every day, accept them as neighbors and quit hiding behind the skirts of women and children I am sure they would enjoy a good life, but I believe this will never happen. It is not in their nature and if they didn't have Israel to confront they would be fighting each other. America has no friends in the middle east save Israel. I am no a Jew nor do I have any relatives or friends that are Jews, this opinion has been formed by what I have seen in the news reports.
Sincerely,
M.B.

Thank you for your comment.

At times one is compelled to look deeper than what the news papers and other media decide to give us. I would strongly suggest that you read former Congressman Paul Findley's book (*They dare to speak up*) or Jimmy Carter's book (*Palestine*).

During WW II when Germany bombed London or when the allies bombed Dresden, the "culprits" were not hiding behind skirts. They were ordinary citizens who bore the brunt of savage attacks. That is exactly what is happening in Gaza today.

For you to think that it is in the nature of Palestinians to fight, how come there were no problems in Palestine before 1948?

I thank you for taking the time to write.

Amjad Hussain

Via email, January 12, 2009
Thank-you for your article regarding U.S. foreign policy regarding Israel. I wish the Blade *would allow comments to be posted. I am also questioning many government policies that involve trusting with unconditional support and never questioning things that are going on*

within the U.S. government. We not only trust and never question Israel, but we do the same with our finances.

We trust the FED and the Treasury Dept. on economic policy. We are expected not to question the new administration's policies as well, just trust that any decisions that are made will be good decisions. Is there no longer such a thing as prosecuting hubris?

Our Constitution was suspended under Bush's Patriot Act and our liberties may never be restored. That was done for our 'protection'. Habeas Corpus is suspended. Posse Comitatus is also suspended.

What is the policy on immigration? Does the U.S. have one? Ellis Island is no longer a touch stone for new arrivals, so is there any form of tracking system with regards to the U.S. population?

Great thought provoking article. By raising the questions you have, I wouldn't be surprised that in the near future, your contributions to the Blade were no longer needed.

I ask these things rhetorically, and continue to search for answers.
No need to reply.

Via email, January 12, 2009
Dear Dr. Hussian,

I read your latest editorial in the Toledo Blade regarding the Palestinian-Israeli conflict. I appreciate your courageous input and boldness as it most needed at this time. Thank you for your efforts and please continue to spread truth in this matter.

Via email, January 13, 2009
Tell your Hamas buddies to stop firing their missiles into Israel and abide by their own agreed-to cease fire. Then perhaps Israel would reconsider their position. But then, that wouldn't fit your agenda, would it.

I do believe that if terrorists (oh yes, I forgot, freedom-fighters) were firing missiles into southern California from Tijuana, Mexico or into the northern US from Toronto, there would be a strong US response.

Use your talents to persuade your Islamabuddies to truly seek peace. But then, if they did, they may just find it and that would not follow their agenda of destroying Israel.
R.J.

Thank you for your rather insightful and profound comments.

If truth be known I have never met any Hamas members. I also never met any members of African National Council either but wrote about the dehumanizing Apartheid policies of White South African government.

I wish you peace and blessings.

Amjad Hussain

Via email, 13 January 2009

DR. YOUR JUSTIFICATION OF HAMAS ROCKETS AND HAMAS REVEALS YOUR TRUE FEELINGS ABOUT AMERICA'S SUPPORT OF ISRAEL AND YOUR BELIEF THAT TERROISTS CAN PREVAIL.

THE MORE ISRAEL GIVES THE MORE THE RADICALS WANT AND THE ANNOUNCED OBJECTIVE OF DISTROYING ISRAEL BY HAMAS, HASBOLLA, IRAN AND OTHERS CAUSES ME TO WONDER WHAT YOU ARE: A PEACEMAKER OR CLOSET TERROIST ?

LOOK AT THE TRAINING OF CHILDREN AND WOMEN TO KILL CIVILIANS AND TELL ME HOW TO BELIEVE THE JEWS (I'M NOT ONE) ARE TO REACT TO EFFORTS TO KILL THEM.

NO WONDER THERE IS NO PEACE POSSIBLE IF HIGH GRADE PEOPLE LIKE YOU SAY AND BELIEVE WHAT YOU WRITE.

TELL YOUR FRIENDS TO LIVE PEACEFULLY AND THEY WILL ENJOY THEIR LIFE A LOT MORE THAN SHOOTING/ KILLING JEWS.

F.M.H.

Thank you for your comments.

I wonder who were you referring to when you asked me to tell my friends to live peacefully. Please do know that I do not know any Hamas member and have not met any. Similarly I never met any member of African National Council but I wrote about the plight of South African blacks under the Apartheid. I guess if telling the truth and showing a mirror makes me a terrorist then perhaps in your wisdom you should redefine what terror and brutality is.

I wish you well.

Amjad Hussain

Via email, January 14, 2009

SIR, I MEAN NO DISRESPECT TOWARD YOU BUT WHEN I HEAR OR SEE MUSLIMS SCREAMING TO THEIR FOLLOWERS, THAT KILLING INNOCENTS IN THE NAME OF GOD IS WRONG, THEN I WILL RESPECT THOSE OF YOU WHO WHO ARE NOT TERRORISTS BUT SEEM TO EXPLAIN AND JUSTIFY THEIR ACTIONS.

WHEN YOU AND MULLAHS SHOUT DOWN IRAN'S IDIOT THAT THE DESTRUCTION OF ISRAEL IS A CRAZY SELF DESTRUCTIVE GOAL, AND SHOUT TO HIGH HEAVENS "LET IT BE" AND WORK TOGETHER TO IMPROVE THEIR LIFE AND BE PART OF THE WORLD, NOT A SLAVE TO AN OLD BOOK WHICH IS SUBJECT TO MISINTERPRETATION, THEN SOMETHING USEFUL WILL BE DONE.

IF YOU SUPPORT THOSE WHO ADVERTISE THAT THEY WANT TO KILLS JEWS AND CHRISTIANS, THEN WHAT ARE WE TO BELIEVE ABOUT YOU ??

F.M.H.

There are a lot of assumptions in your statements.

I condemn terrorism and have been writing about it for a long time. I despise those who incite others to be violent and that goes for religious as well irreligious people.

I invite you to read my columns I have written against religious terrorism.

Peace,

Amjad Hussain

Via email, January 14, 2009
I LIKE MOST OF YOUR COLUMNS.
PEACE
F.M.H.

Via email, January 14, 2009
I agree with you on that one!
Even Jimmy Carter said Israel was justified in attacking Hamas

Via email, January 13, 2009
Dr. Hussain
I believe then Sir, that neither of us have the facts. "Sound bite"
indeed!
J.L.

Via email, January 14, 2009
Dear Dr. Hussain
The moderate voice of Jewery was stilled when the moderate
Palestinians lost the election to Hamas, who is hell-bent on destroying
Israel.
J.L.

It makes a good sound bite but the facts are otherwise. Even before
the victory of Hamas I did not hear any moderate voice from the Jewish
community here in Toledo.

Thank you for your comments.

Regards,

Amjad Hussain

Via email, January 13, 2009
Dear Amjad,
What has Israel done in Gaza that is different than what the United
States did in Iraq?

The voices of dissent are out there, "crying in the wilderness". But
they are drowned out by the deluge of complicit media. And where is
the justice? Muslims are constantly being asked, "Why don't you speak
out against violence?" But where are the Christians and Jews speaking
out against this violence?

I think that the chain goes like this. There are certain groups that
benefit from the current state of affairs. They are extremely powerful in
many ways. They can buy influence in governments around the world
for favorable laws and public money. Through direct ownership and
advertizing money leverage, the few media conglomerates that exist in
our world, waste our time with mindless drivel and propaganda. Truth
is not profitable for them. (The Blade printing your articles is an
exception)

President Eisenhower warned us about the military industrial complex. It is the most voracious consumer of public money on earth. It is a hammer always looking for a nail. Peace is its enemy. And now Israel has moved into the security industry. War is good for their economy. Pictures of the horrid wall are free advertizing. And what we are seeing is the worlds possible dystopian future of endless low intensity conflict and the security industrial complex.

What they do not have on their side is truth, human decency, informed public opinion, or desire for the common good.

Peace be upon them, Moses led a slave revolt. Jesus was executed by the Empire of his day. And Mohammed spoke a reforming truth that changed the world. They were truth bringers against the unjust powers of their day.

My prayer is that "Oh though the wrong seems, oft so strong, God is the ruler yet." (an old Christian song)

But we have to do our part. Thank you for writing this article.

Peace, Ed

Via email, January 13, 2009

Amjad Sahib Salamu Alaikum;

I have been receiving your articles . But I have not been able to reply because I was sick in bed. Your latest write-up " Gaza Carnage" is a forceful and strong statement, to say the least. Jazakullah khayrn. I have shared it with other friends of mine in Memphis.

MU

Via email, January 12, 2009

Sir

One can only give credence to your arguments if one gives moral equivalence to the Palestinians. Civilized people protect their women and children. They do not use them as human shields and they do not glorify them as suicide bombers. Wild animals in the forest have more respect for their young and protect them better than do the Palestinians. When Israel withdrew from Gaza, the residents had an historical opportunity to demonstrate to the world that they could construct a functioning society and be good neighbors at the same time. There are several miles of pristine ocean coastline ripe for the development of resorts, hotels and businesses. International investors would have flocked there to be part of such a venture. The PA was too corrupt to take advantage of this opportunity and Hamas, being openly dedicated to Israel's destruction, had no interest in helping its people achieve stable and progressive government. Gaza until the current military operation was not occupied--the West Bank is occupied because Israel cannot allow hostile forces so close to its heartland. Is there a solution? Perhaps. It would require a complete renunciation of the goal of Israel's destruction by Hamas, Fatah and Hezbollah, demonstrable proof of civilized governance by these organizations, rejection of all support from Iran and Syria, Israeli withdrawal from West Bank areas, trade agreements, exchange of ambassadors to the newly constituted Palestine and the goodwill on both sides to make it work.

S.S.

Jacksonville, FL. Former Toledo resident (UT '61)

Thank you for your comments.

The views you express about dignity and civility are right but what is good for the goose ought to be good for the gander as well.

I draw your attention to the terrorist attacks Jewish gangs carried out against the British and the native Palestinians leading to the establishment of Israel. I do not believe they considered Palestinians worthy of any respect or dignity. You must know that the British had a bounty on the head of Mr. Begin and that his visit to the US was opposed by none other than Albert Einstein.

It is an old adage that if you treat human beings like animals they would act like ones.

I am grateful you took the time to write.

Regards,

Amjad Hussain

What I have read of Menachem Begin's life in Mandate Palestine before Israel's independence, his struggle was against the occupying British authority – British soldiers, not civilians. Yes, I am familiar with Deir Yasin. There have been no occupying Israeli forces in Gaza since the pullout. I can justify the Palestinian struggle against Israeli forces in the West Bank but sending suicide bombers onto busses and into restaurants and public places is barbaric and is pure terrorism as

are rockets indiscriminately launched from Gaza. It eventually comes home to bite you back. This can also be seen in Iraq where the suicide bomber, originally applied against the Israelis in Israel is being used regularly by Arabs against Arabs. I wish I could see the end of it but I do not. When the Palestinian people accept the fact of Israel's permanence, this abject militancy should tone down and recede and perhaps a new generation on both sides not so inflamed by events can work out a peaceful and equitable solution. Thank you for the courtesy of your reply.
S.S.

We may disagree on many things but I agree with the last part of your statement:
When the Palestinian people accept the fact of Israel's permanence, this abject militancy should tone down and recede and perhaps a new generation on both sides not so inflamed by events can work out a peaceful and equitable solution.
Thank you for your comments.
Amjad Hussain

Via email, January 15, 2009
Dr. Hussain
It is important that we find and explore areas of agreement if the future is to hold any hope of resolution of this long conflict. Everyone benefits from peace and a chance to create prosperity. I may be in Toledo in late July for my wife's 50th high school reunion. Perhaps we can share a few moments over a good cup of coffee.
Sincerely,
S.S.

Via email, January 12, 2009
Good God (Jesus) what a pile of Mohammedan rubbish and al-Taqiyya.
Because the United States is a Judeo-Christian country, NOT Islamic - THANK GOD! The Middle East should still be Judeo-Christian but for 7th century AD false prophet Mass-Murderer-of-Jews-and-Christians Mohamet and his band of brainwashed marauding minions. Islam has always been the Religion of Terrorism:

Bukhari (52:177) - Allah's Apostle said, "The Hour will not be established until you fight with the Jews, and the stone behind which a Jew will be hiding will say. "O Muslim! There is a Jew hiding behind me, so kill him."

Bukhari (52:256) - The Prophet... was asked whether it was permissible to attack the pagan warriors at night with the probability of exposing their women and children to danger. The Prophet replied, "They (i.e. women and children) are from them (i.e. pagans)."

Bukhari (8:387) - Allah's Apostle said, "I have been ordered to fight the people till they say: 'None has the right to be worshipped but Allah"

Bukhari (52:220) - Allah's Apostle said . . .. 'I have been made victorious with terror.'

You see from the 2nd above quote in the Hadith that Mohamet had no compunction about killing children. And women. What a Hater. Sorry, no true Prophet of God murders people, or is genocidal (3rd quote from the Hadith above). What no-brainers. Mohamet's just a military Warlord who used "al-ilah" from pagan Arabian mythology to claim prophethood. "allah" doesn't exist. A "God" that commands "Kill the Infidels" and "Slay the Unbelievers" (Koran) for-all-time, never-ending, eternal mass-murder commands? Yeah, right. That's no "God," - that's a devil. Thank God "allah" doesn't exist (except in the minds of brainwashed Mohammedans).

Hamas is not a "so-called" Terrorist group - It IS an Islamic Terrorist group whose stated goal is to "destroy Israel." Israel has EVERY RIGHT to fight back against the Islamic Terrorists.

Bravo Israel, surrounded on all sides by Barbarians. Keep defending yourselves and your civilized country from them.

Best Wishes, and have a great day.

Thank you for your note. You raise important questions. However I would like you to read the Bible and see if there are passages that are brutal, incite to kill and are contrary to modern thinking. A letter to the editor of *Blade* a few weeks ago addressed this issue by a Christian minister Ed Heilman. I am sure you will be able to access the letter from Blade archives.

I wish you peace and blessing.

Amjad Hussain

Via email, January 14, 2009

I read your article with great, great dismay.

It is a true perversion of the facts.

The real truth is that HAMAS, a terrorist organization that has caused unspeakable horror both among the israelis and among it's very own palestinian people, never stopped firing, there has never been a real cease-fire to begin with. Alone, during the so-called "lull" in 2008, Hamas fired well over 200 rockets into sovereign israeli territory.

Second, there is no carnage in GAZA. This is pure and unabated propaganda.

By the PA's own statistics, 900 GAZANS have died in the current war against Israel, half of them civilians. For the benefit of the doubt, I will say that 500 of those dead Gazans were indeed civilians, in spite of the fact that is a common and cowardly technique used often by Hamas and also by Hisb'allah to hide it's fighters in civilian clothing.

There are 1.5 million residents in Gaza.

$500 / 1,500,000 = 0.033\%$, or one third of one tenth of one percent. That's it.

The normal mortality rate in the PA is 0.353% per year, or 10.6 times more than the current deaths due to the war.

So, the word carnage does not fit. And very few of those citizens would die were Hamas to a.) stop breaking the Geneva convention by using human shields and shooting from schools and nursing homes, and b.) would build air-shelters for it's people, as Israel does.

<u>Two days</u> after Israel left Gaza, terrorists were already putting up rocket launchers, in direct violation of the agreement struck between Eretz Israel and the PA. The synagogues in those Gaza settlements were burned to the ground. Lovely human behaviour from people who claim that their religion is one of peace.

"There is an extremely thin line between a terrorist and a freedom fighter."

No, there is not. A freedom fighter is willing to put on a uniform and fight by the Geneva convention. A terrorist kills as many civilians as he can take with him.

"Surprisingly, a great majority of the world has endorsed a two-state solution along 1967 borders in the form of U.N. General Assembly resolutions. All Arab countries have endorsed it. Even Hamas has expressed its willingness to accept that broad solution."

No, it has not. Read the Hamas charter and see that this is impossible. And you well know this. Or one Hamas official says he may consider the idea, only to have five others categorically say NO. Cat and mouse game, and totally facetious to boot.

And perhaps we moderate jews, which make up the vast majority of judaism, yes those of us whom muslims call dogs and pigs and the like, are tired of being fired upon by people who do not want peace nor are they willing to define peace the way the rest of the civilized world does it.

You want to free GAZA? Then help to eradicate HAMAS forever. Stop firing rockets into israeli territory and stop chanting for the deaths of jews everywhere.

The 1st amendment to the constitution guarantees your write to write this kind of hogwash that I just read, but it also gives me the right to call it out for the uneducated horseshit that it is.

You should be ashamed of yourself, truly. By writing this junk, you obviously do not understand the freedoms that our american forefathers fought so hard for, for you support a system, which, had it the power to do so, would destroy these freedoms. You truly disgust me. And the Toledo Blade deserves better than this.

M.R.

I am in receipt of your rather angry note but I am grateful that you took the time to write.

Palestinians and Israelis have their own narrative that could at times be self-serving. In Palestine a great injustice was done in 1948 when in the process of establishing the state of Israel a reign of terror was unleashed by the militant Jews. Revisionist history puts all the blame on victims who abandoned their homes voluntarily.

I believe there is an outline of a peace plan that most people would accept. This will involve giving up West Bank and Gaza and removing illegal settlements on Palestinian land. Israeli politics is in the clutches of 5% of electorate-settlers and right wing fanatics – and I don't think Israel would ever agree to cede even an inch of occupied land.

Here is my question and challenge: Why can't peace-loving Jews join other voices for a settlement according to 1967 borders?

It is one thing to think with a cool mind and fairness and quite another to foam at the mouth and spit at others.

Again I am grateful for your note.
Amjad Hussain

Via email, January 14, 2009
Mr. Hussain:

I say Mr. because you lack credibility to be called "doctor". But insults and disrespect aside your article about US - Israel relations is completely flawed. You ignore the constant barrage of rockets fired into Israel and you attribute every hostile act to Israel. There is NO legal basis for the Israeli government to allow the free access into Israel of any foreign person. Saudi Arabia does not permit Jews to step foot in their country. Jordan does not permit Jews to own land in their country but that is not a problem for you. Why does the West Bank have to be "Jew free" for there to be peace? Yet Arabs live in Israel and have more rights than in ANY Arab country? Why do you ignore the stated aim of Hamas to KILL every Jew and skewer Israel for defending itself? Why do you give Hamas a free pass for using women and children as human shields? Why do you ignore the FACT that when Israel allowed free entry to Arabs the suicide bombings were constant and now that the border is closed there are NONE? The Israelis ceded Gaza to the Arabs and left the infrastructure intact. A horticulture industry which contributed roughly 10%to Israel's GDP was paid for by left wing Jews so the Gazans had a source of income. The Arabs destroyed it and the houses that Jews lived in. There is only one obvious answer to your ignorance: you are as anti-semitic as those you defend. Who can expect an Arab to stand up against Hamas when you openly agree with them. Why don't you write about the failures of the Arab countries (except Dubai) to move forward with civilization? I have nothing but contempt for you and your kind. Until you can condemn your own kind for their evil acts you have no right to judge anyone; especially a country that has shown more moral character than ANY country on this planet. In my view you are Hamas!!! Rot in Hell.
    M.S.

Thank you for your comments.
It seems most of my detractors are reading from the same script that blames the victim for the carnage.

It is hard to carry on a civil conversation when people start foaming at the mouth.

I am not Hamas, I am not an Arab but I sympathize with oppressed and disenfranchized people everywhere and that included South Africans under the Apartheid.

From your last sentence condemning me to rot in hell, I assume you are a person of faith. In return I wish you peace and blessing.

Regards,

Amjad Hussain

Via email, January 14, 2009

You sympathize with oppressed people everywhere? I am not foaming at the mouth as you so immaturely wrote. BTW "disenfranchise" is not spelled "disenfrechized" but why would I expect a thoracic surgeon to know how to spell. I am wondering how many articles you have written condemning the incessant suicide bombings of Israelis prior to the fence being erected. Or about the oppression that Arabs in Arab countries suffer everyday from despotic rulers interested in their own greed. I am sure you have not written any. You are not anti-semitic; you are just anti-Israel. Oops some foam just got on my keyboard. Look in the mirror and if you can't find the time to write against Arab persecution of their fellow Arabs or about the lack of rights in any Arab country then you have no right to write about Israel's legal right to defend themselves. And if you believe Hamas, they are actually winning this war as they sit comfortably underground in their bunkers while the people they purport to govern are forced to act as human shields. Perhaps these same people should realize who their friends are and who their enemies are. Perhaps if people such as you were tor write against Hamas then maybe there would be a chance for true peace. Oh well this is like banging my head against the wall! There is zero chance for someone like you to view things objectively. It is time the World stops thinking that the Jews have a right to die for no reason. The World hates a Jew that fights back and does not walk silently into the gas chamber. 22 Arab countries and that is not good enough to overcome the fact that one tiny Jewish country exists. Arabs must be allowed to live in Israel but not ONE Jew is allowed to live in an Arab country. Women have ZERO rights in 22 Arab countries yet Israel is the apartheid state. It is incredible how you can state that you

*are motivated by defending the oppressed when you conveniently
ignore facts.*
   M.S.

   Via email, January 14, 2009
   AA,
   *I couldn't agree more. The world, including the self serving Muslim
nations watch silently as the carnage goes on. When you last wrote
about Terrorism in South Asia, I thought that although ,the events in
India were wrong, the way the western nations responded was so
different than when something of the sort happens in Pakistan. We
might have a flawed view of things & are probably not doing enough to
condemn extremist views . . it's starkly clear that the difference is only
of religion. This world ,sadly is becoming divided in two groups.*
   Shafaq

   Via email, January 14, 2009
   *I just read your article on Israel, and I just wanted to let you know
that you are a **supreme FAGGOT**.*
   <u>*Have fun being fucked in the ass by 72 demons in hell, you fucking
loser.*</u>

Dear Sir,
   I am thankful you took the time to send me an articulate response to
my column. As you probably know the last refuge of a demagogue is to
descend into the gutter.
   Peace and blessing.
   Amjad Hussain

   Via email, January 15, 2009
   *You are also going to experience a descending experience, one
straight to hell you muslim cocksucker.*

   Via email, January 14, 2009
   *Your article is being circulated around the nation! Here in NYC we
have spoken to over 15 officials and none will speak publicly even in a
"balanced" way including the suffering of Palestinians.*

By the way we here at MCN are starting up a program to discourage smoking among Muslims, funded by America Legacy and in partnership with IMANA.

Seeing that you are a doctor, I wonder if a bit later it might be possible to advise how to promote our project? I will attach our proposal and also for some basic visual see attached flier: http://muslimsagainstsmoking.wordpress.com/

A.C.

Muslim Consultative Network (MCN)

Via email, January 14, 2009

Islam will not stop until it rules the world. Any kind of truce is just them re-arming themselves. Most of us know the truth of jihad Dr. I wish they would take your column out of that shit newspaper.

R.P.

Thank you for taking the time to write. Obviously we are not in agreement.

Regarding the 'shit' newspaper, perhaps you will impress upon the management of the paper to take me off the pages.

Regards,

Amjad Hussain

Via email, January 15, 2009

Dr. Hussain,

I thought your article was thoughtful and well written.

I wish the US would strive to be a fair broker in a peace agreement, instead of a shill for Israel.

Via email, January 15, 2009

The truth is lacking from your editorial. An opinion based on incorrect assumptions must be wrong.

Hamas and other jihadist groups never stopped firing, either during the "truce", or since its inception in 1987. Hamas is an illegitimate regime, marked decidedly by terrorists. If Hamas fancies itself the ruling power in Gaza, it is either impotent or simply unwilling to control rocket attacks by other jihadist groups like Islamic Jihad, when Hamas itself is not behind the rocket fire. Moreover, Hamas' conduct

on many levels is not acceptable right down to its very reason for exist-
ing: the destruction of Israel in favor of a state governed by sharia law.

Rockets are not justified, and they are bad policy, of which Gaza's
residents are victims (along with being used as human shields by their
supposed champions). If those who cared enough inside and outside the
Israeli territories had desired, the amount of funding sunken into the
cause of "Palestine" could by now have turned those areas into
replicas of Dubai, Monaco, or Manhattan. Instead, they chose not only
war, but wars repeatedly conceived in suicidal overconfidence and
triumphalism, beginning with the initial attack of Arab countries on
Israel in 1948.

Islam as a political, social and economic ideology has proven time
and again to be an utter failure; producing corrupt dictatorial regimes,
grinding poverty, illiteracy and intellectual backwardness, misogyny,
hatred of the Other, debilitating fatalism, dysfunctional individuals,
institutionalized hypocrisy and nihilistic terrorists. **That is Islam.** *Islam*
= Evil.

Hatred renders its students intellectual cripples, brooding only on
past perceived injustices and lust for revenge. The purveyors of hatred
and victimology enslave their immature, naive disciples, captivating all
their creative energy to build a mentality of resentment. Thus the
"martyr!" The alleged oppressors, that these mentors assail, are
usually the ones trying to free the youth from their mental bondage.
Intellectually imaginative and inventive people belong to societies that
nurture lives of future potential and constructive achievement. All
societies and cultures have lamentable episodes in their history.
Successful societies, with constructive and happy people are those that
encourage their youth to rise above the abuse of the past, whether
intolerance, prejudice or racism, and create a laudable future. Hatred
and victimology create cerebrosclerosis. Hardship creates an
opportunity for achievement

Perhaps you don't know this or are unwilling to acknowledge these
facts.

Israel has the highest ratio of university degrees to the population in
the world. Israel is the only liberal democracy in the Middle East. In
1984 and 1991, Israel airlifted a total of 22,000 Ethiopian Jews at risk
in Ethiopia to safety in Israel. When Golda Meir was elected Prime
Minister of Israel in 1969, she became the world's second elected

female leader in modern times. When the U. S. Embassy in Nairobi, Kenya was bombed in 1998, Israeli rescue teams were on the scene within a day - and saved three victims from the rubble. Israel has the third highest rate of entrepreneurship - and the highest rate among women and among people over 55 - in the world. Relative to its population, Israel is the largest immigrant-absorbing nation on earth. Immigrants come in search of democracy, religious freedom, and economic opportunity. Israel was the first nation in the world to adopt the Kimberly process, an international standard that certifies diamonds as "conflict free." Israel has the world's second highest per capita of new books. Israel is the only country in the world that entered the 21st century with a net gain in its number of trees, made more remarkable because this was achieved in an area considered mainly desert. Israel has more museums per capita than any other country. Israel leads the world in the number of scientists and technicians in the workforce, with 145 per 10,000, as opposed to 85 in the U.S., over 70 in Japan, and fewer than 60 in Germany. With over 25% of its work force employed in technical professions. Israel places first in this category as well. Israel has the highest per capita ratio of scientific publications in the world by a large margin, as well as one of the highest per capita rates of patents filed. In proportion to its population, Israel has the largest number of startup companies in the world. In absolute terms, Israel has the largest number of startup companies than any other country in the world, except the US (3,500 companies mostly in hi-tech). Israel is ranked #2 in the world for VC funds right behind the US. Israel has the highest percentage in the world of home computers per capita. Other than the United States and Canada, Israel has the largest number of NASDAQ listed companies. Israel has the highest average living standards in the Middle East. The per capita income in 2000 is over $17,500, exceeding that of the UK. With more than 3,000 high-tech companies and start-ups, Israel has the highest concentration of hi-tech companies in the world (apart from the Silicon Valley). The cell phone was developed in Israel by Motorola-Israel. Motorola built its largest development center worldwide in Israel. Windows NT software was developed by Microsoft-Israel. The Pentium MMX Chip technology was designed in Israel at Intel. Voice mail technology was developed in Israel. AOL's instant message program was designed by an Israeli software company. Both Microsoft and Cisco built their only R&D

facilities outside the US in Israel. The city of Beer Sheva in Israel has the highest percentage in the world of Chess Grand Masters per capita – one for every 22,875 residents. On a per capita basis, Israel has the largest number of biotech start-ups. Israel has the largest raptor migration in the world, with hundreds of thousands of African birds of prey crossing as they fan out into Asia. Twenty-four percent of Israel's workforce holds university degrees – ranking third in the industrialized world, after the United States and Holland – and 12 percent hold advanced degrees. What have the Arabs done?
A.J.W.

Via email, January 15, 2009
Dear Amjad:
The sole reason for Israeli invation is not for the defeat and elimination of Hamas. This is a laboratory experiment for their planned next attack in Lenanon where Hisbollah is a formidable enemy. They are using controlled atmosphere of Gaza laboratory to learn methods and problems of unban warfare by invading and fighting poorly armed Hamas in their city in order to invade Lebanon next. This genocide is only a prelude for coming Lebanon war.
T.O.

Via email, January 15, 2009
AOA Agha Ji,
May you continue to be a voice of conscience and justice.
N.Z.
Memphis

Letter to the Editor, January 18, 2009
Dear Sir/Madam,
Kudos on having the fortitude to publish Dr. Hussain's article on 1/12/09. In the backdrop of the brazenly lopsided and unintelligent pro-Israel bias of the coverage of events in the US media, this op-ed is indeed refreshing. That said, I wouldn't be at all surprised if the savagely powerful Israel Lobby now sets about destroying Dr. Hussain's career as a courageous correspondent for your newspaper.
Also, somehow there appears to be a significant disconnect between the title of the article and the contents, leaving the casual reader

wondering if the editors might have gutted the original version for the sake of political correctness.

In any event, do keep up attempts at restoring some semblance of fairness to the coverage of matters Middle-Eastern.

N.A.

Medord NJ

Via email, January 22, 2009

I guess we should expect nothing less from you than accusations of the US being "held hostage" by Israel's "whims."

You may think that the Arabs would be happy with a two-state solution. You say "even Hamas has expressed a willingness to accept that broad solution." Well then, we should ALL be happy about that because we know Hamas is such a trustworthy organization! Hamas & Hezbollah (& Iran) have made it clear that their intention is to get rid of Israel altogether. They are not interested in allowing Israel to have ANY part of the land. Your mention of "rag-tag terrorists" not posing a threat to Israel is ridiculous! Indeed they are a threat to any civilized people! Hamas and their ilk are horrid evil uncivilized people who will not stop at anything. Of course you wouldn't refer to them as a powerful terrorist organization. Let me guess where you stood after 911 – I'll just bet you came out publicly and loudly condemned the evil scum of the earth coward terrorists – sure you did, and pigs can fly!

I know Who has given Israel the land. Many probably wonder how Israel has survived all the assaults over the years. God is in charge, Mr. Hussain, and your ranting and raving about the US stance will change nothing.

President BHO will likely change US-Israel policy but it will not change God's plan. God always has His Plan in place. It might even appear that the Arabs will win in the short term. But they won't win anything in the long term.

None of what goes on is a surprise to God. In the end, God's people will have all the land!

B.H.

Via email, January 22, 2009

I am left to wonder what people of conscious say about Hamas firing rockets into Israel for 6 months during a cease fire?
D.S.

Thank you for your comments.

I thought the ceasefire between June and November 2008 was observed by both parties.

Perhaps you are misinformed or mistaken.

Regards,

Amjad Hussain

Via email, January 24, 2009
Doctor,
You raised a very good point as to why U.S. foreign policy is being held hostage by Isreal. I'm not pro-isreali or pro-palestinian, just an American citizen who is appaled at what Isreal did in the Gaza Strip recently. It was nothing short of genocide. I love my country but I don't understand our blind loyalty to Isreal either.
I enjoyed your article. It was an insightful piece.
Sincerely,
TR

Via email, January 24, 2009
Dear sir,
Are you aware of the territorial discrepancy between Israel and Arab owned land in the Middle East? Israel occupies 1/800th of the Middle East and for you Arabs that is still too much. Israel has changed their borders 10 times to appease Arab radicals who claim "land for peace" yet where is the peace? Do you recall that 3 days after Israel expelled its own people out of the Gaza in Sept 2005, Palestinians using their newly acquired land as a launching point for kassam and kartusha rockets into Israel? How dare you blather about the "trickle" of humanitarian aid Israel has allowed to enter Gaza. Israel sent 60 truckloads of food and medical supplies into the area themselves. I doubt this letter will make any difference to you, but I wanted you to know that not everyone buys your line of bloviating. Shame on you. Your disinformation and lies are an outright disgrace. I cannot believe you're a doctor. The land owned by Israel is

equivalent to a matchbook on a football field and the rest of the field is owned by Arabs. Why don't you spend sometime discussing the human rights violations of your brothers in Saudi and Syria instead of betraying the Western democratic values that make your success possible. My grandfather served in WW1, my father in WW2, my great uncle saw severe fighting in the Pacific theater in WW2, I served during Desert Storm. Where have your fathers fought? How have they helped build the country you vilify. American foreign policy held hostage by Israel, please. It was Israel that helped save American lives by training them in desert combat and house to house fighting. How dare you criticize the Jews, a race that has amassed 10 times the amount of Nobel Prizes that Arabs with 10 times fewer resources and population. If you are so supportive of Hamas then I urge you, get out of the country me and my fathers built and go live with your friends, Hamas, Fatah, Al Asqa Martyr Bridgade, ad nauseum. Get out and live the way you think is right, where women are not allowed to show their faces in public and children are mere property and ignition switches.

L.J.

write back if you have the guts

It does not take guts to malign and insult. A civil discourse among educated people does not have to descend into a gutter.

The size of a country has nothing to do with how a country behaves or conducts itself. Please remember Israel is a country and thus is subject to criticism for some of its policies.

Kindly do know that I am not an Arab. I trace my roots to Indian Subcontinent and yes, members of my family did fight in WWII as part of British India army.

Now the interesting thing is that the rest of the world including Europe, Asia and South America has condemned the high handedness of Israel. I wonder what kind of label you will use to describe them?

In am truly grateful that you took the time to write and vent.

Peace.

Amjad Hussain

PEOPLE

Planting a new forest can be a task for one man
May 4, 1997

On the recent Earth Day, I was reminded of the story of a French shepherd and his oak forest. The story was related by Jean Giono, a French writer and outdoorsman.

During his wanderings in the mountainous Provence region of southeastern France in 1913, Mr. Giono came across a coal mining areas of abandoned hamlets, dried up streams and scanty vegetation. In the few remaining villages life was miserable. Under the perpetual grind, meanness and rivalry were common; suicides and insanity ran rampant.

Mr. Giono saw a lone shepherd in a small stone cottage reclaimed from the creeping desolation where he lived with his dog and a flock of sheep. Used to solitude the shepherd was not very talkative and his dog was equally quiet and unassuming.

The visitor watched with interest when the shepherd brought out a sack of acorns and poured out a heap across on the table. One by one he inspected the acorns with great attention and chose one hundred of the best. Next morning he put his precious sack of good acorns in a pail of water.

The shepherd left the dog in charge of the sheep and climbed the side of the mountain to a ridge a mile or so away carrying the pail of acorns and an iron rod. He would thrust the iron rod into the ground, put an acorn in the hole and cover the hole with dirt. With the greatest of care he planted the hundred acorns he had so carefully picked.

Elzeard Bouffier was his name. He was 55 and had moved from the low lands after the death of his wife and only son. He saw a devastated land and decided to reclaim it. He didn't know if the land was private or public. From the 100,000 acorns that he had planted in three years, 20-thousand had sprouted and he expected only half of those to live.

He was also growing birch trees in a fenced in nursery by his cottage. He was going to plant birches in the valley where he thought there was moisture few yards below the surface.

After a gap of five years Jean Giono, the visitor, went back to the area. The First World War had not disturbed the shepherd and he had continued to plant his trees. The oak trees now covered an area eight miles in length and two miles in its greatest diameter and some of them stood at man's height. And there were birch trees in the valley. The forest had retained enough moisture so that water now flowed in small streams. With trees and the water the wild life appeared. So did the government officials who, not knowing how the forest had sprung up, warned the shepherd not to light fire outdoors as it might endanger the forest.

In 1942, when he was 75, he built a shack eight miles from his cottage so he would not have to walk back and forth. Three years later he was planting 20 miles from his cottage.

People started coming back to live in what were the ghost villages. As the land transformed so did the people. Harshness and meanness of earlier times gave way to gentleness. Whispering soft breezes blew where strong naked winds used to howl. Ten thousand people now lived in the area. The forest echoed with the laughter of children.

In a short span of 35 years the shepherd had transformed a desolate land into a beautiful forest full of life. He had accomplished something that only gods are supposed to do.

Elzeard Bouffier died peacefully in a hospice in Banon in 1947.

Darwin suffers our stone-age thinking
September 6, 1999

Poor Charles Darwin. He got lynched again; this time in Kansas.

The Kansas School Board, in a split decision, eliminated the teaching of evolution in their state.

Kansas is not the first state to take a stab at science and rationalism. In the 1920s several states had banned evolution from the classroom. In 1968 the Supreme Court threw away those laws on First Amendment grounds. More recently, in 1987, the Court did the same to laws in Arkansas and Louisiana that required the teaching of "Creation Science" in public schools.

In a creative legal maneuver, the Kansas School Board did not ban the teaching of evolution but simply eliminated it from the curriculum. It could still be taught on demand. No doubt this Stone Age thinking will be challenged and this latest assault on science will be thrown into the dustbin of history.

The unholy alliance between religious zealots and opportunistic politicians would be laughable, were it not so detrimental to the education of our children. When the zealots tout their simplistic and literal interpretation of the Bible, politicians are always in tow to say a loud "amen." Our environment and science-friendly Vice President Al Gore is a good example. With an eye on next year's presidential elections, he has nodded approval of the Kansas decision. The demands for prayer in school is one thing; turning the clock back to the Dark Ages, quite another.

When Charles Darwin, a 22-year old English naturalist, boarded the ten-gun brig *Beagle* in 1831, he was a firm believer in the story of creation. He was invited by the fundamentalist captain of the ship in the hope that a traveling naturalist might gather geological evidence to refute the evolutionary views that were beginning to shock the religious believers in Europe. For more than five years, through 40,000 miles of travel, some through almost inaccessible lands, Darwin studied animals, plants and geological formations in South America, the Islands of the Pacific and South Atlantic, Australia and South Africa.

He was amazed at what he saw.

He found marine fossils at 12,000 feet in the Andes, saw woodpeckers in a land where there were no trees and observed geese with webbed feet that never enter water. He could have dismissed his observations with the catchall phrase that this is how God has willed it. But he saw a much bigger canvas where the Garden of Eden occupied the entire world and in that Garden were diverse life forms that had evolved from a common source.

Upon his return to England in 1836, Darwin studied and sifted through the voluminous material he had collected. It took him another 23 years to publish his now famous book *The Origin Of Species* in 1859. The book was sold out on the first day of publication.

The opposition to his epic theory was instantaneous. In disbelief the wife of the bishop of Worcester exclaimed, "Descended from apes! My dear, let us hope that it is not true, but if it is, let us pray that it will not become generally known."

It did. And it transformed the world into a huge classroom where inquisitive biologists, geologists, paleontologists and anthropologists kept finding the missing pieces to the great puzzle of how life evolved on our planet. For over 140 years Darwin's work has stood on its merit and has been called the most fundamental of all the intellectual revolutions in the history of mankind.

Science and religion are two distinct but intertwining disciplines. One is based on reason, inquiry and facts. The other seeks to explore spirituality and helps understand the philosophical basis of life. They are not contradictory or mutually exclusive.

But the Kansas School Board, in their medieval wisdom, thought otherwise.

Via e-mail, September 6, 1999:

Isn't it interesting, letters to The Blade *are limited to 300 words while rebuttals are accorded 2 . . .4 . . or 100 times that limit. It took you some 700 words to repeat Darwinian GIGO you were told or read. You cannot personally testify to or verify Darwin's original studies or findings. You accept the evolutionary concept on faith. So much for intelligence, or ability to recognize truth or rationalize. Possibly you should question or review the validity of your credentials or motives...*

In your article in The Blade *on 09/05/99 you used the following derogatory descriptions of non-evolutionists: stone age thinking, medieval wisdom, zealot, unholy alliance, opportunistic, denigrated.*

Christianity: simplistic.

Any more denigrating adjectives? Does this denote integrity and responsible professional writing? It seems to me that you are the illogical and disturbed antagonist.

The events or scenarios you excerpted, for supposed proof of evolution, illustrate the paucity or falseness of the evolutionary ideas and position.

Provide proven, valid, verifiable, specimen, evidence of true evolutionary change from the beginning to the present. If you cannot do that, then admit your beliefs and fantasies are not all that important. In addition our children will be spared the brainwashing and exposure to perverse fables.

Evolution is subject to "reducio ad absurdem" to the nth degree. Review your evidence and admit the truth.

"qwintus"

Via e-mail, September 6, 1999

Please write in your next column, exactly what "facts" about the missing links in Darwin's Theory of Evolution have been found. Have these facts been replicated by the scientific community you wrote about? Five definitive examples will be enough for me to make an educated decision to "believe" in Darwin's Theory of Evolution (that all living things evolved from a single organism).

Unbeliever in Bowling Green,
J.O.H.

Via e-mail, September 6, 1999:
Dear Dr. Hussain,

Congratulations on an excellent editorial. I agree with everything you wrote. Please keep pressing the ideas you wrote about, especially to politicians and religious leaders who keep their minds closed and try to close the minds of others too. Thank you,
K.V.O.

Via e-mail, September 20, 1999:
Hello,

I liked your article on Darwin at the PNS site. I am a graduate student in astronomy and I am involved in teaching a course on critical

thinking and revolutionary ideas in science. When we talk about Darwin, we generally have 1 or 2 students get up and leave. But the majority (35-40) stay and appreciate his ideas.
S.H.

Via e-mail, October 1, 1999:
Dear Dr. Hussain,

I was going through your article in Pakistan Link, and found your view liberating. However, I must tell you that a few of the paragraphs are taken verbatim from The Origin of Species *by Charles Darwin, mostly from the preface and general introduction to the book. It would have been more appropriate if you had provided proper reference for unsuspecting general readers. General readers would take it for granted that some of those phrases as your own, which they are not.*

Hope you would add little correction to your article, and make it appear more original, by providing necessary reference.
Thank you and regards,
S.B.

Dear friend:

Thank you so much for your note.

Those passages were in quotation marks when I transmitted my piece. As you probably know sometimes quotations marks change to numerical letters during electronic transmissions. Those were most likely deleted during editing.

Your point is valid and I must be more careful in my quotes.

I am grateful that you took the time to write.

Sincerely,

S. Amjad Hussain

Via e-mail, October 5, 1999:
Dear Amjad,

I came across your article, "Darwin again suffers our stone-age thinking" dated September 5,1999, and as kindly as I can put this, you are sadly misinformed, at least as far as can be divulged from your article.

First of all, the Kansas State Board struck only MACRO-evolution from the required curriculum – MICRO-evolution is still required, and

MACRO-evolution can still be taught if the local school boards so desire.

This much you sorely misreported in your article. Your personal views on the actual debate surrounding evolution are another issue. No scholar of any sort could debate the occurrence of MICRO-evolution. It happens. It is observable. MACRO-evolution is not. It has much greater implications and is the real source of debate today. Plain and simple, there is NO substantial evidence to support it. In fact, the most widely known documentary evidence in the evolutionist's playbook is the infamous finch-beak study which is merely a well-documented case of MICRO-evolution, which also by the way has since reversed itself, but that isn't reported in most outlets either. And though many will make claims that evolution is the foundation of biological sciences, it violates a most fundamental "law" of science, the Second Law of Thermodynamics. The fossil record has produced not a single "missing link" and anthropological and paleontological "finds" have time after time been proven to be frauds and/or of laughable speculation. Indeed, you offer none of these "facts" in your article, though you state that the THEORY, like all scientific theories, is "one based on reason, inquiry, and facts."

On the other hand, there is mounting evidence to support the theory of intelligent design. Try, for instance, to explain how Darwin's "natural selection" accounts for the "development" of an eyeball, which provides no benefit to its parent body until it has "attained" a level of irreducible complexity. Or, how do Darwinian mechanisms account for the semantic character of biological information and biological information processing systems? The root of these questions are more than unanswerable by the Darwinian mindset; it is evidence for intelligent design.

Evidence for intelligent design will not go away because it is truth and because it is all around us. We are all without excuse. I urge you to reconsider and explore the full body of evidence out there – it could have serious implications for your eternal destiny.

Regards,
M.M.

Thank you so much for your note. The debate is old and the arguments pro and con older still. I do not think science can come up with the kind of evidence that will satisfy the creationists.

I am a practicing Muslim and have a firm belief in one God, the creator and sustainer. Evolution does not negate His presence. I am very grateful that you took the time to comment.

Sincerely,

S. Amjad Hussain

Woman touched community with spirit
January 19, 1997

Virginia Secor Stranahan died two weeks ago. She was scion of the pioneer Secor family that helped found our town. Her life and her work were as that of the French shepherd Elzeard Bouffier who single handedly planted a forest in the Provence region of southeastern France in the early part of this century. As the shepherd, Mrs. Stranahan took an idea, nurtured it and lived to see it blossom.

The story of Virginia Stranahan's multifaceted and unconventional life is fascinating. It is difficult to comprehend her vibrant and full life and it is equally difficult to draw a circle around it.

She attended exclusive schools and graduated from Smith College. Her marriage to Duane Stranahan in 1929 brought two prominent families of this area together. It was a life of charm and privilege and would have continued that way had it not been for her overwhelming urge to share her wealth and herself with the community.

She was raised by parents who fervently believed in civic service and passed on that tradition to their children. Public service and the use of private wealth for public good became part of her creed. As her son Stephen Stranahan recalls, commitment to public service was passed along with potatoes at the family dinners. Public service was as much part of her life as were skiing, tennis or traveling to remote places like Antarctica or working on a farm in Norway.

The sharing and serving started early on in her life. She helped her mother in founding the visiting nurse association. She served on many institutional boards including Maumee Valley Country Day School and Bowling Green State University and helped found the junior league and league of women voters. But her definition of sharing went well beyond the narrow and limiting definition of public service.

It started out in bits and pieces soon after the Stranahans bought twelve acres of river front property in Perrysburg in 1940. First it was an invitation to the neighborhood children to enjoy the grounds. When a potter came to teach her children, neighbors' kids were included too. A summer camp, Hob Haven, was started. Over time beehives were added, an arts center started and a mushroom shaped geodesic planetarium brought from Colorado.

Thus over time slowly and methodically, some say serendipitously, the sprawling property was transformed into a marvel of hands-on nature and art center, a park and a retreat, where a visitor could walk through the trails, watch birds, study bees and examine all kinds of plants under the geodesic dome. The property at 577 East River Road became the 577 Foundation, and was entrusted to the community in perpetuity.

She wanted that place to be a place to come to. "If I didn't do this," she once observed, "I'd just be a little old lady sitting on the edge of the Maumee." Considering her insatiable intellectual curiosity and tenacious benevolence, that was never an option for her. Like the French shepherd, her life was a mission and she lived it accordingly past her 90th birthday.

On a snowy morning a few days after her passing, family and friends gathered at her spacious home at 577 East River for a memorial service. Family members and friends talked about Virginia's legacy and related touching and heart warming stories of the remarkable woman. There were many in the audience, this columnist included, who had never met her but had been touched by her spirit.

"It is something to able to paint a picture, or carve a statue," wrote Henry David Thoreau, "and so to make a few objects beautiful. But it is far more glorious to carve and paint the atmosphere in which we work, to affect the quality of the day. This is highest of the art."

In so many ways, Virginia Stranahan fit that description.

The "doctor" dispenses self-righteous advice
July 23, 2000

I cannot figure out Dr. Laura Schlessinger. The other day she was talking to Mark, a 30-year-old alcoholic gay man who has AIDS. Instead of berating the "sinner," she was civil and a bit sympathetic to the hapless man.

I could not believe she was the same self-righteous Dr. Laura who would not cut a millimeter worth of slack to working moms, gays, lesbians, or anyone who does not subscribe to her gospel of morality.

By definition, self-righteous people do not change their minds or their stripes. So why this newfound compassion?

I do not know for certain, but it might have something to do with the controversy over her forthcoming television show on CBS. According to newspaper reports, many advertisers, including Procter and Gamble, Geico Insurance, Xerox, and Toys 'R' Us have pulled out their support. The show will debut on Sept. 11. Why does this 53-year-old, sharp-tongued diva of daytime radio invoke such passionate response in people? Because while preaching a gospel of tolerance she berates, cajoles, and shames her callers with the gentleness of a sledgehammer.

She labels gays and lesbians as biological errors, dysfunctional and deviant. When the Gay and Lesbian Alliance against Defamation responded to her venomous uttering, she was devastated. She said she cried more times than she would like to admit. But hers is a self-inflicted pain.

For three hours every weekday, Ms. Schlessinger dispenses her sound-bite-sized advice to the confused multitude who call in to seek her advice on such monumental problems as who to invite for a family get together, how to deal with stepchildren, or how to deal with having a child out of wedlock.

In a terse one-sided conversation, she tells them to get a life and live it as God (her god) had intended them to live. In her black-and-white view of life there is no discussion, no argument, no doubts, and definitely no room for mitigating circumstances. Dare to question her and she gets testy and belligerent.

Considering her past, it certainly takes guts to do what she does. After all, not many people have the chutzpah to condemn others for indiscretions in which she herself has indulged. She has, by her own confession, indulged in premarital sex and posed nude for the camera. Her revealing pictures are posted on the Internet. While she condemns working mothers, she herself is one.

Her qualifications are also in question. The "doctor" in Dr. Laura comes from a doctorate in physiology. It probably qualifies her to teach human physiology or biology. But to preach and psychoanalyze under cover of an unrelated doctorate is not only dangerous, it is fraudulent. One wonders about her staying power and the staying power of other purveyors of intolerance on radio and television.

From Rush Limbaugh to Howard Stern, the airways are awash with intolerance and bigotry. Such shows always attract the curious, the insecure, and the mindless. The more outrageous the show, the better the ratings.

Dr. Laura claims to be "the lone voice standing out there for Judeo-Christian principles." Apparently compassion, understanding, and acceptance of others are not part of her abridged scripture.

Via e-mail, July 23, 2000:

Dr. Hussain,

Your argument against Dr. Laura is old and trite. Why does the Blade *let you get away with writing such over-used, boring vitriol? Her detractors have been criticizing her the way you did in your column for years. Where have you been? Perhaps you could spend your time writing unique stories that would in fact further the very socializing you claim Dr. Laura limits: understanding, compassion, and tolerance, instead of babbling negatively about another.*

Furthermore, how dare you claim that I am insecure and mindless because I am interested in listening to Dr. Laura or Rush Limbaugh. Who's the intolerant one now, "doctor?"

D.J.

Austin, TX (former Toledoan)

Thank you so much for taking the time to write. Obviously we disagree on Dr. Laura. I have been listening to most of the "shock jocks" on radio and television. I am appalled at their brazenly bigoted views. Now those in the choir would most certainly say amen to whatever these hosts dish out but there are others who are not amused by their views. We mortals have been at it for over 5000 years and still cannot figure it out.

Life is a bit more complicated than clearly demarcated heaps of right and wrong. I apologize if I offended you but I stand by what I wrote.

I sincerely thank you for writing.

Yours truly,

S. Amjad Hussain

Via e-mail, July 24, 2000:

I recently found it necessary to chastise Mary Lou Johanek for being a lazy commentator when she blatantly misrepresented some facts about Rush Limbaugh that were easy to check out. Columnists are entitled to their opinions, but are not entitled to "make up" facts.

I share some of your opinions on Dr. Laura Schlessinger's self-righteousness.

However, there are many facts that you have misstated, probably because you have not listened to her enough, or have not taken the trouble to read her many books on morality.

Firstly, I do not believe that her Orthodox-Jewish morality is much different than yours or mine. As an advocate of children she is somewhat dogmatic about one or the other parent "being there" for the kids in their formative years. Do you disagree? She does not define the stay-at-home parent as being the mother, as many critics, including you, seem to think...

It is true that she was not brought up religious because her Jewish father and Catholic mother were not religious. She was also promiscuous in her early youth, and had a brief marriage before she was twenty. She had an epiphany along the way during which she became an observant Jew, and changed her ways, and met and married her current husband.

There is no evidence that she has been immoral since then, so her critics, including yourself, are reduced to demonizing her with the cheap-shot tactic of citing her early years, giving her no credit for realizing her mistakes and changing her lifestyle...

Less than 1% of people are reported to be gay, which is Dr. Laura's rationale for calling their BEHAVIOR deviant, i.e. different from the norm. I don't think you will find any evidence where she called the individuals deviant, as you have written in your column...

Your unfamiliarity with the specifics of her beliefs on gays is probably why you were surprised that she showed "compassion" to the alcoholic, gay man with AIDS. Though she is often blunt with people, she often shows compassion, especially with people who are seriously trying to improve their lives.

Dr. Laura always asks people to study and understand their own religion. I have heard her talk several people into giving their own religion a chance rather than change their religion because they do not understand their own religion. So you indulged in another cheap shot with your comment, though you well know that there is virtually no difference between the moral teachings of the Qur'an and the Torah. In fact, most of your prophets are the very same people . . .

M.G.

Via e-mail, July 27, 2000:

Dr. Hussain,

I could probably start my letter with the same name calling of you, that you direct at others. However, I am above that. You are just one more reason I quit reading the editorial page of the Blade *on a regular basis. It is constantly filled with unqualified, so-called journalist like you. The list is endless. And why is it that you, as a left-wing liberal, must use labels and name calling when speaking of others who you don't agree with?*

Now, I am certainly not a defender of Dr. Laura, far from it. But her staying power is not challengeable, even if she might be a purveyor of levels of intolerance in your eyes. What really pissed me off was your combining the names Rush Limbaugh in the same breath as Howard Stern. Sir, you couldn't carry Rush Limbaugh jock strap! Your evident dislike for him only shows your dislike for the truth, as all liberals fear.

Furthermore, to call his listeners as only the curious, insecure and mindless is an insult to my intelligence.

I only hope, for the well being of your patients, that your surgical skills are above your liberal, left-wing writing skills.

D.L.D.

Thank you so much for your e-mail. It is apparent we look at things with different glasses and do not agree with each other.

I write with conviction and passion. I also do the background research on the subject I address in my columns. In the case of Dr. Laura, Rush Limbaugh and Howard Stern, I have spent years listening to them. In fact I was listening to Limbaugh when he was not a household name. Therefore permit me to say that I stand by my words.

I am not a left leaning liberal. In fact it is rather difficult to squeeze people in cubby holes with defined parameters. I stand for equality, respect, compassion and understanding. Certainly these are the attributes that all religions and cultures teach.

Regarding surgery, I do the best I can. I have been in practice for over 25 years and have had good relations with my patients and their families. Whether my skills as a surgeon are better than my skills as a writer is hard for me to judge. The views expressed in my words are out in the open for every one to judge. Two-thirds of those who wrote about Laura column agreed with me.

It was very kind of you to take the time to write. It is the hallmark of a civil society.

Sincerely,

S. Amjad Hussain

Via e-mail, July 23, 2000:

Thank you, doctor, for your thoughtful article about Dr. Laura in the Toledo Blade. *Although we are Californians, we have relatives in the Toledo area who need to hear messages such as yours.*

Many thanks, keep them coming!

Gary and Julie

Chico, CA

Via e-mail, July 24, 2000:

Dear Neighbor:

You describe Dr. Laura as "self-righteous." This has become the "politically correct" label for anyone who defends traditional morality.

She has not said she was any saint, and I would describe her as "abrasive" and "abrupt" but I have always enjoyed her show when I have to drive in the morning. And I am not "mindless."

She IS sometimes rude and impatient and other times compassionate and understanding . . ., Perhaps it is PMS with her – I have thought so at times – or maybe it is simply because she is not a Christian with what I call "Christian temperament," but an orthodox Jew. (It is my observation that there are four characteristics of Christians – Christian temperament, Christian faith, Christian convictions and Christian disciplines or lifestyle. Not every Christian has all four, but should.) However, I have never heard her be rude to gays about being gay. She is sort of rude as she points out the fact that most solutions to human dilemmas are SIMPLE and obvious except for our willful desire to do what we want to do rather than what we OUGHT to do . . .

Christ also says sin has eternal consequences and he did not change the definition of sin which was shared by Jews and Moslems alike. As for sex, he said a man is to leave his parents and CLEAVE to his wife – not wives plural and not harems and not same-sex spouses. Adam and Eve were God's ideal, necessary to start the human race, and He gives us no alternatives . . .

Don't you think you sound "self-righteous" in your attack on Dr. Laura and her audience? In your attack on her view of homosexuality? You are saying that you are more compassionate and therefore more righteous than she. Maybe it is not compassionate to encourage homosexuals in a lifestyle that has been labeled recently by the CDC as "high-risk" – any male with male sex behavior was categorized "high-risk" along with any promiscuous conduct, IV drug use, etc. If the ancient prophets truly wrote God's Word, then it is NOT compassionate to make people feel that being gay has no eternal, dastardly consequences along with the well-documented health risks in the here and now . . .

Not that I think it is appropriate to say God "hates" homosexuals. The Bible clearly says it is the same-sex acts which God hates – because they are against the body's design and purpose. The purpose is not to have orgasms any way one can think up but within the context of marriage and for the purpose of godly oneness and procreation. Sex is pleasurable for a purpose – and heterosexual monogamy, as God designed it, is HEALTHY. All the human-designed deviations from God's ideal are NOT healthy. So why is an MD like yourself seemingly encouraging the lifestyle? . . .

As for Dr. Laura's degree – she earned it. Even though hers is not in psychology, Dr. Dobson's is (of Focus on the Family – he used to be on staff at UCLA) and also Dr. Paul Cameron's (of the Family Research Institute, which has printed several objective articles in scientific journals on homosexuality research. Both say there are many who successfully become heterosexual after years in the gay community . . .

We are told that Social Security as it is will collapse because there are not enough workers to sustain the aging population. Would that be so if men were making babies with women instead of bed-hopping with each other? Would it be so if we had not aborted millions of people since 1973??

The Religious Right is not called RIGHT for nothing. And they are certainly no more "self-righteous" than the "Irreligious Wrong".

I am not being self-righteous – I just have a strong faith and yes, confidence, that the Bible is true. We are saved by Christ's atonement on the Cross – it is His work and not ours that justifies us in the eyes of the Heavenly Creator/Father. Nevertheless, He did tell us we need to repent and to do that we are accountable to agree with God about the nature of right and wrong and are accountable to strive to be worthy of the free gift of salvation we have.

To truly love my neighbor is to wish that you would come to know Christ as the living Lord and Son of God. For if the Gospel of Christ is true, He is the only way to the Father. Today, we are told that it is bigotry to believe that our religion is the true religion. Bigotry is when I HATE you for not agreeing with me and refuse to let you have the same liberties and benefits I have. Just saying that Christ is the Truth and homosexuality is sin – that's not bigotry.

Sincerely, your neighbor,
B.R.

Thank you so much for your note. It is always a pleasure to hear from you. Just for the record I am a practicing Muslim and am a heterosexual. I am also a man of science.

Almost 10% of the population (some will say less than that) is gay. It is how they were born. They have no control over it. I do not think I have the right to say that they are aberrant, deviant or less than others. What they do in the privacy of their own home is not my business. I think God is compassionate, understanding and forgiving. It is between the person and Him. For Dr. Laura and her followers to pass judgment on them is wrong.

You say that our salvation is only through Jesus Christ. Suppose I say salvation is only through Islam. Wouldn't that create a conflict between you and me? We could never prove the other person wrong. We both could quote from own scriptures to prove our own point of view. And we both could be equally right or equally wrong. I have no difficulty with the Judeo-Christian values. The values are very close to what I believe in. But I do not condone the likes of Dr. Laura berating others who happen to disagree with her or subscribe to different values.

I do not promote different lifestyles, as you seem to say; I let them be and do not condemn them. Your concluding paragraph is amusing. You were kind to invite me to Christianity. By doing that you assumed that the faith I believe in is not as good as yours and that I can only be saved through your faith. This is pretentious. Incidentally my faith dictates that I respect all other religions even if those religions are at variance to my own.

Thank you, once again, for taking the time to write.

Sincerely,

S. Amjad Hussain

On a quiet summer day, personals open new world
August 13, 1997

Whittling away a long summer afternoon can be taxing and exhausting. After reading few hundred pages of an action packed thriller, assorted magazines and the daily newspaper I realized that the *Wheel of Fortune* and Vanna White were still three hours away on the evening television. It was in that somnolence that I discovered a section of the newspaper I had not paid much attention to in the past. I discovered "Personals." It made the most exciting and stimulating reading.

For those of you who are ill informed about certain parts of your daily paper, "Personals" or "The Meeting Place," as the section is called, is the repository where for a fee the lonely (and perhaps not too lonely) flirt with the idea of finding a companion, a friend, a match or a lover. It is a picture gallery of thumbnail sketches where eager and willing people seek out other eager and willing people. Browsing through the section, I was reminded of the elaborate courting and mating rituals among the birds and other animals on Discovery Channel. The "Personals," however, give you only a glimpse of the plume or the comb and leave a lot to imagination. Armed with a vivid imagination the seekers walk through this unique market place that is the computer age version of a fruit stand, a meat market, a diary queen and a fashion parade.

There are obvious differences in the way women and men advertise. Women claim to be decent, upright, sensitive, caring and honest. They also claim other equally desirable attributes like fun loving, sense of humor, and being down to earth. Not too down to earth, I hope. Too much down and there is danger of being walked on or trampled over by those who are not that close to the ground.

Men on the other hand are not into the sensitivity thing. They, like the birds, lay it out, in bold colors, what they have to offer: sports, wealth, status, athletics, outdoors, and intelligence. Yes, intelligence. Men in these ads seem to think they have corner on intelligence and smarts. Little do they know.

Most personals tend to be monotonous Xeroxed pen sketches. But occasionally, one comes across a zinger. Here is one:

"Divorced, overwhelmed, fat, sassy mom of three troubled children in search of distinguished professional to save me from my miserable existence. Co-dependency a must. All responses subject to approval of ex-husband."

This could qualify as the ultimate truth in advertising. I feel sorry for the guy who, while carrying on this heavy rescue mission, will have to be anointed by the mission controller – the ex-husband. Here is an example of male colors:

"Reasonably intelligent male, 68, in good health, like(s) exciting things, home, romance, cooking, birds and ladies. I know there is some-one for me. Is it you?"

I hope not. Who would want to be cooked along with the bird? Instead of a tenuous comma between cooking and birds, this reasonably intelligent man should have placed an unambiguous period. Then there was this spartan ad, to the point and direct. No colorful plumes here:

"Man on a mission with God, seeking a woman for friendship and companionship. Hallelujah!"

This was my first introduction to the underworld of romance and mating. I had barely scratched the surface when it was time to watch Vanna White turn letters on the *Wheel of Fortune*. But before long I must visit other parts of the "Market Place" also. There are galleries, I have learned, where men seek men, women seek women and couples seek an extra kick (side kick?) in their lives. It should be interesting fall reading.

Political storm now buffets Elian
January 23, 2000

A six-year-old Cuban boy has become a symbol of what is wrong with this country. For the past two months since the boy was plucked from the sea, interest groups – Cuban-Americans, politicians, and the Cuban government – have exploited the situation to their selfish gains.

The U.S. immigration laws are simple enough. The surviving parent, in this case the father, has the right to the boy's custody. But Cuban-American lobby, opportunistic politicians and the right wing anti-communists have made it complicated.

The Cuban-Americans, 700-thousand strong, have a profound hatred of Cuba's long time ruler Fidel Castro. They seldom miss an opportunity to humiliate him. Now it is being done on the back of an innocent boy. Ever since the failed attempt to invade Cuba in the early 60's, the Cuban-Americans have dictated public policy towards Cuba. We are the only country without diplomatic relations with Cuba. Any efforts to normalize relations with Cuba have been sabotaged by this powerful lobby. Through federal legislation enacted in the 60's the Cuban refugees enjoy a preferential treatment for residency and citizenship in this country. The Cuban-American lobby hopelessly stuck in the murky waters of the Bay of Pigs is still dictating our foreign policy towards Cuba.

Adding fuel to the fire are our opportunistic politicians particularly the Republicans. Messrs Giuliani, Bush, McCain and the old ideologue Senator Helms have thrown their weight with the Cuban-Americans. The Congress is planning to pass legislation to grant U.S. citizenship to the boy. Never mind the boy is a minor, cannot speak for himself and the only person who can – his father – has been totally ignored.

It is amazing that the legislatures, who wish to grant citizenship to Elian, conveniently ignore the plight of other refugees who make the perilous journey to our shores. Recently 437 Haitians were deported to Haiti without any fanfare. Refugees from other countries are routinely sent back into the clutches of the regimes they had fled from in the first place. In this new era we return the "wretched refuse of your teeming shore" of Emma Lazarus's *The New Colossus* and keep a Cuban poster boy for our selfish political gains.

Why should Elian stay in this country? The proponents say that the boy will have a bright future in this country. They also invoke the ultimate sacrifice his mother gave in rescuing her son from Castro's Cuba. Powerful stuff, but blatantly untrue. The boy's mother left Cuba, not for the future of her son, but to follow her lover who had planned the boat trip and perished at sea with others.

It must be déjà vu for Castro. While imprisoned in the early fifties by the Batista regime for his revolutionary ideas. Castro's divorced wife took their six-year-old son Fidelito to Florida. Castro wrote powerful letters from prison demanding his return to Cuba. A few years later when Castro was in exile in Mexico the boy did come to see him on a temporary visit. Fearing that Castro would keep the boy with him, the boy was kidnapped and returned to his mother in Florida. It was not until 1959 when Castro came into power that the boy returned to Cuba to live with his father. A geophysicist by profession, Fidelito Castro still lives in his father's Cuba.

When and if Elian will be reunited with his father is hard to tell. But one thing is very clear: we must engage Castro and normalize our relations with Cuba. All the posturing and rhetoric of the Cuban-American lobby aside, the path to diplomatic recognition does not have to pass through Miami's Little Havana. It will be better for this country and for the people of that poor island.

Via e-mail, January 23, 2000:
Mr. Hussain:
Thank you for your article in The Blade. *I have been going to Haiti on short term mission trips annually since 1987 helping to build schools, clinics and churches. Through this experience I have come to dearly love the Haitian people.*

As you stated, "It is amazing that those who wish to grant citizenship to Elian ignore the plight of other refugees who make the perilous journey to our shores." It really tore me up and made me extremely disturbed when the recent boat load of refugees from Haiti, China and the Dominican Republic were deported to Haiti without any fanfare, questions or comments, in spite of the one pregnant lady repeatedly asking about her children who were on the boat.

It's a sad state of affairs when the treatment of human beings turns into a political show like this.

It is time that the 1960's federal legislation granting Cuban refugees preferential treatment should be removed from the law books and Cuban and Haitian refugees, as well as others, be treated in a fair and equal manner.

B.W.

Via e-mail, May 1, 2000:
I wrote you sometime ago when I disagreed with your opinion. So it's only fair to commend you for your views about the custody of Elian Gonzalez.
I agree completely!
P.A.

Via e-mail, April 14, 2000:
Dear Dr. Hussain,
Monie was kind enough to forward me a copy of your editorial after I had voiced similar opinions in an email to him. Your article couldn't resonate more with my thoughts and opinions regarding this issue. Thank you for adding a voice of reason to this publicity fiasco and an interesting historical perspective to Elian's unfortunate plight.
Hope all is well in Toledo and say hello to Mrs. Hussain for me.
Fondly,
L.P.

Via e-mail, May 1, 2000:
Well spoken. I have written to Senator Hatch and others asking them to stop embarrassing themselves and blowing taxpayer dollars politicizing this matter.
F.Z.
Oviedo, Florida

Via e-mail, May 1, 2000:
100% correct!!! The boy goes to the father, period. The Miami kidnappers (a.k.a.: relatives) should be thrown in jail for 60 days.

It did exhibit the political clout of a well-organized minority. South Florida should be renamed NuCuba as our gutless senators & congressmen treat it as an independent nation.
J.S.

Via e-mail, May 1, 2000:
Thank you for the excellent editorial in the Blade. *You have expressed what many Americans feel about this unfortunate incident. It is clear that the Cuban community cares more about its continuing war with Castro than the welfare of a little boy. It is certainly ironic that those who raise the issue of "family values" abandon their views so quickly when it doesn't suit their immediate goals.*

Please continue speak out on this and other issues. It is refreshing to have area editorialists write with such insight and clarity. Thank you for saying what needs to be said.
D.O.

O Sodom, O Gomorrah! Casual dress has limits
August 31, 2003

On a recent Sunday, I saw one of my saner colleagues making hospital rounds dressed in a T-shirt and shorts. While in these permissive and anything-goes times I should not have been startled (and dismayed) but I was. Casualness has its limits and I always thought there was a clear distinction between the place of work and a Sunday afternoon stroll through the park.

It took me a while to get used to the society norms when I arrived in Toledo almost 40 years ago to the month. On that first day I was invited to a party in one of the apartments on the hospital campus. I appeared dressed in a three-piece suit thinking of a hot cup of tea and a piece of cake. Instead I entered a noisy and raucous pizza and beer party where young residents and nurses were having a merry good time dancing to the tunes of the Monkees and the Beatles. For a moment I thought I had entered the kingdom of Sodom and Gomorrah. But the shock of young women wearing Bermuda shorts wore off in time and from our present vantage point that wildness was sedate and placid indeed.

Since then I have been witness to the slow erosion of dress code in our society. Bermuda shorts that so startled me are now replaced with plunging necklines that merge with ascending hemlines and in the process bare various anatomic assets along with a few shiny body rings. Or a dude showing his biceps and pectorals and other attributes through a breezy tank top and a Speedo.

But those spectacles are usually seen on the outside the rarefied confines of professional places of work. There has to be some distinction between the street and the work place. As my fellow *Blade* columnist Rose Russell lamented in one of her fine pieces last year, casual wear has become so common that dress-down days occur almost every day.

Professionals – physicians, lawyers, business people and the like – used to conform to a workplace dress code that included jacket and necktie for men and business attire for women. While the latter two professions still adhere to that time honored tradition, the medicos are slipping. Slowly but surely they are trading their white coat, tie and jacket for casual wear. Now, if you enter any hospital the chances are the man dressed in blue denim jeans with frayed cuffs, tennis shoes and a wrinkled shirt could be a surgeon or anesthesiologist rather than a visitor. I can't imagine a lawyer appearing before a judge in a similar outfit to plead a case. (Though truth be known, I have seen one local judge who leaves a lot to be desired the way he presents himself on the bench.)

When I was a resident in surgery training there was an unwritten rule, strictly enforced by the chief, that everyone on the service had to wear a clean shirt (not necessarily pressed) and a necktie. Violators were asked, not too politely I must add, to leave the hospital and return only when they were properly dressed. Dr. Marion Anderson, the late chief of surgery (and also one time president) at the Medical College of Ohio, had a simple explanation. It was a privilege to take care of patients and with that privilege came the responsibility to present oneself properly. I also know of a well-known surgeon at the old Mercy Hospital who was asked to leave the hospital by the nun-administrator when the gregarious surgeon appeared in tennis outfit to make rounds.

Now I am not pleading a return to the stuffy and starchy days of the past where every public appearance would dictate a pressed suit, necktie and a button down shirt. I did that faithfully to the point where a colleague of mine once remarked that if I were Adam in the Garden of Eden I would be sporting a button down fig leaf. Alas, age has a way of changing one's perspective and I have over the years become a bit lax by abandoning the tie and jacket for my weekend rounds.

But I still cannot bring myself to appear on the bedside of my patients wearing my squash outfit or a tank top.

In the Toledo Blade Readers' Forum, *September 21, 2003*
"No one bothers to dress appropriately"
Like Dr. Amjad Hussain, I have wondered what has happened to our ideas of how to dress appropriately.
When we attend church, even the minister looks as tough he's going to a picnic or to play golf, so casually dressed is he.
My mother always said, "Church is God's house to meet us, we should give our best to the Lord." Somehow, blue jeans, shorts, tank tops, etc., don't seem to me like you're looking your best.

Not only has the church been changing its appearances, but it seems everyone is changing to where there isn't a dress code anymore. As Dr. Hussain said, we used to look up to those who were neatly dressed and were noticed.

There is a distinction between the street and the workplace. Slowly, people are changing so there is no emphasis on how you look, or where you are going, or what you do.

It's a privilege to present yourself in a manner matching the occasion. Give the best of yourself to those around you.

You not only look better when you dress for the occasion, but you feel better. You act the way you are dressed.

How about getting back to looking "classy" and "neat," and being admired by ourselves, as well as others?

E.B.

Wauseon

Frank McCullough: Right man at MCO
July 7, 2002

It was with sadness that we learned last month that Dr. Frank McCullough, the president of the Medical College of Ohio, has gone on an extended leave of absence because of recurrence of prostate cancer. His many well-wishers, including this writer, fervently hope and pray that he will regain his health and eventually return to MCO. His sudden departure is a great loss for MCO and the community.

Dr. McCullough's rise to the MCO presidency six years ago came unexpectedly and under the most unusual circumstances. After the retirement of Dr. Richard Rupert in 1994, the MCO board brought in Dr. Roger Bone, who was the dean at Rush Presbyterian Medical School in Chicago, to head the college. While the concept of bringing in an outsider with new ideas and a fresh outlook is usually healthy, this particular appointment turned out to be a mistake.

Dr. Bone embarked upon a controversial plan to sell the financially strapped MCO hospital to ProMedica Health System in a deal that was to create a "world-class medical center" in Toledo.

There was, however, one important element missing. Neither the MCO community, from the higher ups to the lowly workers, nor the medical community outside MCO, bought Dr. Bone's grandiose idea. The proposed marriage broke up amidst acrimony without the parties ever taking the first step toward the altar. By this time the MCO board, having realized its folly, placed Dr. Bone - at that time suffering with recurrent kidney cancer - on forced leave of absence and appointed the executive vice president, Dr. McCullough, interim president.

He had his work cut out for him. With diligence, perseverance, and hard work, he picked up the pieces from the MCO-Toledo Hospital wreck that had littered the distance between North Cove Boulevard and Arlington Avenue.

Frank McCullough was the right man at the right time to salvage the situation. He knew the institution - he had been there since 1978 - knew the staff, understood the dynamics, but above all was great at working with people and not dictating to them.

He surrounded himself with talented individuals and went about restoring the image of a tarnished institution and instilling confidence in a demoralized staff.

And then the proverbial second shoe dropped. Annoyed by the proposed MCO-St. Vincent Children's Hospital merger, ProMedica in a fit of retaliation severed its 33-year-old academic links with MCO.

It was perhaps Dr. McCullough's greatest challenge to look for alternate sites for training residents and medical students. Somehow he managed the crises and ensured a smooth transition for continuation of training at other sites.

Even though the loss of ProMedica facilities for training was a severe blow, Dr. McCullough kept the lines of communication open, and it is to the credit of both Frank McCullough and Allan Brass, the ProMedica CEO, that the academic relationship has been re-established, even if on a smaller scale.

During his presidency, Dr. McCullough was also able to reunite the faculty and re-focus the institution on the core values of education.

He reformed the curriculum, instituted programs to teach the teachers how to teach, and expanded the pool of quality students applying to the college.

Realizing the fact that MCO had always been a community resource, he strengthened the ties with the medical community outside MCO.

In the face of ever-shrinking state aid for higher education, he instituted fiscal restraints to keep the institution solvent.

And perhaps he was also able to deflect efforts in Columbus of some ill-wishers who had advocated the closing of some medical schools in Ohio, including MCO. All in all he served the institution and the community with understanding, dedication, sincerity, and grace.

Now another experienced hand at MCO has taken over the institution.

Dr. Amira Gohara is a homespun physician, pathologist, and administrator.

Her journey from Egypt to Maumee Valley Hospital in the 1960s and her journey from that venerable institution in South Toledo to the pinnacle of a medical university just a mile away is a remarkable accomplishment for an immigrant woman from the Third World.

She has proven her mettle, and hopefully she will continue the overall direction set by her predecessor.

Thank you, Frank McCullough, for a remarkable job. Our prayers and thoughts are with you.

Via e-mail, July 11, 2002:

Dear Dr. Hussain,

I just read your column regarding Frank McCullough's tenure at MCO. Our thoughts and prayers are also with Frank and his family.

Thank you for acknowledging the effort of Dr. McCullough and I put forward to re-establish academic ties between our organizations. It is an important part of what we do for this community and as part of continued medical education in this country. However, I feel I must clarify the reason we were able to come together was, in part, due to the unbundling of our old contracts. Many years of changing relation-ships, expectations, actions and leadership left these arrangements unproductive. Only by creating a new, solid foundation we were able to once again reach agreement in philosophy and principle on how best to provide academic opportunities to medical students.

ProMedica Health System remains committed to our current relationship with MCO, and will continue to make decisions on acade-mic affiliations based on the needs of the facilities and communities we serve.

Sincerely,

Alan W. Brass, FACHE

President and Chief Executive Officer, ProMedica Health System

Via mail, July 18, 2002:

Dear Dr. Hussain,

My family and I appreciated your article on Frank and his tenure at MCO. He is really a modest man. There has never been a time that we have saved newspaper articles about him. However, he asked me to save your article – for his grandchildren. Thank you so much from all of us. It meant a great deal to us.

Sincerely,

L.M., Perrysburg

Biologic Russian roulette can endanger
July 20, 1997

Recently Dr. Karen Wetterhahn, a chemistry professor at the Dartmouth College, died of a freak lab accident. Her death underscores the risk laboratory researchers and health care professional face in their work.

Dr. Wetterhahn, age 49, was studying the effects of dimethylmercury, a rare synthetic mercury compound, on cell metabolism in humans. Somehow a few drops of the deadly compound seeped through her intact rubber gloves and penetrated her skin. Four months after the exposure she came down with the symptoms of mercury poisoning and despite the best medical efforts she died six months later. She probably would have survived if struck by a bullet through her chest.

The history of scientific inquiry is replete with examples of intentional and unintentional exposure to chemical and biologic toxins. John Hunter, an 18th century surgeon and biologist, accidentally became inoculated with syphilis. He elected not to treat himself and instead studied the development of syphilis rash on his skin. He went on to publish a classic description of syphilitic ulcers, which carry his name. He died of heart attack years later but not until he had contributed enormously to the scientific knowledge in as diverse areas as surgery, anatomy, physical sciences and dentistry.

William Halsted (1852-1922), a world-renowned surgeon at Johns Hopkins University, was another pioneer who came close to losing his life and reputation while experimenting with cocaine as a local anesthetic. Later he not only kicked the habit but went on to publish a paper detailing the use of cocaine as a local anesthetic in over 1,000 cases.

In 1929 a German physician Wener Theodore Otto Frossman wondered if one could pass a tiny tube through one of the veins in the arm and advance it to the heart. He wanted to inject antibiotic solution through the tube to treat life-threatening infections. Conventional wisdom maintained that the heart would respond by going into fatal abnormal rhythm. Sitting in his hospital office, Frossman introduced a small catheter into his vein and advanced it towards the heart. The catheter dangling from his arm, he walked to the radiology department and asked the radiologist to confirm that the catheter was in the heart. It was. That daring experiment by a single-minded physician led to the development of heart catheterization and in turn opened up the new field of heart surgery.

Today, scientists and researchers do not expose themselves willfully to unlock the secrets of diseases. But the risks of inadvertent exposure to life threatening illnesses as AIDS, hepatitis and virulent infections remain a threat. During surgery, for example, it is not uncommon for the surgeon or the assistant to be poked with a needle or a sharp instrument. On the hospital floors, nurses and other care givers can and do get splattered with patients' blood and body fluids. The same is true for lab technicians in the process of handling tissues and fluids.

Take AIDS for example. Handling known cases of AIDS is usually not the problem since people are very careful. But there are millions of others who silently harbor the virus and do not know it. Legal and ethical constraints prevent giving everyone an AIDS test upon entering the hospital.

Compared to the large number of health care workers who get exposed to the AIDS virus only a few go on to develop a positive HIV test. Still there have been 159 such cases where nurses, lab technicians and surgeons became HIV positive as a result of such exposure.

Researchers and health care workers take enormous risks in their daily work. While the majority of them remain safe, a few unlucky ones lose out in this deadly game of biologic Russian roulette. Dr. Karen Wetterhahn, the chemistry professor, was one such victim.

Sadly, honor killing remains common in the Middle East
June 5, 2007

Six weeks ago another deplorable and degrading inhuman spectacle was staged in Iraq. This time the venue was not the usual centers of violence Fallujah, Baghdad or Tikrit; it was the relatively peaceful northern Kurdish area of Iraq. A young girl of 17 years was stoned to death in the streets by the frenzied mob. Her crime: illicit sexual relations.

Before we get carried away with the here-is-yet-another-example-of-a-religion-gone-crazy chorus, let me emphasize that what happened in Bashiqa in the Nineveh province of northern Iraq was not religious punishment but an old tribal custom of reclaiming honor when, according to tribal code, a woman of the family has violated that code.

The punishment for sex outside the marriage is whipping, not stoning. And that is only when there are four credible eyewitnesses. Only fools and crazies would indulge in such kind of sexual relations in public.

In this particular case, the Kurdish girl belonged to the Yazidi religious sect which practices a mixture of Islam, Judaism and Christianity as well as Zoroastrian and Gnostic beliefs. The boy, also a Kurd, is from mainstream Islam. She is reported to have converted to Islam and married a Sunni young man. After receiving assurances that she would not be harmed, she returned home to the confronted by the mob that also included her own family members. The police stood by idly and allowed the frenzied and crazed mob to torture her to death.

Honor killing has been part of many diverse cultures and societies and is still practiced with varying frequency throughout the world. It is a phenomenon of patriarchal societies where the women are considered the honor of the family or a clan. Any violation of that honor, willingly or unwillingly, by a woman, would automatically condemn her to death. The practice is particularly common in the Middle East and around the Mediterranean. But it is also practiced in as far away places as Afghanistan, Pakistan, India, Bangladesh, and Africa and even in South America.

In different countries and cultures it takes different forms but the end point is femicide whether for violating family's honor or a man's masculinity. In South America it is the absolute power of man over a woman that has been source of murders in Bolivia, Brazil, Columbia, Peru, Mexico and Guatemala.

In India the brunt of cruelty has been on new brides who do not bring dowry as expected by the husband's family. In the Punjab and Haryana states of India, according to the *Daily Telegraph* of London, one out of every ten murders are honor killings.

The savagery of the lynching led to threats of retaliation. This part of Nineveh, though outside the jurisdiction of the Kurdistan Regional Government (KRG), is strongly under its influence. The murdered girl and her intended husband were Kurds. The KRG's President, Massoud Barzani, held meetings with Yazidi leaders. Kurdish officials in Mosul said at the time that they had the situation under control. The KRG is now calling for an investigation into what happened, though the central government in Baghdad has little authority in the north of the country.

Having said that, I am appalled at Muslim religious leaders in this country and abroad that they have not come out as forcefully as they could have against this barbaric practice.

Via e-mail, June 8, 2007:
Dear Dr. Hussain,

While I admire your defense of the Qur'an, I sometimes get the feeling that is what you think many of us non-Muslim people are angry about. It's not about the Qur'an – it's about the behavior of people who profess to follow the religion of Islam. I could care less what the Qur'an says or doesn't say. I feel the same way about the Bible, which many know has some language in it that would be considered criminal in today's society. Whether the Qur'an speaks to honor killings or not, the fact of the matter is that Muslims, and others who practice this barbaric tradition, are doing so in the name of Allah. Religion develops the culture of a society. I see a very strong correlation between the countries that practice honor killings and the people who practice Islam. I see the same correlation between other acts of brutality and discrimination toward non-believers and women. I really don't think you can separate them as easily as you want to do so. Technically, I'm willing to believe what you say about the Qur'an. Practically, I have major doubts.

I do agree with you that moderate Muslim leaders have to do more than give lip service to the peacefulness of the Qur'an. I fail to understand how schools that preach hatred can be tolerated by any religion that calls itself peaceful for any reason whatsoever. The same is true of the criminal treatment of women. I fail to understand the need for an Imam to have a militia. We see innocent people murdered everyday by intolerant Muslims. We see Muslim leaders condemning the action, but we do not see any justice against the perpetrators or an effort to stop it. They seemingly shake their heads and move on. Maybe I'm wrong, but I always thought a Muslim was a person who practices the Islamic faith. I don't want to be at war with a Muslim or Muslims. But, there are millions of Muslims who advocate and actively pursuing war against my beliefs. Who gives a damn if it is in the Qur'an or not? It's a real threat. I consider myself a very compassionate man. I don't understand why someone wants to kill me simply because they cannot tolerate the way I live. You talk a lot about the discrimination of the Muslim populace. What about the discrimination of Muslims toward non-Muslims? Do you really think it doesn't exist? Do you really think I would be welcome in a crowd of Muslims?

As I have said before, I think you are a peaceful man with extremely good intentions. But, you can't wipe away the brutality of Muslim culture and/or behavior with words. Even if the Qur'an does not specifically condone many of the brutal actions we witness, I have got to believe that somehow it plays a major role in the attitudes of the brutal perpetrators of hate.

Peace.

R.J.

Oregon, OH

I am neither defending the Qur'an nor I am being an apologist. I am saying that honor killing is a worldwide phenomenon, cuts across ALL cultures and is deeply rooted in tribal traditions. Religion gets blamed but it is not religious.

In case you overlooked, I condemn this practice no matter who does it. I also point a finger at Muslims who should condemn the practice in no uncertain terms.

I am however surprised at the tone of your letter. On this issue at least I would have expected you to agree with what I said.

By saying that technically you agree with me but have big issues with the Qur'an you slip into the same 'we' versus 'them' trap. Since 10% of all homicides in the Indian states of Punjab and Haryana are honor related and the majority of the people in those states are not Muslims, with whom would you have the problem there? Or for that matter with the killing of women in South America and Africa for the same reason?

I am sorry but I am beginning to believe your mind is already made up and nothing I can say would make you change that.

I wish you peace.

Sincerely,

Amjad Hussain

Via e-mail, June 8, 2007:

Dear Dr. Hussain,

You are not defending the Qur'an? I see you defending the Qur'an in everything you write, but maybe that's just me. And, of course, you are certainly entitled to do so.

Is it not true that going back 2,000 years all major religions preached intolerance and discrimination toward women? Where do you believe current day tribal attitudes toward women got their root? I believe they started with religious attitudes at that time and are tolerated today merely out of tradition and ignorance.

I did not overlook the fact that you condemn the practice of honor killings nor that you expect more out of Muslims to condemn the practice. I agree with everything you said in the article. The only point I was trying to make is that "this mess" is not about what the Qur'an (see the first sentence of the fifth paragraph in your article) says or doesn't say. However, I do believe that the attitudes are linked to ancient religious beliefs regardless of what major religion you want to talk about.

And, yes, my mind is not going to change until I see Muslims leaders giving more than lip service to condemn the horrific acts. To the best of my knowledge, large populous of Hindus, Catholics, and non-Muslim Africans are not openly calling for violence as a solution to anything.

Regards,
R.J.

Via e-mail, June 11, 2007:
Bismillah as-Salaamu 'alaykum,
    "The practice of honor killing is common in the Middle East and around the Mediterranean. It is also practiced in Afghanistan, Pakistan, India, Bangladesh, Africa, and also in South America."
    And here in the United States. One only need to turn on their local news any day of the week to hear some variant of similar so-called honor killings.
    M.F.

Thank you for your note.

Honor killing is defined when a family thinks its honor has been violated.

It does not include revenge killings, jealousy killings etc. You are right, there are women being murdered in this country by irate husbands and male friends but they fall in a separate category. I hope you are not, by pointing a finger at the U.S., condoning this horrible practice.

Regards,
Amjad Hussain

Via e-mail, June 5, 2007:
What a horrible "religion" you fools endure. Honor killings, maiming men and women. . .my god what a pathetic religion you sadists have. Having checked other religions, yours is the absolute WORST! ....you idiots hate Jews, Christians, Hindus, and EVERY and I mean EVERY religion out there!!! And you sick bastards are the religion of "peace"?? What moron thought that lie up? .. .. and it ain't going to change until GW teaches you heathens a great lesson!!
    M.C.
    "hollandbenefits"

In the Toledo Blade Readers' Forum, *June 14, 2007:*
"Old Testament reference gratuitous"

The horrific behavior, the murderous conduct of a Kurdish com-munity toward a young girl who followed her heart was appropriately excoriated by S. Amjad Hussain in his column dealing with honor killing in the Middle East.

His gratuitous reference to Old Testament law concerning the death sentence for sex outside of marriage as well as bestiality reflects upon his evidenced attitudes. It is true that the Old Testament does require the death penalty for certain social excesses. It is also true that no one has been stoned in some 2,000 years. Judeo-Christian law and practice have matured.

It may well be that the Qur'an does not proscribe a death sentence reflecting upon the honor of a family. Nonetheless, it is common in Muslim lands. Obviously, there are many Muslims who mouth the words of the Qur'an and practice the customs of barbarism. To compare the ancient religious text of the Hebrews with the present horrendous practices in Muslim society is specious and demeaning.

Rabbi A.M.S.

Man on a mission brings hope to needy
October 9, 2006

One main reason for the prevailing anti-American sentiments around the world is that people fail to differentiate between the American government and American people. Working through this potentially deadly fog of confusion are some brave Americans who at great risk bring relief and comfort to millions of needy people around the world. For the most part they go unnoticed and unappreciated. Greg Mortenson is one such American.

It was by sheer accident that this lanky west coast nurse got involved in building schools in a remote area of northern Pakistan called Baltistan and also in Afghanistan. The accident in this case was a potentially fatal wrong turn he took while coming down from the base camp of K2 in 1993.

His hopes of scaling the summit were dashed when he helped rescue a sick team member at 22,000 feet. The 36-hour ordeal left him totally depleted and exhausted. After resting for a few days in the base camp, he started the seven-day trek over the Baltoro Glacier to reach the town of Skardu.

The fateful wrong turn took him to the tiny village of Korphe by the edge of the glacier, which he reached by crossing a roaring river in a basket suspended from a steel wire strung between the rocky banks. While he was recuperating in the village, he inquired about the schooling of their children. Yes, there was a school, he was told, but the teacher came a few days a week and the rest of the time the kids were on their own.

The school was a flattened rocky outcrop where children sat on the icy ground under open skies. They used the ground as the slate on which they wrote with twigs. An idea was born.

The journey to build a school in Korphe turned out to be more perilous than climbing the world's second highest mountain. It would be full of frustrating twists and pleasant turns. Back in the United States, he worked as an ER nurse in the San Francisco area and saved money by sleeping in his old car. He told his story to anyone who would listen and sent 850 letters of solicitation to celebrities and well-to-do people. He received one reply – from NBC anchor Tom Brokaw

– with a check for $100. Children in one school started a "Pennies for Pakistan" drive and raised a few thousand dollars.

In an unexpected twist, a mountaineer friend put Mr. Mortenson in contact with Jean Hoerni, a reclusive Silicon Valley physicist and a one-time trekker to the Karakorum Mountains. Once convinced of Mr. Mortenson's sincerity, the man gave him $12,000 - the amount Mr. Mortenson had chased unsuccessfully since his return from Pakistan.

The villagers had one more request when he went back. While they needed the school, they also needed a bridge over the river to get supplies into the village. The frustrated American returned to the U.S. to raise additional funds. Again the reclusive scientist, now on his deathbed, came through. He created Central Asia Institute with a gift of $1 million and asked Craig Mortenson to head the organization.

In all the organization has built 55 schools in Baltistan and Afghanistan. It has not been easy. Mr. Mortenson was once kidnapped in the Pakistani tribal areas of Wazirstan, but was released unharmed. In Baltistan he had to face the wrath of village mullahs who decried that girls' education was against the religion. A timely fatwa in support of his work from the Shia religious hierarchy in Qom, Iran, defused the situation.

The head of Mr. Mortenson's host village, an elderly grey beard, had once told him that the first time an outsider shares a cup of tea with a native in Baltistan he is considered a stranger. The second time he becomes an honored guest and the third time a family member. He had attained that status now. The account of Greg Mortenson's mission to educate the poorest of the poor is chronicled in a recently released book he co-authored with Oliver Relin. Appropriately titled *Three Cups of Tea*, the book is published by Viking.

Amid the cacophony of anti-American rhetoric emanating from all corners of the world, Greg Mortenson exemplifies the indomitable American spirit. As the book's subtitle says, "His is a one-man mission to fight terrorism and build nations . . . one school at a time."

I applaud his work and celebrate his accomplishments.

Via e-mail, October 11, 2006:
A beautiful story so very well told.

There is no doubt that so many U.S. citizens do so much for the needy people of the world and as you so aptly state all this in general goes unnoticed.
    K.B.

Via e-mail, October 11, 2006:
Dear Dr. Hussain,
Three cheers for Greg Mortenson and three cheers for your writing about him.
Now all we have to hope is that the Taliban doesn't kill him.
    R.J.
    Toledo, OH

Via e-mail, October 11, 2006:
Thank you, Dr. Hussain. It was with deep pleasure that I opened the Blade *this morning to your wonderful review of Greg Mortenson's book and your thoughtful closing remarks about him. I have been telling friends today about your article. As I write this my husband, John, is on an errand to buy extra copies of today's* Blade.
    When we entered the ballroom of the Missoula, MT Holiday Inn where Greg was making his presentation, I had the opportunity to meet Greg briefly, handed him your card and tell him you were writing an article about him and his work in the Toledo newspaper. He was most appreciative and tucked your card into his pocket. Greg spoke to a packed, standing-room-only, crowd who gave him a tearful standing ovation at the conclusion of his talk. Greg urged us to get his book into our public libraries so his message will spread. An interesting opening comment in Greg's talk: he had just returned from a meeting with his publisher. At the meeting Greg strongly objected to the jacket statement "One man's mission to fight terrorism . . .. " He wanted the statement to read "One man's mission to build peace . . .. " The publisher argued that the book would only sell if the word terrorism was used.
    Greg is leaving Nov. 8 for Pakistan for 6 months. He is leaving his family, a wife and two young children, in Bozeman. I am mailing him your Blade *article.*
    With my appreciation for your splendid article...I hope you receive many e-mails about it.
    L.S.

Via e-mail, October 10, 2006:

Dear Dr. Amjad Sahib,

I am writing to compliment you on your excellent article in The Blade *reviewing* Three Cups of Tea *and Greg Mortenson's unique achievement. I have read many articles on this topic but none as focused, succinct yet comprehensive. I am a member of the Board of Directors of the Central Asia Institute and have the honor of working with Greg. I am originally from Lahore, Pakistan, and have been a professor of English and Interdisciplinary Studies at City College of San Francisco. I thought that in the process of complimenting you on your article, I might as well introduce myself.*

Best wishes,

A.J.

Thank you so much for your very kind words. I believe people like Mr. Mortenson need our support and our appreciation.

I trace my roots to the old walled city of Peshawar and have, in the past 25 years, written for the *Blade* and some other publications.

Warmest regards,

Amjad Hussain

PLURALISM

Misconceptions feed fanatic view of Islam
June 5, 2006

At a recent speaking engagement in a church, I was asked the inevitable question that somehow always finds its way to the podium: Why does Islam teach intolerance and militancy? I would have liked to ask the questioner, just to prove a point, if he still beat his wife. I was, however, amused by the widespread assumption that Islam is inherently a violent religion and Muslims are a fanatic bunch.

This and many other similar questions have been raised rather frequently in the post-9/11 climate in the western world. These assumptions also include that Muslims keep their women under wraps, they look down upon all other religions, and they believe it is against their religion to have non-Muslim friends. These are legitimate questions and Muslims ought to address them not with a knee-jerk defensive response but with knowledge of their sacred text, the Qur'an, and understanding of their surroundings.

The Qur'an is the compilation of divine revelations that Prophet Muhammad received over a period of many years from 612 to his death at age 63 in 632. Most of the revelations came in response to a particular need of the nascent Muslim community, first in Mecca and then in Medina.

While certain passages are eternal, others are topical and dated. The latter were revealed to address a certain situation and their presence is only of historic significance and thus cannot be applied to current times.

Of particular interest is one passage (5: 57-58) that when read without proper context appears to prohibit Muslims from having friends among non-Muslims. There are many xenophobic Muslims who still think that this injunction holds true today. They ignore the fact that it was directed toward those who were determined to wipe out the new religion at its inception. Had this injunction been meant for all times the world would have not seen the great flowering of the arts and sciences that happened through interaction of Islam with Christianity and Judaism in Spain under the Moors (711-1492) and in the Ottoman Empire under the Turks (1342-1924) and also with the Hindu religion in India during the Mughul period (1508-1857).

Another misconception still being perpetuated by many Muslims and non-Muslims is that the Qur'an condemns and rejects all other religions. There is an all-encompassing and clear declaration in the Qur'an that there is no compulsion in religion (2:256). This should have put to rest the controversy about the Afghan man who converted to Christianity and any Muslim who chooses to leave Islam for another religion. Religion is a personal and private matter and the society or the state has no say in anyone's personal religious preference. Perhaps Islam is more tolerant and accepting of other faiths than some of them are of Islam.

Why then do such misunderstandings continue in the present? The fault lies squarely with the Muslims themselves. Instead of adopting a more reasoned approach toward their faith, many Muslims are comfortable in accepting centuries-old commentaries and explanations even though they are repeatedly reminded by the scripture to think and understand the world around them. Saudi Arabia is a good example where school textbooks still teach superiority of Islam over other religions and advise Muslims not to have non-Muslim friends. No wonder such intolerance was the incubator for the self-righteous and xenophobic beliefs of the 9/11 hijackers.

There is an interesting debate going on among the Muslims in the West. A good many of them still believe in literal interpretation of the sacred text and are content in living in their comforting and comfortable self-created cocoons. Others with a more moderate and pluralistic attitude want to look at their faith and understand it according to the times we live in. This debate that is rather familiar to other religions is relatively new for Muslims.

Time will tell whether Muslims will want to live in the soothing world of the status quo or forge ahead as confident citizens of this world at ease and at peace with themselves and with the followers of other religions. Their faith will not diminish by being inclusive.

Via e-mail, June 5, 2006:
Dear Amjad,
Nice to see you back on the front page of the Sunday editorial section. Liked your article. Particularly the part about how we need to be ashamed about what happened. Your assessment about how our

nationalist and religious feelings about those events getting in the way of reconciliation is right on.

Looking forward to next week,

N.A.

Via e-mail, June 5, 2006:

Dear Dr. Hussain;

Having just read your article on line I must comment that not only must some Muslims interpret the words and meaning of the passages in the Koran so should Christians and any others who seek to condemn others for not following the true word....

We live in a different time, a different world; we must remain open to understanding and change. But the basic message is the same: be kind and do good deeds to one another.

Originally posted in Writers Forum at YahooGroups:

"This is an article written by a well-meaning person, who wishes to correct misconceptions amongst non-Muslims and also simultaneously counter some of the misinterpretation of the holy book by extremist elements within Islam. However, after reading several such articles, I am convinced that such an approach will really lead nowhere. By challenging the extremist in terms of interpreting the Qur'an, the liberal:

a. plays in the playground of his/her opponent. The opponent has much more willingness to condemn the liberal as being a heretic/apostate/kafir than vice versa. Additionally, the opponent often has more credibility in matters of religion than the liberal who is often seen as irreligious even by those who don't necessarily consider them heretics. It is an unequal battle.

b. opens himself/herself to the charge of being just as dishonest as the extremist. This is because, like many other holy books, there are multiple injunctions in the Qur'an. By selectively quoting those which support the liberal position, while either denying or suppressing those which support the extremist position, the liberal does not do much justice to his/her cause. For instance, Dr. Amjad Hussain, in the quoted article, refers to some verses as being applicable only for 7th century Mecca/Medina and not for today. That may well be the case. But since there is no clear guidance in the Qur'an itself of which verses are for all times and which are not, this becomes a matter for open interpretation by everybody. And it conflicts with the view held by most Muslims (at least to the best of my knowledge) that the Qur'an is the unalterable word of God for all times to come.

c. limits the debate to the realm of religion, when the issues are actually mostly political and secular in nature.

I think a better position for a liberal is an appeal to humanism rather than religion to counter the extremist's point of view. This would imply playing in his/her own playground instead of the opponent's. And it would be free of the contradictions that the use of religious logic entails.

The fight against extremism in other religions has been successfully fought (or is being fought) only through recourse to universal human values and not to religion itself. As others have pointed out on the forum, Martin Luther's "reforms" did not lead to the spread of fundamental rights and freedom. The ideas of Voltaire did. Well-meaning reformers like Vivekananda or Ramanuja did not effect the liberation of the Dalits in Hindu society. Ambedkar did. I don't see how the situation is going to be any different in Muslim society."

Regards,
Girish

Via e-mail, June 7, 2006:
Often we hear that Islam is a religion of peace. Is it only a religion of peace if one agrees with its teachings? My understanding is that Muhammad received his revelations in Mecca. Because his teachings were not accepted there, he moved to Medina where he did gather a following. Then he and his followers went back to Mecca with swords and forced his teachings onto the people of that town. Was that being a people of peace?

It's certainly true that most Muslims are not terrorists. However, do many Imams incite their followers to terror with their teachings? How about all those Islamic schools where the students are taught to hate western and Christian cultures? There are certainly countless examples of where these Islamic extremist resort to violence if they don't get their way . . .

Criticism of these radical tendencies by we non-Muslims is not effective. I believe that Muslim "leaders" need to speak out and con-

demn all acts of violence. Why don't the Imams preach that terror is against Islamic principles? Maybe the peaceful leaders need to take out full page ads in our newspapers condemning these acts of terrorism and list the names of the Imams and others in authority who agree with the ad.

I believe the Islamic people need to stand up and show they support America and our culture. Several years ago there was no American flag flying near the Islamic Mosque in Perrysburg. A friend of mine had Islamic contacts and I suggested to her that the Mosque should have a American flag to show where they stand. She relayed this to her Islamic connections and several weeks later a small flag was installed on the property but not near the Mosque. I don't know if my comments had anything to do with this. The flag is small and not close to the Mosque. Was this installation merely to appease critics of the Mosque policy? I say that if they really want to show that they are American and support American policies, get a big flag and fly it on a tall pole close to the Mosque. It's probably against Islamic rules, but if it were mounted atop on one of the Minarets, it would really show allegiance.

B.T.

I am pleased to receive your comments on my recent column and am also pleased to respond to your allegations.

Your understanding of Muhammad going to Mecca with swords drawn and forcing the people of Mecca to his religion is totally off base and wrong. He not only declared general amnesty for everyone, he gave them the choice to accept or not accept Islam. (Please do read the biography of Muhammad by someone who is not biased and has impeccable scholarly credentials. I recommend John Esposito and Karen Armstrong. Both are non-Muslims.)

Your second paragraph is pure conjecture. I was educated in Pakistan and I never learned (in school or at home) to hate other religions. I wrote the piece to show people like you that not all Muslims are violent and terrorists. I tried to explain how true teachings can be distorted to fit any agenda. I gather that you are not going to be satisfied with no matter what the moderate Muslims say or do. Perhaps you would like me to condemn Islam and the Muslims. It would be akin to you condemning Christianity for the actions of Nazi Germany. After all Hitler used to quote the Bible in support of his brutality against the Jews. I hope you understand the difference.

Regarding the flag at the Islamic Center in Perrysburg you are mistaken. Mr. Nasr Khan donated the flag and the mosque leadership accepted the gift with gratitude. The flag predates 9/11. While some Muslims might object to the flag as a non-religious symbol in a religious institution (just as the Mennonites) an overwhelming majority at the Center support the idea. Please do know (hard as it is for a person of your mind set) that most of us take pride in our religion and in our adopted homeland.

Though I disagree with the premise of your e-mail I am, none-theless, very grateful that you took the time to write.

Sincerely,

Amjad Hussain

Via e-mail, June 16, 2006:

Hi, Dr. Hussain,

Once again, I enjoyed reading your article of Mon. June 5.

You are right, revelations in the Qur'an need to be read in the proper context just like we Christians need to read the Bible in the proper context. St. Paul tells us in Ephesians Chapter 4, that we are to live with humility and gentleness, with patience, bearing with one another through love . . . with one God and Father of all who is over all and through all and in all. Maybe one day we children will get it right.

M.B.

Turkey can teach the world about Islamic government
November 24, 2002

Recently, a major earthquake hit the traditional political establishment of Turkey, and its reverberations were felt in all the capitals of the western world. In a national election the Turks threw out all the major political parties and their heavyweight politicians and gave a clear majority to an Islamic party.

The victory of the Justice and Development Party (AKP) under the leadership of Recep Tayyip Erdogan, a one-time mayor of Istanbul, has created some very interesting dynamics in that nation of 68 million people.

Present-day modern Turkey emerged from the debris of the Ottoman Empire at the end of WWI. Mustafa Kemal (called Ataturk or "the Father of Turks"), an army general under the Ottoman caliphs, picked up the pieces of a devastated empire and established modern Turkey in 1923. In a clear break with the past he set his country on a westward course. He gave women the right to vote, changed Arabic alphabets to Latin for the Turkish language, closed religious schools, and banned the wearing of headscarves by women and the fez by men. In a secular democratic Turkey, he surmised, religion would play no role in public life and in effect would be discouraged. While throwing out the bath water, he tossed out the baby as well.

Or at least that is what he thought.

It is evident that the majority of Turkish people do not subscribe to that gospel of extreme secularism and have remained attached to their faith and their age-old traditions. There has always been a disconnect between the elite in Ankara and Istanbul and the common folks in the country. The importance of Turkey's religious identity became apparent when in 1995 Necmettin Erbakan succeeded in forming a coalition government with the help of the centralist True Path Party to become the country's first Islamist prime minister since the days of the Ottoman caliphs. But not for long. After two years the powerful army brass had him forced out of office and banned his Refah, or Welfare, Party. In Turkey, the fiercely secular and decidedly anti-religious generals consider themselves the custodians of Ataturk's legacy and do not hesitate to impose their will on the government. Their shadow has loomed high over the civilian governments.

In Turkey, the official restriction on the display of religion in public life is rather bizarre. For example, girls in public schools and women in government jobs are forbidden to wear headscarves. A few years ago an elected member of the parliament, 31-year-old western educated Merve Kvackci, caused a stir by going to the parliament wearing a headscarf. She was expelled from the parliament and stripped of her Turkish citizenship on a flimsy technicality that forbids dual citizenship. She had acquired American citizenship while studying in the United States. The leader of the victorious AK Party, Mr. Erdogan, had to send his two daughters to Indiana for education because the girls could not wear the scarf in schools in their native land.

The ouster of Mr. Erbakan in 1997 did not dissuade Turks from abandoning their Islamic identity. After five years they have now sent an unambiguous message to the generals by giving AKP a clear and decisive majority.

Unlike the Taliban of Afghanistan, the ayatollahs of Iran, or the religious politicians of Pakistan, Mr. Erdogan is a pragmatic man who understands his country's secular traditions and has vowed to uphold them. At the same time he has shown pride in his country's Islamic identity. If he becomes prime minister, he would not abandon Turkey's ties with the West but would most likely strengthen ties with the Islamic world. Already he has done the rounds of European capitals, allaying their fears of an Islamic government in Turkey. He would also push for the resolution of the Cyprus issue that has stymied Turkey's relations with Greece and in turn with most of the Western Europe. He would also push for Turkey's admission to the European Union. On the domestic front, he would allow the Kurds the freedom to use their language in schools and in broadcasts.

However, there is a big hurdle in his way to become prime minister. He was banned from contesting elections because of a conviction for reading a poem in public that according to authorities promoted religious hatred. Unless the president of the country intervenes or the constitution is amended, he would be denied his rightful claim to become prime minister.

Turkey has an unprecedented opportunity to show the world that an Islamic government can govern according to democratic principles. It would be a shame if Mr. Erdogan were denied that opportunity.

Via mail, November 25, 2002:

Dear Dr. Hussain,

May I please attempt to respond to your article in the Blade *on Turkey?*

I suggest that an "Islamic government" is a concept as illogical, contradictory and out of date as is a Christian government. It seems to me that no good government can be guided or controlled by religious concepts. Is it not true that religious concepts are based on faith in the unknowable, the unproveable? One hopes that the concepts of good government are based on human experience in this world and some demonstrable logic.

While there are good and wholesome principles taught by all religions, I suggest that no religion is qualified to govern. A couple of examples support my point. Only within the last decade has the Catholic Church revoked its ban on Galileo's 1632 Dialogue, which was seen to contradict the Church's concept that the earth is at the center of the universe. Some Christian "scholars" are still searching for the remains of Noah's ark! There is still discussion about the authenticity of the cloth of Turin, which supposedly covered the corpse of Jesus.

If an old western man of the 21st century like me can challenge these items of Christian faith, how can he take seriously a government which is "Islamic?" Am I correct in understanding its fundamental belief that Mohammed, in a trance, led by Gabriel, ascended on a winged white horse through the seven heavens, where he met the earlier prophets, to have a meeting with Allah? How can faith in that be squared with good government of an earthly country? How can the question of women's scarves be a matter for government concern?

My concern, sir, is that for the next x years or centuries this world will be engaged in religious conflicts and wars without a winner and for which there will be no logical explanation. It is a world of imperfect men and imperfectable governments. Man has not yet evolved to the state of general acceptance of peaceful coexistence on earth. His animal instincts lead to fighting.

Sincerely,

M.P.

Toledo

Thank you so much for your letter dated 11/25/02 commenting on my recent column about the victory of an Islamist party in Turkey.

While I agree with the thrust of your letter and the arguments made against a religious government, I do disagree with certain points.

In my view, religion is a set of principles that guide the believers through their lives. If such principles do not infringe upon one's personal freedom, then a government can be guided by those principles.

Every government is based on certain principles. It is only by adhering to coherent laws formulated under these principles that such government can function and be successful.

All religions are peaceful in their core and as such can coexist with each other. The same is true of governments. I happen to believe that a government based on broad religious principles cannot only function well, it can inspire and enlighten.

I am grateful for your note.

Sincerely,

Amjad Hussain

Dear Dr. Hussain,

I am honored to have your hand-written response to my letter, which I did not expect. Thank you.

A final thought or two. We do not know enough about each other's religions. I am ashamed and offended by the cruelties committed (e.g.: the Inquisition, the Crusades) and wars fought in the name of Christianity. I like to think that such atrocities would not be tolerated today in the name of Christianity.

In your letter, you state that all religions are "peaceful in their core." Is that really true? If so, why does enmity exist? Am I wrong in my understanding that the Islam religion was imposed by acts of war throughout Arabia, the Mid-East, and northern Africa? That Mohammed was a military warrior and leader? That the religion promises heavenly rewards to Muslims who are killed in fighting the infidels? I see pictures of thousands of men kneeling in their prayers, but my feeling is that all of them are taught to hate me!

If your peaceful and kind outlook is generally accepted throughout Islam, why is it that to my knowledge no leader, no spokesman, no cleric, no intellectual, no person of stature from that part of the world has openly and publicly expressed opposition and antipathy to the acts of terrorism, the acts of murder which are condoned and supported by the likes of Bin Laden which have changed life in this country and threaten peace in the world? I can understand that they may be afraid to do so.

Why do I feel that my country and its people are cordially hated by Muslims? It was recently reported that the father of the boy who had killed himself in a bombing in Israel was proud of the boy, proud that he had acted during Ramadan, proud that he had followed the teaching of Mohammed as expressed in the Qur'an? Is it true that the parents of such "martyrs" are rewarded with payments of money? I used to travel in, feel welcome and enjoy such countries as Lebanon, Jordan, Syria, Egypt, and Morocco. I would now be afraid to do so. Would I be wrong?

How can there be peace, a live and let live philosophy, in a world where such violence and hatred is encouraged and supported by leaders? Have the great majority of peace-loving, moderate Muslims been captured, co-opted by the minority of haters and killers? Hitler may have started in the minority, but he ended in control. Stalin was a pathological killer, but he dominated. Ditto Castro, Pol Pot, et al.

Kind regards,
M.P.

Muhammad's life and deeds still resonate
November 10, 2002

Faced with worldwide protests and condemnation, the Rev. Jerry Falwell has tendered a half-hearted and lukewarm apology for insulting Prophet Muhammad. In an interview on CBS' *60 Minutes* he had called the Prophet of Islam a terrorist. He said he reached that conclusion after reading Muslim and non-Muslim sources.

There is a large body of work, by both Muslim and non-Muslims writers and historians, about the life and times of the prophet. Had the reverend bothered to look beyond his religious xenophobia he would have not labeled him a terrorist.

Unlike many other figures in history, the life and deeds of Prophet Muhammad are well documented. Most of what the prophet said and did was recorded by earlier Muslim historians like Muhammad Ibn Ishaq (d. 767), Muhammad Ibn Saad (d. 845), Muhammad al-Waqidi (d. 820), and Abu Jafar at-Tabari (d. 923). Their objective narratives are devoid of any selective bias and have been used by contemporary historians to understand and reconstruct the history of that era.

So who really was this man?

Muhammad was born an orphan in the southern Arabian town of Mecca in 570 A.D. He grew up in the mostly pagan environment that prevailed in the Arabian Peninsula. He had no formal education and was said to have shunned most of the adolescent and youth pastimes that were the norm in Meccan society at that time. As a young man he made business trips to Syria on behalf of a rich widow whom he later married. He would often retreat to a mountain cave in the valley of Mecca for reflection and contemplation.

It was during one of his retreats that he received the divine call through the Archangel Gabriel. Like many others before him, his message of change and the worship of one God was rejected by the polytheistic pagan community of Mecca that included members of his own extended family and his tribe. Relentless persecution at the hands of his own people forced him and a small group of his followers to flee north to the city of Medina where he found a receptive audience for his message.

For the next 23 years he preached and led the people of the Arabian Peninsula as their spiritual leader as well as head of the nascent Islamic state. At the time of his death in 632 at age 63, the entire peninsula had accepted his message. Qur'an, the sacred text of Islam, is the compilation of divine revelations he had received during his prophethood.

Here are some of his quotes:

"The first thing created by God was intellect."

"The most excellent Jihad is the one waged for the conquest of self."

"Women are the twin halves of men."

"Assist the oppressed whether Muslims or non-Muslims."

These certainly are not what a terrorist would have preached. So why is the Prophet of Islam denigrated by the likes of Mr. Falwell?

British author Karen Armstrong in her 1991 biography of Muhammad traces this to times when the fear of Muslim expansion into the heart of Europe led many a writer to cast Islam and its prophet in the most degrading terms.

They called him the Great Pretender, a false prophet and an Antichrist. They turned him into a bogeyman to scare unruly children.

Some people just cannot get out of the dark ages of their own making. However, for Muslims, Arabs and non-Arabs alike, Muhammad remains an ideal, and in their own lives they strive to live up to that ideal. So when someone, out of ignorance or hatred, heaps abuse on a man revered by one billion people, it touches them to their core.

Jerry Falwell should have known that.

Via mail, November 12, 2002:

Dear Dr. Hussain,

I always read your articles and I think I would like you if I ever met you, but I can't agree that Islam is an enlightened religion.

When 9/11 hit, I was as baffled as everyone else. What kind of people are these? Since I knew next to nothing about Islam I went on the 'net to look it up. I decided to read what Islam scholars had to say about it and found a site that offered insights on many subjects. The site is al-islam.org/al-tawhid/islam-know-conc.htm. I clicked on two subjects – knowledge and women – and read lengthy discourses on them. I came away with two principles. On knowledge, the position seems to be that true knowledge leads to Islam and any knowledge that does not is not true knowledge. On women the aim seems to be to support stability. When everyone knows his/her role from birth, that creates stability. My thought on that was if you want stability, go to a graveyard. There's stability. Since then, I have also learned that Islam does not encourage children in creative thinking and activities since creation is the province of God.

Personally, I feel that all three major religions are oppressive and none of them have histories to be proud of. I follow Buddhist thought myself. It is the only school of thought that has a stainless history behind it. Hope this doesn't offend you. I think you are probably a very nice and kind person. I just wanted to say that the precepts of your faith don't seem to support tolerance and compassion.

P.B.

Port Clinton

Thank you so much for your note of 11/12/02.

The people who masterminded 9/11 were no different than the fringe elements in any other religion. These people take bits and pieces of their religion and use them in a distorted way to justify their narrow, evil agendas. Most other major world religions like Christianity, Hinduism, Sikhism, and Judaism have their own who could pass for Al-Qaeda. Just as we cannot condemn these religions for the misdeeds of some of their followers, we cannot condemn Islam either. The instability you mentioned in your note is caused not by the majority, but by a vocal, virulent, and militant minority.

If you are interested in learning about the history or the teachings of Islam, I would recommend a few non-Muslim writers who have written about Islam with objectivity. These include Yvonne Haddad, Michael Hart, John Espisito and Karen Armstrong. These writers (and many others like them) are not in any particular camp.

I am grateful that you took the time to write.

Sincerely,

S. Amjad Hussain

In the Toledo Blade Readers' Forum, *November 26, 2002:*

"So many religions claim to be the way"

Dr. S. Amjad Hussain's column in defense of the Prophet Muhammad was both well-written and justified. I would like to assure Dr. Hussain and those of the Islamic faith in our area that Jerry Falwell and most other televangelists do not represent me or the God I've come to know and love.

The Taliban is to Islam what the Ku Klux Klan is to Christianity – a fraudulent representation. No group of people enjoys being judged by the actions of a few.

Religion is an emotionally charged topic. Men need to come to the table of discussion calmly and respectfully, with a thirst for truth and an appetite for humble pie.

The Qur'an offers some profound doctrine. As do the teachings of Buddha, Confucius, and Hinduism. From Aristotle to Einstein, great minds have offered words of wisdom. Jesus offers words of eternal life.

Good people don't go to heaven; saved people do. So the question is not how to be good, but how to be saved.

From this Christian's perspective, Jesus – the sinless one – shed His blood on the cross for the sins of the world. If that's true, then it's true if people believe it or not. Christian theology dictates our responsibility is to accept His sacrifice, then be buried with Christ in baptism. For if we die with Him, are buried with Him, then likewise we will be raised with Him.

So many religions and philosophies claim to be the way. Say what you will about Satan, one thing we can all agree on is that he is nothing if not clever. Where, except in a forest, could he hide the tree of life?

D.G.
Franklin Avenue

Via e-mail, November 11, 2002:
Hello, Mr. Hussain,
Nice short history of Mohammad. Did he ever go back to Mecca and kill people? Was that the first thing that he did once he got power? Is this another case of religious xenophobia? The inference from your article is that Mohammed never harmed anyone. According to your newspaper Muslims and Hindus fought in India over Jerry Falwell's statement. Why would Hindus ever fight over that? Was that the supposedly worldwide reaction to Falwell's statement? Which religious leader told his followers to kill Jerry Falwell?
Pope John Paul II
Billy Graham
A rabbi

A religious leader of the peaceful Muslim state of Iran.

Who was the first person arrested for the bombing in Bali? This person was arrested by the largest Muslim country in the world when it was forced to take sides against terrorism. It was forced to take sides, not by the United States, but by its neighbors in Asia. Why does Hamas, Islamic Jihad, etc. all have religious leaders to advise them? Are they advising them about peaceful living? Yassar Arafat condemned the killing of a murderer by Israelis during Ramadan on the very same day that Palestinians killed an Israeli solder. Is this Muslim logic? Sorry that I ramble, but Muslims have no credibility with me. It looks like the fanatic minority of Muslims is growing every day and that scares me.

    D.J.

Via e-mail, November 11, 2002:

Mr. Hussain,

Your apology for Muhammad certainly omitted some important information. You didn't point out that Muhammad Ibn Ishaq wrote the prophet's biography 120 years after his death (although you did give some death dates) or that we only have access to his work because of Ibn Hisham who died more than eighty years after he wrote it.

Why didn't you mention Muhammad's slaughter of the people of Banu Qurayza or his treatment of Kab ibn al-Ashraf or Kinana or of his relationship with Zaynab? Perhaps we can't call Muhammad a terrorist in the modern sense, but do you consider his treatment of other humans honorable?

    T.H.

Thank you so much for your e-mail.

I did not write an apologetic column. I really do not feel I need to apologize for anyone present or past. I hope you are familiar with the scholarship of Karen Armstrong, John Espisito and Yvonne Haddad who have painstakingly reconstructed the events of that era. They are not apologists for Muslims or Islam. Perhaps you will care to read any one of these to get a fair idea of the events you mentioned in your e-mail.

It has become fashionable to apply contemporary standards to events that happened 1400 years ago. Can we apply a contemporary yardstick to events narrated in the Old Testament? You would agree that some of the people and Prophets mentioned in the Old Testament could also be called terrorists. As a practicing Muslim I consider all the prophets mentioned in the Bible as honorable and worthy of our utmost respect and devotion.

I do thank you most sincerely for taking the time to write.

S. Amjad Hussain

Via e-mail, November 12, 2002:

Dr. Hussain,

You said, "I hope and pray that you would accord me the same courtesy." I find it interesting you would ask me this. If we were living in a Muslim controlled country, you would not be able to grant me this sort of courtesy. An individual living in a Muslim country isn't free to worship as he/she pleases (as you are here). I would be jailed or probably executed in a Muslim country. Islam is a religion of peace?

Let me ask you another question. What Islam-controlled country would you prefer to live in over the United States? I cannot think of a single country where Islam has control that would be a remotely desirable place to live. Afghanistan? Pakistan? Sudan? Syria? Jordan? Iraq? Iran? Turkey? What has Islam done for these countries?

I don't need to grant you the courtesy to believe as you wish. You have that right already because you live in a country founded on the principles of the Bible and Jesus Christ (although it no longer is). You are free to worship as you please. No one is going to execute you or put you in jail because you refuse to worship Jesus Christ. That is your choice.

You must be made aware however that refusing to accept Jesus Christ as your Lord and Savior, will have eternal consequences. Jesus Himself said, "I am the way, the truth and the life. No one comes to the Father except by me" (John 14:6). Your own scriptures reveal Jesus Christ as a prophet and incapable of lying. Therefore, you must consider these words of His carefully. Your eternal destiny depends on it.

Sincerely,

A.S.

Christmas is Christmas
January 2, 2006

The year 2005 was an eventful year. The news was rife with on-going conflicts in different parts of the world, natural disasters and the triumph of human spirit in the face of unprecedented calamities. But the controversy around Christmas was the one that interested me the most and for some very good reasons.

There was a lot of controversy about the so-called secularization of Christmas. People took exception to replacing the word Christmas with the generic name "holiday." The Christmas season is now holiday season and the Christmas tree has now been christened the holiday tree.

Why?

Many reasons are given, but none are very good or convincing. Some say the word Christmas is offensive to secular Christians and to non-Christians. To that I say a loud "nonsense."

Christmas is a Christian holiday and since the majority of people in this country are Christians they have every right to enunciate it and celebrate it. They have not insisted, at least for the past 40 years that I have lived amongst them, that I give up my religion and become a Christian. Except for the minority of self-righteous Christian evan-gelists who are always ready and willing to bring a stray sheep into their flock (a rather common streak in some other religions as well) the majority of Christians are quite content with their faith and are willing to live and let live in peace.

Although the trend to secularize Christmas has been going on for some time the tinsel hit the fan this season when someone in Boston City government called the 48-foot spruce "the holiday tree." The people of Halifax, who have for many years gifted a spruce to Boston, were not very happy.

While the airwaves were abuzz with the Halifax-Boston story, someone in the office of Canada's Governor General added insult to injury by saying that Madame Michaëlle Jean, the Governor General, would light the Holiday Tree at her official residence. She promptly reassured Canadians that the tree at her residence is the Christmas tree. In Washington, Congress also weighed in and passed a resolution not to tamper with the name Christmas. According to Speaker Dennis Hastert, the Capitol tree will still be called the Capitol Christmas Tree.

For many years now "Holiday Season" and "Season's Greetings" had become accepted alternatives to "Merry Christmas" or "Christmas Season." But the efforts to be inclusive have gone ridiculously too far when "Christmas" is being air-brushed out of the "Christmas Season." Why would non-Christians take offense to a Christian holiday? Would any Muslim, Hindu or Jew like to have his or her religious holidays made generic? And they ought to know also that in countries of their origin any effort to secularize religious holidays would most certainly be met with violent protests. Religious sensitivity has to be a two way street.

Against this backdrop it was amusing to see the paranoid ranting of people on Fox News who seized the opportunity and started blaming the liberals for this trend. The banner headline on Fox News "The War on Christmas: How the Liberal Plot to Ban the Sacred Christian Holiday Is Worse Than You Thought" had all the elements of intrigue, paranoia and self-righteousness. From their Foxholes, however, they could not see that the very paragon of conservative religious/political correctness Bill O'Reilly himself was undermining Christmas by peddling "holiday gifts" on his web site. They promptly became Christmas gifts once he found himself on the wrong side of the argument.

Another inhabitant of the Foxhole, John Gibbon, according to the *New York Times*, blamed Jews and other religious minorities who are out there to kill Christmas. Earlier on Christian Radio he had said that all non-Christians are following the wrong religion but he promised to be tolerant of them "as long as they're civil and behave." Mr. Gibbon seems to believe the age-old myth that when-in-doubt-blame-the-Jews.

Fox News had nothing to say about the White House greeting cards that the President and First Lady sent out bearing "Happy Holiday Season."

All the contradictions and double talk aside, Christmas should stay Christmas and we non-Christians should not be embarrassed to wish a Merry Christmas.

So, a belated MERRY CHRISTMAS to all of you, and also a very prosperous and Happy New Year.

Via mail, January 2, 2006:
Dear Dr. Hussain,

A note to thank you for your article in today's Blade – *"Christmas is Christmas." You put into words what many of us are thinking and trying to explain to others.*

Thank you, again.
Sincerely,
J.M.P.
Toledo, OH

Via e-mail, January 2, 2006:
Dr. Hussain:
Thanks so much for yet another honest, in-depth column, "Christmas is Christmas!" How true that "religious sensitivity has to be a two-way street!"

And how right you are about the "paranoid ranting of people at Fox News." My wife & I gag with laughter when we happen upon Fox News and listen to the "no spin zone" and the "fair & balanced" rantings of the likes of Bill O'Reilly, John Gibson & co.

Keep up the good work - we look forward to your column!
Lou & Deb

Via e-mail, January 2, 2006:
Amjad Hussain:
I was SO happy to see your article, "Christmas is Christmas" in the Toledo Blade *today. Thank you for expressing what so many Christians feel. I think, coming from a non-Christian, it will be better-understood and taken to heart. I especially like the point you made that in other non-Christian countries the "effort to secularize religious holidays would most certainly be met with violent protests." Great point!*

It seems to me, though, that it's not those who practice another faith, but those who have NO faith at all that seem to object to "Christmas," those Christians who have lost their faith that want to secularize society.

Thanks, again, for your bold stand on this matter.

Tell Dottie I said "hello." May both of you have a great new year full of prosperity and peace.

(And a belated Merry Christmas to you, too!)
Sincerely,
G.C.

Via e-mail, January 3, 2006:
Dear Dr. S. Amjad Hussain,

I would like to take this opportunity to thank you for your column on Christmas. It was not only refreshing but enlightening to hear. I believe we can all live in this country peacefully if we can learn to let others believe and exist in their own way. The sanctity of life should not revolve around one's religion; all life is sacred. Thank you again.

Respectfully,
K.T., R.N.
St. Anne's Hospital

Via e-mail, January 4, 2006:
Hello, Mr. Hussain,

I very much enjoyed, and agreed with, your editorial in the Toledo Blade, *"Christmas is Christmas." I am a Christian and certainly share the sentiment you mentioned, "content with their faith and are willing to live and let live in peace."*

Thank you for your courage in putting these feelings in print!
T.K.

Via e-mail, January 3, 2006:
Amjad:

I am amazed by your sensitive article about Christmas. I had a hard time taking seriously my conservative Christian followers when they criticized our culture for being against Christmas. These people would be the last to criticize the central issue of the marketplace being a "god" of its own in our world of the USA.

It was healing to have a follower of Islam be so open to another faith and I am sure other Christians are quietly blessing you for your thoughtfulness as well.

Blessings to all in the New Year,
G.C.E.

Afghans need medicine, food, not religious zealots
September 2, 2001

The Taliban are in the news again. They are being chastised for arresting eight members of an aid agency, including two Americans, for their attempts to convert Afghans to Christianity. I applaud this action of the Taliban.

Afghanistan under the harsh religious rule of the Taliban has suffered tremendously. Its economy is in shambles, education system a mess, and health care almost non-existent. And now because of Afghanistan's refusal to hand over Osama bin Laden, an avowed enemy of the United States, the U.N. Security Council, over the objections of Secretary General Kofi Anan, has imposed the most stringent economic sanctions on the country. The most vulnerable - women and children - are dying of famine, disease, and a prolonged drought. Humanitarian help of any kind is needed and is welcomed.

But most of this help comes with religious strings attached. Aid agencies, mostly Christian missionaries disguised as aid workers, arrive on the scene with a loaf of bread in one hand and a Bible in the other expecting to barter bread for their souls.

This is how it works. While the entire world is forbidden to deal with Afghanistan, aid agencies can get in the country on humanitarian grounds. And most of them enter the country with their own agenda to proselytize and convert. It is, in simple words, an unholy blackmail.

Christian missionaries have a long history of preying on the most vulnerable. For centuries these self-anointed purveyors of salvation have been trampling the far corners of the world to convert the poor to their brand of true faith.

In all fairness, Christian missionaries are not the only ones who indulge in conversions but they are the most organized and well funded. Muslims and Hindus have fought each other over conversions that have led to communal bloodletting and together they have fought the advances of Christian missionaries.

Afghans are no strangers to such overtures. In the early 19th century, Anglican missionaries set up hospitals and schools along the turbulent western frontier of British India. A missionary surgeon by the name of T.L. Pennell spent 20 years dispensing medicines with a hefty dose of his religion to the tribes. He called his effort "extraordinary Christianizing, civilizing, and pacifying influence into some of the darkest abodes of cruelty and superstition on the face of God's earth." To him ancient Hindu practices were nothing but "superficial philosophies and dogmas; rites, and ceremonies from the hoary Vedic ages." Upon his retirement he lamented that in 20 years he was able to convert only one Afghan to his religion.

It was one convert too many.

Compare Dr. Pennell and other missionaries' self-righteousness with the selfless mission of Mother Teresa of Calcutta. She gave comfort to the street people at the end of their life without attempts to redirect their departing souls to a different destination.

Religion is a personal choice and one should be free to practice any religion one prefers or none at all. It should not be shoved down the throats of desperate hungry people when they are most vulnerable. Freedom of religion and conversions under duress are not the same. To say otherwise is to turn sublime into profane.

The West owes a debt to the Afghans for their efforts in defeating a super power and starting the process of disintegration of what Ronald Reagan called the Evil Empire. Today the country is laid waste from that struggle. What Afghans desperately need is food, medicines, and assistance to build their country. They do not need proselytizing by a bunch of zealous missionaries.

Via e-mail, September 7, 2001:
Dear Dr. Hussain,
First, I want to say that I have thoroughly enjoyed your column and articles in the Toledo Blade *for years. I have felt like I was personally traveling with your companions as I was taken away by your giftedness of the pen, storytelling of places I could only imagine getting to. Time and again I have felt compelled to thank you for such articles, but alas, the words were only composed in my head until now.*

Your Labor Day column surprised me a bit with the almost "anti-Christian" flavor that it had. To applaud any behavior of the Taliban is somewhat disconcerting! I reread the column several times to truly see if I was not missing something.

I, too, do not care for anyone "shoving" religion down the unsus-pecting throats of others. However, the words of my savior, Jesus Christ instructed all disciples (followers of Christ) to "Go, then, to all peoples everywhere and make them my disciples: baptize them in the name of the Father, the Son, and the Holy Spirit . . ." Matthew 28:19. For Christians anywhere, to do otherwise is not being a true Christian.

Could you imagine anyone writing against your Qur'an and its teachings in this same manner as you have written about these so called "zealots"? What has your prophet instructed the faithful to teach and display as their pillars? Open-mindedness and dialogue are where our efforts should be to emphasize the oneness of humanity. There is, after all, only one true God. I do not agree with the harsh sanctions we (The U.S. government) have imposed on these innocent people of Afghanistan. It is deplorable that it has gone on for so long. What is worse, however, is the power of the Taliban on these same people. Maybe this *is the story that you should concentrate on!*

As you well know, the power of the pen (and the media) can be mighty persuasive. Please, be very, very careful.

Sincerely, a faithful reader,

C.M.W.

Thank you for your very nice letter. I deeply appreciate that you took the time to write.

Now to the subject at hand. If the followers of every religion believe that every one else is on a false path and start converting others we will have chaos in this world. Or take the example of your own town of Findlay. Suppose every Sunday a bunch of missionaries from other denominations would show up at your church and start preaching their brand of gospel? And suppose every Sunday we have this tug of war between different churches to convince others to convert. It would not be a very pleasant situation.

All religions preach that theirs is the only way to salvation. Who is to say which one is right? The Southern Baptists consider anybody outside their fold, including all Christian believers, to be non-Christians. Catholic church says salvation is only through the teachings of their church. Muslims believe salvation is only through their religion (but they conveniently forget that their holy book says there should be no compulsion in religion and that people are free to choose what ever religion they like).

I firmly believe that religion should be a free choice and conversions should be allowed when there is no coercion. What I have seen in the third world is not free choice but exploitation of the poor and the hungry. Hence, I am against preaching and converting under such circumstances.

The Taliban believe in a brand of Islam that is mostly alien to a person like me. My interpretation is different but I do not think I have the right to tell them that what they believe and practice is wrong.

If the followers of various religions are to live in peace with each other, they have to accept that other religions are as good as theirs. To deny religious equality to others is to assert one's superiority. I cannot accept this.

You did not have to write but you did and I am most grateful to you for sharing your thoughts with me. I consider it a blessing that we can discuss such issues without getting angry or upset and that we retain respect for each other.

Warmest regards,

S. Amjad Hussain

Via e-mail, September 8, 2001:

Dear Dr. Hussain:

Your recent essay in the Blade *misled readers in three ways. First, 24 workers were arrested, not just eight foreigners. The Afghan workers might be executed, since the Taliban leadership has declared that Muslim citizens who convert to Christianity or attempt to convert others will be under the sentence of death.*

Second, contra your assertion, the Shelter Now International aid agency is not merely a bunch of "missionaries disguised as aid workers." In January and February, SNI distributed over 4,000 stoves and thousands of blankets. SNI also operated a bakery, distributing thousands of bread-patties each day. Previously, they constructed about 3,000 geodesic dome residences and ran a factory that produced construction materials. That's some disguise! This week, the Taliban closed down the International Assistance Mission, which ran the largest eye hospital in the country. Are you still applauding?

Third, while some of the people who were arrested might have provided Muslims with access to a movie about Christianity, that would not mean that they are trading bread for souls or provoking "conversions under duress." It would show that a professional relief worker could be a non-professional gospel-sharing Christian. The American branch of SNI has stated that they provide assistance "with no expectation that beneficiaries will convert to Christianity."

If people in Afghanistan want to learn about Christianity and/or become a Christian, they should be able to do so without risking execution. How can you say, "One should be free to practice any religion one prefers," and then commend the Taliban's actions? If anyone in Afghanistan is using force to promote a religion, it's the Taliban!

Sincerely,

J.S.

Minister, Church of Christ

I am grateful for your letter.

Obviously we have a different definition of freedom of religion. I just don't believe anyone – Muslim, Jew, Christian, Hindu or Buddhist – has the right to tell others that they need saving. While I have the utmost respect for every religion (and my writings over the past 30 years prove that), I cannot grant this license to any one.

Just imagine if people from various churches, mosques or synagogues would start visiting each other's places of worship to preach their own religion. It will make a rather unpleasant situation, wouldn't it?

Look at the situation in the world. The Vatican thinks salvation is only through the teachings of Catholic Church. Southern Baptists claim everyone is doomed except them. Muslims consider their religion to be the only way to salvation. Jews have no faith in any book but the Old Testament, which they call The Hebrew Bible.

If a Muslim, Christian or a Jew would like to study any other religion and convert, it should be a free choice. This, to me, is freedom of religion.

What the missionaries are doing in Afghanistan is not exercising this freedom; they are taking advantage of desperate people.

Yes, I applaud the action of the Taliban. The Taliban should expel these workers from their country. As you probably know I am no fan of the Taliban as my three part special report in the *Blade* (July 15, 16, 17, 2001) clearly indicates.

While we may disagree on this issue, I want you to know that I hold your religion in great esteem. I am very grateful for your comments.

Sincerely,

S. Amjad Hussain

Via e-mail, September 9, 2001:
Dear Dr. Hussain:

Thank you for the informative series on Afghanistan earlier this past summer. You filled in many gaps in my knowledge after a lifelong interest in that nation that began nearly 50 years ago when, as an 8th grader in Chicago, I selected Afghanistan as "my country" to research for a United Nations and international series study. At that time, after my writing to the information centre in that nation, they in turn sent me a pamphlet, now lost, and a very kind letter. From then on, I read everything that came my way about Afghanistan. I remember my parents thinking I should go there to study someday. Alas, that was never possible. However, I felt they would "win" the Russo-Afghan conflict/war, and they indeed did. Your series illuminated the terrible cost to Afghanistan of their resistance, and the price they are continuing to pay. A group of French citizens who are very concerned about the women of Afghanistan occasionally send me a listserv notice....

Thanks again. We in Northwest Ohio who have traveled and known so much diversity appreciate your insights, opinions, and information!

Sincerely,
A.Y.

Via e-mail, September 10, 2001:

I was saddened and disappointed reading your above article. I thought you will see the harsh reality that how the Taliban are hurting the cause of Islam by making life so difficult for Muslims under their rule that the poor people started thinking that if this is the true Islam then we are better off without it.

You cannot blame others for the situation created by Taliban. Taliban should create situation that people should be happy that they are Muslim and under true Islamic rule.

I did not expect you to be so blind about the twisted and corrupted religion these Taliban are showing to the world as Islam. I am convinced that it is Allah himself who is punishing them for hurting the True and Great religion of Islam.
S.M.

Thank you for your comments. If you have the time please log on to www.toledoblade.com and use the paper's search engine to find my three-part special report on Afghanistan (published July 15, 16 and 17, 2001). You will get a good idea of my evaluation of the Taliban. I do not agree with their brand of Islam.

Now... the missionaries in Afghanistan. The Taliban are within their right to kick the aid workers out. Unless you are willing to give free reign to the missionaries in the third world, you should also be concerned about the coercion they use to convert destitute people. Their activities are well known in India and Pakistan. I am against religions making claims of superiority whether it is Christianity, Islam or any other religion.

I am grateful that you took the time to write.

Sincerely,

S. Amjad Hussain

Via e-mail, September 12, 2001:
In light of the recent events, I was wondering if you still applaud the Taliban? Perhaps your thriving practice would be better put to service in that country?
Please consider it.
K.C.

Generalizations of any kind tend to ignore the basic issues. It is obvious that I was not able to get my point of view across to you. Perhaps you would care to read my 3 part series on Afghanistan published in the *Blade* in mid-July 2001. If you had read them you probably would not have asked this question.

I made a choice over 30 years ago to make this country my home. It was not done under duress or under any threat against my life. I think I have been a responsible citizen and have contributed to the society and community in many ways. The question whether I would like to go to

Afghanistan and practice among the people 'I applauded' is a knee jerk response to the separate issue of conversions. In all honesty I would not mind helping out the people in Afghanistan just as I have on many occasions worked in the medical missions in Dominican Republic.

I thank you for your comments.

Sincerely,

S. Amjad Hussain

Via e-mail, September 13, 2001:

I don't know when your next Blade *column is due but you'll get an opportunity to offer your insight into the recent terrorist problems. I suggest an explanation about what the Islamic religion does and doesn't stand for. Perhaps a comparison with what is happening in Ireland. Most Christians know that neither religion (Catholic nor Protestant) support the killing and terrorist acts of the IRA.*

You may also help us understand why the U.S. is hated so much.

Finally, how we should retaliate? There is no question that the U.S. will not settle for anything less than a violent response. How would you suggest that a response be directed so as to assure that the proper persons are punished?

Good Luck,

H.H.

cc: Tom Walton - The Blade

Via e-mail, September 19, 2001:

You, sir, are a disgrace. How dare you applaud the capture of those spreading the Gospel? Don't you know they can receive the death penalty? You are a poor excuse not only of a man, but a human being. And I would rather die than for you to be my doctor.

So Afghan does not like the missionaries? Fine! We will be sending a new kind they should like better shortly. They will be wearing helmets and carrying guns. My only disappointment is that you will not be there to see them and hear what they have to say.

The highest insults are extended to you, sir.

D.B.

I sincerely thank you for your comments.

While I do not wish to enter into a contentious debate I must say that no one likes to be forced into another faith under duress. In present day Afghanistan these religious overtures in exchange for food are just that.

I do not think any one particular religion has a corner on salvation. This applies to Judaism, Christianity, Islam, Hinduism and Buddhism. All these religions are part of the American landscape. If we do not begin to understand and accept each other (rather than trying to convert each other by forcing our own brand of religion down each others' throats), we will be in sad shape.

Whatever action our country takes against the Taliban, I hope and pray it will be taken to curb terrorism and not on behalf of any one particular faith. If that were true then Northern Ireland would pose a difficult dilemma.

Obviously we disagree, but our disagreement should not prevent us in discussing important issues in a polite and civil way. I think America, throughout history, has stood for this cherished principle.

Again I thank you for taking the time to write.

Sincerely,

S. Amjad Hussain

Via e-mail, September 19, 2001:

Sir,

I am well aware of the strategies of some Christian missionaries. The ministry I am involved with has complained about it for years. However, I do not believe such mistakes merit your conclusion that you are happy to have missionaries arrested, especially not the ones who recently have been.

They could be put to death, and you know that. It is hard for me to be civil with a man who approves of an organization that would do this. I think you are expecting a little bit too much in that vein.

I am also aware of how some push their faith on others, and I detest that strongly as you do. But to assume that ALL missionaries do that is the same as assuming all people of a given group are bad because some are. That is prejudice and bigotry. And how is it that you are so against Christians "pushing" their faith on others, yet so in favor of the Taliban, who are destroying Buddhist statues? Is that not pushing their faith on others also? Is not their terrorists destroying the WTC because we do not think as they being just a little pushy on their part?

Were I to say that I was glad that Muslims simply sharing their faith with others were jailed, you would be the first to go on the warpath. These particular missionaries were not bartering food for the soul, either. But you throw them into your bigoted stereotype as if they have nonetheless. How do you expect anyone to respect that?

Those in the East like to complain about the evil Christians and their medieval Crusade. At least we had a Reformation and cleaned up our act quite a bit. Looking at the actions of the Taliban, I'd say Muslims were about due for one. And those Muslims who strictly follow Islam are calling for precisely this at this time.

Do you think I am happy to write such things? I am not, I would much rather speak things which bring harmony and peace. But articles such as yours sadly need addressed, because unless they are we will never get there. I certainly hope you come to terms with your prejudice and bigotry. It does not become you.

    D.B.

Let me make on thing very clear: I am not an apologist for the Taliban. I have written against their harsh rule and the version of Islam they practice. My writings on the subject speak more loudly than I can tell you in this brief conversation. At least check the detailed three part special report I wrote for the *Blade* in mid July.

I am against any conversion that even remotely takes advantage of poor people. This goes against Muslims as well. When, a few years ago, Christians were persecuted by some bigoted Muslims in Pakistan, I wrote about it in the Pakistani press and raised the issue in a personal meeting with the then-Pakistani Prime Minister Nawaz Sharif in New York. At this very time efforts are underway by a number of Pakistani Americans to raise funds to help rebuild a church that was destroyed in rural Punjab during communal violence a few years ago.

Often I have been asked by Muslim zealots as to which side I am on. My answer is I am on the side of the downtrodden and persecuted. I am certainly not on the side of zealots of any religious persuasion including Muslim zealots.

I am very conformable with my faith. I will never impose it on others. If someone wants to learn more about my faith I will point them to the available sources but never make myself part of their personal quest. If some one would like to talk to me about my faith I would try to make time but will not enter into a debate. Religion is too precious and sublime to be the bone of contention among decent people.

I hope the above would be of some help.

Sincerely,

S. Amjad Hussain

Dear Sir,

Your explanation certainly does help. In fact, it is what I suspected, or at least hoped. You are no more in favor of a religion taking advantage of others than I am. Now that we have come to this, I can make the real point with you that I want to make. Your basic underlying perspective is a good and fair one, but your choice of how you express your sentiments is sometimes not so good. That is not prudent, especially in these times. It took two letters to find out we are actually in agreement on this issue, at least in terms of the principles involved (that is to say, that the imposition of one's religion, and the persecution of another for their religion are both wrong). The only point I would care to make in which perhaps we have may still a difference is that, while imposing one's religion is wrong, throwing someone in jail or killing them for doing so is inappropriate. For example, when the misguided Christian missionaries in India were up their tricks, India simply refused them entrance into India at all. This is better than jailing them or killing them. Just boot them out when you find them....

All this being said and finally discovering what your positions really are, I rescind my decision that you could never be my doctor, I apologize for giving you a high insult, I am glad you are over here in America instead of Afghanistan, and would only say please, especially in these times, be careful to fully examine what you are going to say making sure you are really explaining yourself and what you think. I got the impression you were glad Christians were in jail and want them to die because they were sharing the good news. What you were really trying to say was that Christians sometimes get these results because of how they present their message. What a difference between the two impressions!! I know it is easy to do this by mistake, and find myself also doing it all the time. But I must do better, for these things cause needless misunderstandings, of which there are enough of in the world already.

Please watch how you present yours. I do not want you to get harmed in these times by some nut.

Have a nice day.

Thank you for your note. I appreciate you took the time to hear me out.

What I do in a very minuscule way on behalf of other minorities is something very personal. I shared that with you only to make you understand that I take a rather broad view of religion. My religion also demands that I invite others to Islam. I just do not believe that is practical or justified. We can learn from each other, respect each other's faith and together contribute to a better world.

It might surprise you but I have attended church services on many occasions with my Christian friends and have enjoyed them. The last time was yesterday evening at the Corpus Christi Church on Dorr Street where my wife and I joined some of our friends for a service.

Sincerely,
Amjad Hussain

Time for Taliban to roll up the welcome mat
September 16, 2001

There comes a time when an overwhelming feeling of outrage and grief leaves us speechless. The wanton and cowardly act of violence against our country and the free world have left us stunned and has changed us all in ways we cannot understand or comprehend.

The meticulously planned and masterly executed attack against the United States has no historic reference point or precedent. The Pearl Harbor and Oklahoma City bombings pale by comparison. Long after the rescue and cleanup, the image of two commercial planes plowing into the World Trade Center twin towers will remain seared in our consciousness forever.

While it is early to point an accusing finger in any one direction, it is easy to realize that this was not the work of a few lunatics avenging their real or perceived grievances against the United States.

There are very few organizations capable of pulling off an act of such mammoth proportions. The prime suspect has to be the Saudi fugitive Osama bin Laden. He has money, controls an elaborate international network of terrorists, and has the loyalty of committed followers. His past behavior and his often-repeated threats against the U.S. leave little room for doubt.

Osama bin Laden lives in the Kandahar region in southern Afghanistan under the protection of the Taliban.

Caught in a time warp, the Taliban are totally oblivious or willfully ignorant of the workings of their guest. In my discussions with the Taliban leadership nine months ago in Kabul they denied his role in any terrorists attacks against the United States and rejected out of hand the evidence this country had provided to them through Pakistan.

It is time the Taliban face reality and abandon their grandiose ideas of molding the world in their own image. For the sake of their own suffering masses, if not for any other reason, they must pull the welcome mat from under their "honored" guest and hand him over to the international community.

It is also an opportunity for Pakistan to mount a cleanup operation and curb the rising tide of militant Taliban-style movement within its borders.

In the past few days the word Islamic has been used in conjunction with terrorism or terrorists groups. Islam has nothing to do with acts of violence by some of its followers just as Christianity has nothing to do with the communal violence in Northern Ireland.

A great majority of one billion Muslims in the world have been as shocked and repulsed by these events just as others in the world. Leading Muslim organizations in this country and abroad have, in unequivocal terms, condemned this terrorist act.

At times like these an expression of outrage by the citizens is natural but directing this rage towards one particular segment of the society is not. While some people want to lash out at anyone who even remotely resembles the terrorists either by ethnicity or religion, it is misplaced blame.

When the terrorists hit the World Trade Center, they were hitting at a prominent symbol of America. In that symbol on Sept. 11, there was a cross section of American people. There were in excess of 50,000 Christians, Jews, Muslims, Hindus, whites, blacks and Asians in that place. They all took the hit and many of them lost their lives.

When a hole is blown through the fabric of a society, it damages all segments.

In due course Lower Manhattan will be rebuilt, as will be the destroyed wing of the Pentagon. And in time the gaping hole in the psyche of the nation will also mend.

We will look back and remember the day when terrorists struck a terrible blow to America and all Americans, regardless of their color or belief, stood together in solidarity as one people.

God bless America.

Via e-mail, September 16, 2001:
Dear Dr. Hussain,
Nice job in the Sunday column.
H.H.
cc: Tom Walton - The Blade

Via e-mail, September 16, 2001:
Dr. Hussain,

I realize we are a country of prejudices and I am pleased to see your article. Your outrage is my outrage and we are Americans together. I do not want to see what happen to our Japanese citizens after Pearl Harbor. The more we hear from our Arab citizens, the more people realize you are Americans.

I come from Tiffin and actually know very few minorities. But, since I am one of those liberals, I feel for those that are different and have to suffer due to prejudices. I pray that our country will stand tall against the prejudices of those that cannot see that America is more than white. We are a splash of colors and no one color stands taller. Even whites have their terrorist groups, such as the KKK.

Keep writing and showing who you are: an American citizen.
Sincerely,
J.J.

Via e-mail, September 17, 2001:
Excellent argument regarding the IRA and Christianity. I've been using that one myself. Our country needs to understand the more we let these events eat at our national psyche and cause us to turn on each other the more Bin Laden wins. I have no doubt it is of amusement to him and makes him feel, and to some, look more justified in his actions.

Thank you for your words.
S.H.

Via e-mail, September 19, 2001:
Dear Amjad,
It takes a lot to depress me but I am not a happy camper right now.

Anyway, first the better news. I hope you have seen the strong and relentless condemnation by President Bush of the ignorant Americans who are mistakenly attacking Muslims, and some Indians, in America. The Arab-American Anti-Defamation League has strongly commended him for his stand. Also, more and more Muslim organizations and countries are joining in the alliance against terrorism saying the attacks on innocent civilians is un-Islamic and cannot be allowed to continue. Iran is probably going to join as well because they have their own Shia-Sunni conflict with the Taliban.

What depressed me was watching 60 Minutes II *last night. They visited a boy's high school in Pakistan. This was not a madrasa. The boys were all wearing sweaters and ties and speaking perfect English, so I could tell that it was an exclusive, upper-class school.   What amazed me was that these well-to-do kids were describing themselves as mujahadeen, expressing blind support for Osama Bin Laden, and had even designed Long Live Osama (in English) screen savers for their desktops.*

I wondered: what do these kids have in common with Osama? Pakistan has always been an ally of the U.S., yet they support a known terrorist, who deliberately kills innocent civilians including women and children, which the Imams say is strictly prohibited by Islam. Obviously they are not being taught the true version of Islam, but the distorted version practiced by the Taliban and militant, extremist Arabs.

Is it because of America's "blind" support for Israel?   Hard to believe, because neither Afghanistan nor Pakistan has anything to do with that conflict...

On the 60 Minutes II *show last night everyone they interviewed in Pakistan and Afghanistan seemed full of bravado that they would prevail because they were strong and willing to die, and Americans were weak and not willing to die...*

Throughout history, when Americans are under physical attack, as they are right now, I believe they will fight ferociously to protect their way of life, precisely because they do not want to die.   They entered and fought two world wars on behalf of other people, and prevailed after losing tens of thousands of their own people.   In addition, they have the economic and military strength to do a lot of damage from a distance.   Now, they also have growing support from many other nations.

Watching the kids in Pakistan last night sent a chill up my spine.   It made me wonder how many people are going to die before this is all over.

Mario

Thank you, Mario, for your concerns. I agree with you.

I missed the *60 Minutes* program. There is a strong undercurrent of resentment against the U.S. in the world. In the new order after the collapse of communism these people do not find a comfortable place.

These include the independent movements the world over. What the boys in Pakistani schools said was what they hear from their parents.

Osama's anti-American stand appeals to them because the past American policies have not brought them any comfort. It is a maze of conflicting and counter-conflicting interests. I hope that after the passions have cooled down, a public debate on the causes of almost global disenchantment with America would ensue.

As ever,

Amjad

Via e-mail, September 19, 2001:

Dear Dr. Hussain,

Although we have only met via correspondence, I just wanted to express to you my deep sorrow that some people have taken it upon themselves to commit acts of violence against Muslims, despite the appeals made by myself and others not to do so. Personal vengeance goes against the message of Christ. Those who carry out such acts are either not Christians, or else, caught up by their emotions; they have forgotten what Christ taught.

I am praying for many people this week. And while I hope that the terrorists will be brought to justice – and surely they will have to answer for their actions, if not now, then on Judgment Day – I also pray for the welfare of Muslims everywhere. I pray that the Taliban will be true to the principles of genuine Islam. I pray that onlookers will realize that those who committed the attacks (and killed some Muslims in the process) do not represent genuine Islam. And I pray that America as a whole will be patient and will put its trust not in military might, but in the living God.

In my theological research, I see many components of Islam and Christianity which are practically identical, and many more which, while not identical, are compatible. Perhaps we may be able someday to work together to cultivate better relations and discuss the things that separate Muslims who adhere to the Qur'an and Christians who adhere to the Bible.

Sincerely yours,

J.S.

Minister, Church of Christ

It was heart warming to receive your note. Thank you for your words of comfort and wisdom. You are absolutely right in stating the

Muslims and Christians have much in common. Perhaps we could emphasize the thread that binds us and set aside the issues that separate us.

Acts of vandalism, as acts of terrorism, have no religious basis. No religion can ever justify plowing loaded jet liners into population centers and no religion can justify damaging a place of worship. These acts are but acts of terrible vengeance committed by misguided people.

Last evening 2000 people came to the Islamic Center to make a human chain around the building. It was a beautiful sight.

I am grateful for your kindness.

Sincerely,

S. Amjad Hussain

Containing the spread of bigotry and hate
September 30, 2001

In the aftermath of terrorist attacks, America has undergone a sweeping change of attitude. A palpable and often visible backlash against those who even remotely resemble the culprits is sweeping the country. This has sent many of our citizens into hiding, has made them shun public places, and has forced them to wonder about their rightful place in our society.

A backlash in the wake of a horrible national trauma is to be expected. Not all citizens are given to thoughtful introspection. Not everyone is familiar with the causes, perceived or real, that fuel a venomous hatred of this country in militant fringe elements in some far away lands. Add to the sickening images of collapsing Twin Towers the refrain "Islamic terrorism" and someone wants to settle the score here and now.

Since Sept. 11, there have been more than 600 hate-related incidents against Muslims and Arab-Americans and even against those who may look like them. There have been four murders, 45 assaults, and 60 attacks on mosques, including the one here in our own community where a vengeful citizen put a bullet through one of the prayer room windows.

While it is convenient to blame such random acts of violence on an ignorant fringe of society, one cannot ignore the overwhelming negative feelings toward Arabs in a sizable number of Americans. In a poll conducted by CNN/*USA Today*/Gallup, almost half of Americans said they would require all Arabs in this country, including those who are U.S. citizens, to carry special ID cards. I hope this "Fortress America" attitude is nothing but a transient overreaction to the tragic events of Sept. 11.

We immigrants may understand this backlash to some extent, but our children do not. They are confused because, being born and raised in this country, they don't have the tugs and pulls of far away ancestral homes that their parents, grandparents, and, in some cases, great-grandparents might have felt. They are committed to America and not to some dubious and quasi-religious causes espoused by terrorists who distort the words of the sacred texts to suit their own agendas and justify their horrible acts.

Here are some revealing facts about Muslims in America. There are 7 million of them in this country, more than Jews, Episcopalians, or Presbyterians. A solid 35 percent of them are African-Americans and the rest are equally divided between Arabs and South Asians. Of the total number of Arabs in this country, 75 percent are not Muslims but Christians. There are 1,372 mosques in this country, including a mosque at the Norfolk Naval Base in Virginia where about 50 American sailors gather every Friday for weekly Sabbath prayers.

Islam is not only a Middle Eastern or Asian religion; it is also an American religion.

Of late, the media have gone into overdrive to contain the very genie of Muslim intolerance and bigotry they unwittingly helped uncork in the first place. The comments by the likes of Louisiana Congressman John Cooksey ("If I see someone come in that's got a diaper on his head, that guy needs to be pulled over") and Rush I-was-just-kidding Limbaugh ("I would like to wipe the smiles off the face of Palestinians who were celebrating after the terrorists attacks") are the kind of inflammatory rhetoric that ignites the fires of communal hatred.

Despite the backlash and the bigotry of some of our fellow citizens, America remains the most tolerant, understanding, and accepting country in the world. No nation in the world, including the countries we left behind, can match that.

The loose change we carry in our pockets has the Latin inscription *E Pluribus Unum*, meaning "From Many, One." While the founding fathers could not have envisioned the present makeup of this republic 225 years ago, they did provide the basis for a diverse and plural society. We will all be served well if in addition to waving the flag we also look at the inscription on those coins.

Via e-mail, October 5, 2001:

Dr. Hussain.

In your recent column, you stated that the media were using "inflammatory rhetoric" to stir up "communal hatred." To support this view, you quote Rush Limbaugh as saying "I would like to wipe the smiles off the face of Palestinians who were celebrating after the terrorist attacks."

As much as I disagree with the mainstream media, Rush was absolutely correct in his reaction to those pictures. My wife and I had a much more violent reaction than Rush did.

We do not tar all people of Arab descent with the same brush. If, however, you are jumping up and down and cheering the death of thousands of innocent men, women and children, you are not worthy of anyone's understanding. This is not bigotry. The friend of my enemy is my Enemy. I would be happy to help wipe the smile off their faces.

Your sympathies should have been directed to the people who lost loved ones in the World Trade Center. I'm sure the Arab-Americans will survive the very few bigots who exist in this country. The victims of these attacks did not survive the bigotry coming from overseas.

J.F.W.

Via e-mail, September 30, 2001:
Dear Amjad,
I see many articles in the media similar to the attached one. I try to rationalize this as the media resorting to its typical practice of skewing and sensationalizing the news. Every community has its ignoramuses and extremists, which the media love to publicize. What I don't see are any articles about Muslim leaders who condemn the terrorists and explain to the community that these people are distorting the Islamic religion and trying to use it to further their own megalomaniacal ambitions...

On the local front, I have not seen a single letter to the editor since September 11 from a Muslim name. Even the Christian Arabs who are normally vociferous on behalf of the Arab cause have fallen silent, people like Marise Mikhail and Mary Abowd.
M.G.

Via e-mail, September 30, 2001:
Dr. Hussain,
I've enjoyed your commentaries and articles in The Blade, *for a couple of years now. I think I've learned more about Middle Eastern culture, from you, than from any other "media source".*

This is a very difficult time for all Americans right now and must be especially so for you and your family. I wish you and your family the best.

It must be difficult to even pick the topic of your articles, given the level of emotions we're all carrying today. I'm looking forward to reading more of your work in The Blade.
Sincerely,
S.L.
Pettisville, OH

Via e-mail, October 1, 2001:
Dr. Hussain:
As an Indian American, I've begun to read the Pakistani press and editorials for the first time in my life. And reading columns such as yours has made me realize there's possibility of a bright future for the Pakistani people. Unfortunately, it is the extremist minority which catches the attention of the ignorant, the sleeping – and the onlookers like me.

Musharraf has a HUGE job ahead. And despite American help, Pakistan may suffer grievously from the refugee problem and the political strife. It is fortunate that Pakistan finds itself ruled by the military; a civilian President would've found it virtually impossible to take a position hostile to the fundamentalists. But once the Afghanistan crisis is over, I hope Pakistan tackles the NEXT step – transition to democratic, civilian rule.
Thanks for a good column.
A.D.

Via e-mail, October 1, 2001:
Dear Neighbor,
I wonder if you saw the religious aid workers, the two American girls and their parents on NBC Dateline last week? They looked like any of your most respectable patients and sweet young American daughters. Have you changed your mind about applauding their imprisonment?

Of course they knew witnessing was against the law, but they must have heeded a higher law. They may have been invited into homes to share Christ, or even entrapped and betrayed. They are now in harm's way and we all hope they don't get used as pawns or get sacrificed because we have to go after the Taliban for harboring Bin Laden. The

Taliban could win some points if they'd let all the aid workers go. Talk about biting the hand that fed them!

I wonder if you wonder where your head was when you wrote that column. Do you still deplore the concept of religious liberty, so basic to American values? Or have you re-thought your earlier condemnation of such liberty, since Arab-Americans are benefiting from it?

I also wonder about a religion that notes American moral corruption while promising its young martyrs that they'll have a rich sex life in the hereafter if they kill American "infidels." They could be smoking and watching strippers in an American bar before doing their heinous deeds to please Allah. Are they merely as un-Koranish as Ku Klux Klanners are un-Biblical? White supremacist groups often claim some Christian identity, but they practice none of Christ's teachings. Is that the way it is with bin Laden? Is he really attracting rather "riff raff" Moslems, as Ku Klux Klan attracts the uneducated, crude, poorly parented, bigoted, poor folks of America. Or is it in both cases a class of people who feel that wealth will never be realized by them because of other groups of people?

Apparently, I have to be content with my one-sided dialogue on these interesting subjects. Wish you had time or motivation to correspond.

By the way, you mentioned Rush Limbaugh's comment as inciting hatred of Arabs generally - but he didn't make a blanket condemnation of "diaper heads" as Cooksey did; he talked about specific Palestinian people who had the gall to celebrate the bombings on camera. We all saw it. We all found it grossly inhumane. Rush only articulated something we all felt upon seeing that scene and others like it from around the Middle East. Don't make the mistake (another one) of doing what you decry – tarring everybody with the same brush who happens to be angry that any peoples anywhere in the world would celebrate these tragedies . . .

Granted, it is not good to fan the flames of bigotry by selective media – nor is it good for media like yourself to celebrate the persecution of Christians for merely expressing their faith and proclaiming God's definition of good and evil. It is popular now to condemn missionaries and Bible believers, saying we impose our way of life on unbelievers in this country. We do impose our democratic ideals in our own country and had best keep doing so. We used to have

laws that supported the morality of the Bible. We neglect those laws (re: marriage, homosex, abortion, promiscuity, etc.) at our own peril, because all of God's moral standards are for society's good – for our physical, emotional, economic and family health.
    Sincerely,
    B.M.R.

I have, on more than one occasion, made my positions very clear. I am afraid I have nothing more to add than what I have already discussed with you on the phone and through e-mails.

I do not represent any particular ethnic group or some sects in a particular religion just as I do not represent Hindus, Sikhs, Christians or Jews. But I have written against the persecution of all of these groups at various times.

Unfortunately I do not have the time or energy to engage in a protracted debate with you. I wish you and your family peace and happiness.

S. Amjad Hussain

Via e-mail, October 1, 2001:
Dr. S. Amjad Hussain:
I read your article "Containing the spread of bigotry and hate" and applaud your comments. Thank you for sharing the facts about Muslims in America. I was somewhat surprised regarding the 75% factor of Christian Arabs. Perhaps it was how you worded this paragraph. How many total Arabs are there in the U.S.? Because this was the factor I believe you were using to state the 75%.

So if you do not read this paragraph correctly you think that out of the 7 million, 75% are Christian. But again I liked your article and prior articles you have written. Always look for your column in the Toledo Blade.

Dr. Hussain, I am a Christian woman, recently retired, after 30 years as a senior staff accountant with a local CPA firm. I now have some free time to share and if I can be of service to a woman from the local Islamic community who would like company to the grocery store or a mall for shopping I will leave my phone number after my name listed below.

May God grant you peace, Dr. Hussain,
A.D.

Sorry for the confusion. Of all the Arabs in this country, 75% are Christians. Globally Christians constitute about 5% of the Arabs. I am very grateful to you for your kind words. It is really very noble of you to offer your help in transporting elderly to the grocery store etc. I will pass on your offer to the people at the Islamic Center.
Sincerely,
S. Amjad Hussain

Via e-mail, October 1, 2001:
Dr. Hussain:
Thank you for writing such excellent columns. When I wanted my students (college freshmen) to analyze and evaluate a piece of writing, over half selected your column over two others. Just after they made their selections, the terrorists attacked New York and Washington. Several of their papers on your anti-proselytizing piece were defensive based on a perception that you were anti-Christian in your views. This led to some excellent discussion about your essay and how you expressed a strong dislike for a particular behavior without making blatant generalizations about millions of people. Even those who struggled with your message said "he makes me think." When one young man told me he has started to read the editorial and opinion pages every day, I decided you should know.
Sincerely, J.B.

Thank you for your note. We all suffer, at times, from the malady called generalization. I try very hard to make a distinction between a particular faith and the behavior of some of its followers. Islam is a noble religion but some of its followers (read the Taliban) are far from noble. The same is true of Hinduism, Christianity and Judaism. I respect and accept all religions but have difficulties with some of their followers.
Perhaps some day I will have the opportunity to sit down with you and your students for a friendly chat.
Sincerely,
S. Amjad Hussain

American Muslims must find their voice
and condemn violence
September 12, 2006

Five years ago yesterday, as we watched with horror, the first of the hijacked planes hit the World Trade Center and the world started to change.

Five years later we are living in a world that is unsafe, unpredictable, and full of strife. The outstanding geopolitical problems that had spawned the terrorist culture are no closer to resolution than they were five summers ago. And amidst all this turmoil Muslims are caught between the hard rock of terrorism and the deep blue sea of suspicion.

Life for American Muslims has not been easy of late. Each foiled terrorist plot makes them more vulnerable to stereotyping and bigotry. Retaliations abound: a Muslim commercial pilot is taken off the flight schedule, a Muslim passenger is removed from a plane because other passengers are fearful of his presence, and a young Arab-American man at an airport is forced to change a T-shirt that had Arabic inscription on it. There is widespread racial profiling of Muslims at the airport and at customs. This not only erodes their confidence in the system, it makes them very angry.

Against the backdrop of this angst one cannot ignore the fear that non-Muslim Americans have of Muslims. Unfortunately, the two groups have been talking past each other instead of understanding their mutual concerns. We all appear to be living in an echo chamber where we only hear the reverberations of our own concerns.

I am a champion of civil liberties and worship at the altar of the Bill of Rights. But what good are civil rights when there is a growing distrust and suspicion between the non-Muslim majority and the Muslim minority? How do you convince the majority that out of 1.4 billion Muslims only a small fraction is responsible for the suicide bombings, beheadings, and other atrocities committed in the name of religion? We will not be able to convince them unless the majority of Muslims living in this country refuse to be linked with the self-righteous murderers masquerading as pious believers.

Some Muslims find it difficult to take that step not because they sympathize with the terrorists, but because of a deep-rooted, but utterly unworkable, utopian concept of a worldwide community of believers, or Ummah, which deters them from speaking ill of other Muslims. After all, the terrorists portray themselves as true believers and use the language of religion to justify their despicable acts. But by remaining quiet, American Muslims invite distrust and misunderstanding by the community at large.

A great majority of Muslims are indeed peaceful and they get their inspiration from the same sacred texts that the terrorists flaunt and quote. The problem, common to other faiths as well, is that two people may read the same passage and draw diametrically opposed conclusions. If a majority of Muslims finds the terrorists' interpretations at odds with their own, then they have to take a visible stand. This might further erode the concept of a unified Ummah, but it has to be done.

By remaining quiet on one hand and complaining loudly about racial and religious profiling on the other, American Muslims are isolating themselves from the majority in this country. They must come out of their self-created virtual cocoons and condemn all those who use their religion to further a hateful agenda. This discussion should happen not only in public (which has been happening with increasing frequency) but also in private. There should be no disparity between private utterances and public posture.

It is also necessary because there are many non-Muslim bigots who do not miss an opportunity to malign all Muslims with a broad brush. The incoherence or silence of American Muslims gives credence to their arguments.

The Muslim majority should make it clear that they have nothing in common with the bloodthirsty jihadists and declare them beyond the pale of Islam. This message has to be repeated loudly and frequently. This will make some Muslims on the extreme right very uncomfortable but they are the ones who have always been quick to label Muslims who do not agree with their interpretation as heretics and infidels.

A parting thought for my Muslim readers: When was the last time you invited a non-Muslim friend to your home for a chat over a meal or a cup of coffee?

In the Toledo Blade Readers' Forum, *September 25, 2006:*
"Where is outrage of Muslim leaders?"

On Sept. 12 Amjad Hussain finally wrote the column I have been hoping he would write about the need for Muslims to condemn terrorist violence. I live not far from his lovely mosque in Perrysburg. When it was built there in the cornfields of northwest Ohio, I marveled at our area's wonderful diversity.

I attended the grand opening, celebrating with Muslim friends. Then came 9/11 and in the aftermath, people of other faiths came and formed a human chain around the mosque to protect it from retaliation. Since that time, the terrorist threats and attacks have continued.

Why should Muslims be at all surprised by the suspicion and racial profiling surrounding them when some of those of their religion, in the name of Allah, threaten our way of life and our very existence? Some of those arrested have even been from the Toledo area.

I don't like the fear and anger I am feeling now as I pass the mosque. The feelings don't come necessarily from my fear of the terrorists but more form a very lack of outrage and condemnation from local, national, and international Muslims and their leaders.

When that response isn't forthcoming, it is only natural to wonder if there isn't agreement with the terrorist agenda. I believe clear condemnation would do more to discourage terrorism than our war on terror.

Will Dr. Hussain's column make a difference in the Muslim world? I hope so.

I also commend him for his articles through the years that help us understand another way of life so that we can all live more harmoniously together.

M.B.

Perrysburg

In the Toledo Blade Readers' Forum, *September 25, 2006:*

"Bringing together all people of faith"

My husband and I as followers of Christ would like to respond to Peter Silverman's Sept. 17 letter and sign the Toledo pledge for peace in the world that he wrote about.

Along with that letter, S. Amjad Hussain in his Sept. 12 column posed a thought to consider for his Muslim readers: "When was the last time you invited a non-Muslim friend to your home for a chat over a meal or a cup of coffee?"

Changing the question just a bit and making it one for all of us to consider would go something like this: When was the last time you invited a person of a different faith background over to your home for a chat over a meal or a cup of coffee?

Dr. Hussain's question has moved me to respond in a way that I believe will help promote peace here in Toledo and around the world.

My family plans to invite a family of a different faith background over for a meal sometime in the next two months. I believe that getting to know each other in an informal setting will help us all love each other and work together for peace regardless of our faith backgrounds.

We commend Dr. Hussain and Mr. Silverman. Let us as brothers and sisters continue to pray and work for peace here in Toledo and in our world.

S.B.

Toledo Mennonite Church

Via e-mail, September 12, 2006:

Dr. Hussain:

I personally want to thank you for the column you wrote for today issue of the Blade. *I believe an intelligent dialogue between mainstream Muslims and non-Muslims would be the most valuable action we as Americans could undertake.*

I also appreciate your comment regarding Ummah. I believe a majority of non-Muslim Americans believe that the terrorists primary goal is the total conversion of the rest of the world to Islam. My uneducated understanding of the Qur'an is that religion is not compulsory. I am a non-Muslim (Roman Catholic) and I sincerely hope that we can all learn to understand each other and coexist peacefully. Do you believe that can be achieved?

D.J.

Thank you for your kind words.

Yes, Muslims and non-Muslims can coexist peacefully as they did in Spain under the Moors. We need to learn about others.

Amjad Hussain

Via e-mail, September 13, 2006:
"By remaining quiet on one hand and complaining loudly about racial and religious profiling on the other, American Muslims are isolating themselves from the majority in this country."

Amjad Sahib,
Your diagnosis is right on the money. We have wasted the last 5 years only complaining about our "right." As though it is our divine right to come to this country to enjoy a life of luxury and at the same time to look down at the "materialistic" Americans.
I think it is about time that we should make a decision. Are we going to be a part of the melting pot or are we going to hero-worship those who want to melt the pot?
A.A.

Via e-mail, September 13, 2006:
Dear Dr. Hussain;
Writing to say that I enjoyed your recent Op/Ed in The Blade.
We, my wife and I, have met and have friendships with Middle Eastern people who happen to be Muslim and your column made me wonder about why we put labels on people with respect to their religion.
What I mean to say is, we do not refer to our dear friend from Lebanon as our Muslim friend, we say, "our wonderful friend who is Lebanese."
Her religion is her own and is not the first thing we concerned ourselves with, although we do enjoy great conversations about her homeland and her experiences as a child in the devastating civil war in Lebanon many decades ago and we have discussed topics that came up with regards to the distortions about the Koran.
I think that we do a disservice to our friends and neighbors, those that we know and those that we have not met yet but one day hope to meet, by labeling them as Muslims...
I think we are perpetuating the bigots deeds by continuing to label typically darker people or people with distinctive accents as this or that, why not refer to them as people first and get to know them and talk . . .

Best wishes,
M.L.

Via e-mail, September 13, 2006:
We've been waiting five years to see some expression such as yours.
Thank you for saying what must be understood and consistently
articulated.
Mr. And Mrs. A.J.S.

Via e-mail, September 13, 2006:
Dr. Hussain,
I often read your column in the Toledo Blade *and most times,*
whether I agree with your point of view or not, find them a good read.
I read online with interest your article today concerning why Muslims
and Non-Muslims don't trust each other, and you state that Muslims
could be helping themselves in the court of public opinion by standing
up against the terrorists vocally.
While I agree with your statement, I would ask the Muslim com-
munity as a whole where they've been for the last 5 years. I've not
heard of very many large or organized groups of Muslims protesting
those of their brethren who commit atrocities. Maybe that is part of the
problem, in that media just do not report Muslims that have made such
protests. At this point, the only clear indication is that many Americans
do not trust Muslims as a general rule, most especially Arabic Mus-
lims. Prejudices run very deep in American society, as has been proven
time and time again. I'd like to believe that the average everyday
Arabic Muslim doesn't deserve to be grouped with the terrorist, but for
most people, the Arabic-looking person at the corner market or at the
gas station is someone that needs to be watched in case they "try any-
thing funny," much like they watch the average young black man, and
for the same reasons...
As for the point of your article as I read it, Muslims who dislike
being grouped as "one of them" should indeed do what they can to
show that they are not. I would not expect any Muslims to suddenly
start celebrating Christmas or Kwanzaa or Hanukah, because even in
today's world, being different is not a bad thing. I would suggest, how-
ever, that in your speaking engagements with various Muslim groups
you advise that speaking out against the daily violence and murders

can only help. Have them also speak up for other issues, such as interest their community. Stress to us "native" Americans that we aren't so very different.

Most Americans should already realize that generally speaking, Muslims do not spend a lot of time in their garages building bombs and putting explosives in the family van, just in case the mood strikes. Those that feel animosity towards their neighbor just because they're Muslim probably can't have their opinion changed very quickly. They also probably have problems with their black neighbor and their Asian neighbor, and probably even the little old Italian lady down the street. Such people, it must be hoped, will eventually see the light of peace.

For the rest of us, the so-called normal people, hopefully we will continue to see the best in people and not the worst. May that enlightenment spread out to those who seem to like to hate so much.

Peace to you, and to us all, Sir.

R.H.

Rossford, OH

Evangelical groups make war on terror look like a Crusade
September 10, 2007

There is a widespread belief in the Muslim world that George W. Bush, under the guise of a war against terrorism, is in fact waging a war, a later day Crusade, against Islam and Muslims. In the waning days of this administration it is becoming more and more evident that there is some truth to that assumption.

An article published in *Los Angeles Times* a few weeks ago outlined a disturbing relationship between Department of Defense (DoD) and Christian Evangelists. DoD has been delivering packages, called Freedom Packages, to U.S. soldiers in Iraq which, contain proselytizing material both in English and Arabic as well as a Bible and an apocalyptic video game "Left Behind: Eternal Forces." In the video game, the soldiers of Christ hunt down enemies.

The packages were supplied by Operation Straight Up, a fundamentalist Christian ministry. This group was also planning to hold a series of entertainment programs for the troops called (symbolically named?) "Military Crusade."

According to the same article another evangelist group, Christian Embassy, has had an unprecedented access to the DoD facilities and personnel for making a documentary. Their cozy proximity to the DoD led one high Pentagon official, Air Force Major General John Catton, to assume the group was a quasi-federal agency.

Proselytizing by Christian missionaries has had a long and checkered history. Burning with zeal to save people around the world, these do-gooders descend with Bible in one hand and loaf of bread in the other and prey on the most vulnerable and most needy. Be it in Iraq, Afghanistan or India the *modus operandi* is the same. Almost a century ago Mahatma Gandhi, the apostle of religious harmony and pacifism, urged Christian missionaries to stop proselytizing in India. To Gandhi, most conversions had little to do with religion and a lot to do with hunger instead of heart.

Surprisingly the freedom of religion does not include freedom to convert others. I would defend anyone's right to practice his or her religion but would oppose any overtures to convert. For the missionaries to believe they have a God-given right to save others is not only arrogant but reduces human spirituality to a cookie-cutter, one-size-fits-all concept of salvation. It tends to turn sublime into profane.

Most major religions carry a Himalaya-size chip of superiority on their shoulders. Each religion thinks it has the answer to life here in the world but also a recipe to secure the hereafter. One wonders what goes through the minds of religious leaders when they gather for their interfaith powwows. They profess equality while holding hands but sing a different tune to their flocks back in their churches, synagogues, mosques and temples. Unless one is a hypocrite, it is just not possible to be equal and superior at the same time.

The recent capture and subsequent release in Afghanistan of Korean missionaries is a case study in ignorance and hypocrisy. Why would these young men and women risk their lives in a strange and dangerous land to convert Afghans rather than putting all their efforts back in their own country? After all, South Korea, a nation of 49 million, still has 36 million non-Christians to convert.

And how about here in America? If every Christian denomination thinks it has the key to salvation then why don't they, in the spirit of love thy neighbor, try converting other Christians to their brand of Christianity? One would think these Christian evangelists would first work to save their own before embarking on saving the rest of humanity.

At a recent interfaith seminar at Lakeside, Ohio a pastor told me that proselytizing is an integral part of Christianity and therefore it may not be possible for most Christians to accord equality to other religions. While this might be a formidable barrier for some, it has not prevented a great majority of believing men and women of all religions to use the age-old concept of faith and reason and move forward from the unattainable goal of painting the entire world in one color. All they have to do it to come down from their celestial high horses.

In a civil (and civilized) society one should have the right to convert but only out of one's own free will. The government has no right to favor one religion over another and use the instruments of the state to facilitate proselytizing to a captive and captured people in occupied lands.

In the Toledo Blade Readers' Forum, *September 16, 2007:*
"Sharing faith is necessary for Christians"

As an evangelical Christian, I apologize for the inappropriate tactics practiced by even well-intentioned Christians in Amjad Hussain's recently published column. At the same time, I feel it is appropriate to add some clarity to following the command from Jesus Christ to "Go into all the world and preach the gospel to all creation." Christianity is the only faith that believes reconciliation between God and man has already occurred through the life, death, and resurrection of Christ. While we have a respect for others' beliefs, we cannot in good conscience hold back from proclaiming and practicing our faith.

When the Apostle Paul entered Athens and saw the various objects of worship to other gods, he did not attack, malign, offend or cause any insult other faiths. Rather, he spoke about an altar that was marked "to an unknown god" and shared his conversion to Christ. What an amazing story his was and still is.

Our sharing the Christian faith is not accomplished by the sword, but by the cross. The humanitarian efforts carried out by countless missionaries across the globe are not a form of nutritional bribery, as suggested, but a tangible way of putting our faith into action. To suggest otherwise is very disingenuous. I would suspect those in need are more grateful than resentful for these efforts. Courageous men, women, and children have been martyred for their compassion and love to follow in the footsteps of Christ. Remember, Jesus was also sentenced to death because He refused to compromise or back down from proclaiming Himself to be the Son of God.

As Christ followers, we will always continue to share His love with everyone. Anything less would be an abandonment of our calling and a betrayal of our Savior.
RW
Forestlawn Road

In the Toledo Blade Readers' Forum, *September 16, 2007:*
"Limiting messages limits free choice"
I was surprised to read that, for columnist S. Amjad Hussain, "freedom of religion does not include freedom to convert others."
I always assumed that freedom of religion meant the right for each individual to choose what they believe to be true. If the Muslim world

insists on limiting what their people hear about God, doesn't that limit their freedom to choose?

To quote the Apostle Paul, "How can they believe in the one of whom they have never heard?"

Dr. Hussain seems to think it is evil to share one's faith with others. If I believe I have found a relationship with God through Jesus Christ, and that this relationship makes all the difference in my life, I think it would be evil not to share that good news with others it might also help.

Are all religions equal? No, I don't think so. I believe there is such a thing as the truth, and I am always seeking to learn the truth. I am not afraid to listen to other views, and I am willing to share why I believe what I believe.

What is Dr. Hussain afraid of? That people will be forced to sign up as Christians in order to receive help from the missionaries? There is no evidence at all that this is happening.

I think Dr. Hussain should consider that there is nothing to be afraid of when people are allowed to hear about other religions, and make informed choices themselves about what they believe to be true.

DJN

Pettisville, OH

In the Toledo Blade Readers' Forum, *September 16, 2007:*

"Jewish faith doesn't try to convert others"

I read the trenchant article by Amjad Hussain on evangelical groups that use some sophisticated methods to take their message of their faith to the Muslim world. It is easy to understand his unease.

I feel uncomfortable when I am approached by Mormon missionaries or Christian advocates. While no Muslim has ever approached me, it is commonly accepted that the largest number of religious converts in our time is to Islam. Therefore, one must assume that there are those in the Islamic community who are reaching out to others to promote the superiority of the faith of Mohammed.

Americans are blessed with a society that can positively accept Justice Oliver Wendell Holmes' concept of a "marketplace of ideas." All are free to promulgate and promote those tenets and religious ideologies that are precious to them. Every person of faith can legitimately believe in the specialness of that religious concept.

Equally, agreeing with Dr. Hussain, each must accord to all others the dignity and worth of their religious beliefs.

I am sorry that Dr. Hussain erroneously included synagogues along with churches and mosques in his diatribe against hypocrisy and conversion. While Judaism lovingly accepts those who would join the Jewish people and the Jewish faith, there is no missionary movement at all seeking converts. Rather, Judaism accords the ultimate freedom of religious thought to all peoples when it affirms the words of the Prophet Micah, "All the nations may walk in the name of their gods; we will walk in the name of the Lord our God for ever and ever."

Rabbi AMS
Pine Ridge Road

In the Toledo Blade Readers' Forum, *September 16, 2007:*
"'Crusade' is to help the world's poor"
In response to Amjad Hussain's Sept. 10 column, "Evangelical groups make war on terror look like a crusade," he makes a good point when he takes notice of the relationship between some so-called evangelical groups and the Bush Administration. Why these groups would include the video game "Left Behind: Eternal Forces" in their "Freedom Package" is beyond all reason. It just shows how arrogant the current administration is.

However, to lump all missionaries into the same category is ignorance at its worst. He sets aside all the good works these dedicated men and women do with the poor and starving people of the world. In essence he is telling them "Stay home and mind your own business." I wonder, do the people who have benefited from the kindness of the ones who give their time and talents to feed and clothe them feel the same way that Dr. Hussain does?

He says missionaries "prey on the most vulnerable and needy with a Bible in one hand and loaf of bread in the other." Well, if I was starving I'd eat the bread and be glad that it was because of the Bible that the bread was there. And I might even wonder what's in that Bible that would bring these people all the way to this place. Dr. Hussain then almost quotes the Bible passage of love thy neighbor. He can't understand why 23 Korean missionaries would risk their lives in a strange and dangerous land. He should read the parable of the Good Samaritan.

I think that if anyone has a Himalaya-size chip on his shoulder, it is Dr. Hussain. If he wishes to call the work that these saintly people do a crusade, then I say, onward Christian soldier.

TER

Glenbrook Avenue

In the Toledo Blade Readers' Forum, *September 16, 2007:*

"Only crusade is one waged on Christians"

There is widespread misunderstanding of the calling and role of Christ followers in evangelism.   Amjad Hussain's Sept. 10 column builds on that misunderstanding.

First, the major evangelical criticism is that not enough is being done in our own back yard.   The Bible is clear.   First spread the Gospel in your own back yard, then the world.

Second, we do not convert; God does.   We are called only to spread the Gospel and then educate those who make the decision to follow Christ.   Note that this is an action of choice, not force.

Third, it is clear from the great commission that we are expected to spread the word.   In many cases this effort is to the unfortunate among us.   So bread and a Bible are natural tools.

Fourth, we believe that Jesus Christ is the only way to salvation, not one way or the best way, but the only way.

The only crusade I recognize is the war being conducted on Christ followers and nominal Christians by the rather radical elements of the Muslim world.

JL

Perrysburg

In the Toledo Blade Readers' Forum, *September 21, 2007:*

"Purpose of talk often is to persuade others"

In his Sept. 10 column, S. Amjad Hussain takes issue with religious proselytizing, stating "freedom of religion does not include freedom to convert others."   Actually, it does.   The freedom to practice religion allows for the sharing of ideas, ideas one believes to be true, in the hope that others might find them believable.

Much of human communication has as its goal the evoking of some kind of change in the other person.   Forcing one's beliefs on another is, of course, wrong, but from soap box to the radio talk show to Dr.

Hussain's column, the goal of the communicator is to change the thinking, behavior, or even the belief system of others by a well-articulated and compelling argument.

I enjoy regular warm and animated conversation at a local coffee shop with a Muslim. I suspect we'll never come to common ground in our beliefs but we'll continue to show respect and care for each other.

Dr. Hussain states that "in a civil (and civilized) society, one should have the right to convert but only out of one's own free will." I agree.

We should never deny a person the free will to believe as they want, and to convert only if they want to do so.

This, however, does not preclude anyone from offering what they believe to be a compelling argument that, when stated out of love and with respect, might prompt the other person to want to convert.

I'm certain Dr. Hussain will continue to try to "convert" people's thinking by his insightful columns, and I will also try to "convert" people's thinking by my writing and speaking.

I'm glad we live in a country where we can both do so freely.

The Rev. DJC

Temperance

In the Toledo Blade Readers' Forum, *September 21, 2007:*

"Freedom of speech includes conversion"

The University of Toledo's newest trustee upped the ante for idiocy in his most recent anti-Christian diatribe. S. Amjad Hussain once again berates Christians for their attempts to "proselytize" Muslims. The good doctor's references to the Crusades indicate his ignorance of history. The Crusades were organized by Europe's royalty to halt the "proselytizing" of "celestial-high-horse" riding Muslims into their countries.

The zenith of Dr. Hussain's unintentional column of irony is "freedom of religion does not include the freedom to convert others." To take his constitutional "logic" further, does freedom of speech not include the freedom to persuade others? Does freedom of assembly not include the freedom to meet in large groups? Does the freedom to petition the government not include the freedom to disagree with the government?

Unfortunately, for millions of people around the world, the idea of certain "freedoms" isn't debated, or guaranteed in a constitution. It's only hoped for.

Fortunately for myself, and Dr. Hussain, the United States does allow all those freedoms – thank God.

JH

Wauseon

In the Toledo Blade Readers' Forum, *September 28, 2007:*

"Christianity has also had a bloody past"

"Christian fanatics don't kill anyone" wrote a Sept. 18 writer to The Blade. *It's true that Muslim fanatics are now carrying out suicide missions against the United States and other western countries and Christians aren't, but Christians have no reason to be proud of their bloody past.*

From 1095 to 1272 (the Crusades), European Christians invaded the Holy Land to kill and expel Muslims. When Christianity was 1,500 years old (Islam is now about 1,400 years old), Spanish Conquistadors were invading the American continents, murdering the local "heathen" inhabitants who stood in the way of their thirst for gold and land. In Spain during the Inquisition from about 1490 to 1700, it has been estimated that from 3,000 to 5,000 people (mostly Jews and Muslims) were burned at the stake or murdered by other means for not accepting Catholicism as the one true faith. During Europe's religious wars of the 16th and 17th centuries, millions were killed as Catholics fought Protestants.

The irony is that Judaism, Christianity, and Islam all worship the same god, the God of Abraham. I wonder what He thinks about the way His children have behaved while invoking His name. The best advice is to "beware the true believer," whatever his faith may be.

RAK

Sylvania

In the Toledo Blade Readers' Forum, *September 21, 2007:*

"All major religions are out of control"

Christian fundamentalists are not benevolent proselytizers as recent critics of columnist Amjad Hussain have asserted. They are overtly trying to control all three branches of government as well as school boards in an attempt to abandon the constitutional separation of church and state and establish a "Christian culture" in America. Christian pharmacists deny women access to birth control and politicians think nothing of violating the privacy of my body to gain votes from Christians who ignore the gruesome reality of what happened to women seeking abortions prior to Roe vs. Wade.

Disguising themselves as Arabs, they go into the Arab world and claim to be converts from Islam to Christianity, further straining our relationship with the Arab community. They used anti-gay, discriminatory legislation to lure Christian conservatives to the polls to vote for a President who is responsible for the death of hundreds of thousands of innocent Iraqis.

All the major religions are out of control, destroying our world and failing to keep their beliefs in their homes and places of worship. Protection from religious fundamentalism is the reason we have a constitutional separation of church and state, and religious freedom also includes freedom from *religion.*

SJK
Sabra Road

In the Toledo Blade Readers' Forum, *October 7, 2007:*
"Columnist gives evangelism a bad rap"
I was bothered by Amjad Hussain's Sept. 10 column.

While he is correct in being concerned about the cooperation of the Defense Department in any promotion of religion, his characterization of Christian evangelism is inaccurate.

The article depicted Christian evangelism as being unloving and hypocritical. Especially offensive was his description of Christian missionaries as "do-gooders who descend with Bible in one hand and loaf of bread in the other to prey on the most vulnerable and needy."

We should be careful about characterizing a whole religion based on extremes within that religion.

Dr. Hussain's column touched on two important tenets of the Christian faith. Christians are called to share their faith with others.

The Bible is filled with admonitions to give an account of one's faith to the world. This is important to believers because Jesus said, "No one comes to the Father but through me."

At the same time it is clear that this is not to be done out of arrogance, but out of love. Most often this sharing is part of a loving dialogue. It is never depicted in the Scriptures as coercion.

A second tenet of the Christian faith is to help those who are in need. It is not to be done as a means to coerce faith, as the columnist implies.

Christians are to reach out to help simply because there are people in need, without expecting anything in return.

Christians do this on a daily basis. This is what moved Christians to help with the flooding Findlay, Hurricane Katrina, and the tsunami.

There are countless Christian organizations in our communities, our country, and the world that offer ongoing service to people regardless of their religion, nationality or culture.

The Rev. SHL
Elmore

Via e-mail, October 7, 2007:
Dear Sir:
I've read and re-read Dr. S. Amjad Hussain's op-ed that has raised so much of a storm in the Reader's Forum lately. Notwithstanding that this writing will be deemed as siding with a fellow Muslim's, I honestly feel that his opinions were based on hard facts open to the public for scrutiny.

In case nobody has noticed, in the past seven years it has become ironically clear that the political system that vociferously preaches the concept of the separation of church and the state has embraced the very ideology. Ironically...these are the same principles which nations 10,000 miles away have been accused of harboring and practicing, and which at times and at best border on the same level of fanaticism that Iran and Saudi Arabia have been accused of by the President and his administration.

Mr. Bush's second term victory was mainly due to the loyalty of the right wing, which thought he was of a higher moral standard than his opponent. And, lo, megachurches popped up all across the mainland and in fact became a very healthy and wealthy enterprise because of faith-based initiative and monetary support given by Mr. Bush. Commendable, if it is an honest attempt to uplift the morality and induce God's fear in a society. But if the LA Times' *account is true, it changes the entire playing field.*

Dr. Hussain was equally critical of the Taliban who force their hostages to convert as the first act of "Godliness." But then, that's a crazy ignorant bunch of cave-bound byway robbers. How does it sit well though with the altruist Christians in particular and the American public in general, if such a plan is concocted by overzealous evangelists in cahoots with DoD (supposedly a 'neutral' entity) and christened Freedom Package? Does this constitute 'morality' these days?

Sincerely,
A-MA
Perrysburg

Jewish religious symbol carries special poignancy
March 9, 1997

This is a story of a religious symbol, a Toledo physician and broken strands of history spanning more than fifty years.

Dr. Blair Grubb is a well-known local cardiologist and a professor at the Medical College of Ohio. A soft spoken and unassuming man he is nationally and internationally known for his work on effects of viral infections on autonomic nervous system and in turn on the heart.

In 1993 Dr. Grubb received a request from a French physician to help diagnose a mysterious ailment in his granddaughter that had baffled her physicians in France. The French physician wondered if the young girl had the same ailment that Dr. Grubb had written about.

Through transatlantic telephone conversations and fax messages the patient's care was directed from Toledo. Once diagnosed and appropriately treated the little girl made a rather miraculous recovery. The grateful grandparents invited Dr. Grubb to their home in Southern France if he ever happens to be in France. The opportunity presented itself last June when the Toledo physician took the time to visit with them while in Southern France for a conference.

After the dinner while they sat sipping their drinks and talked in a mixture of English, French and Spanish, the grandmother asked their guest if he was Jewish. When informed that he was, the lady asked about the Jewish faith and traditions. She was particularly interested in the Jewish holiday of Hanukkah. The couple listened attentively as the guest described the significance of the holiday and the reasons behind lighting the menorah on that occasion. She looked her guest in the eyes and said there was something she wanted to give him. She brought out a package wrapped in cloth and handed it to the guest.

It was a solid brass menorah with eight cups for holding oil and wicks and a ninth cup centered above the others. For hanging the menorah there was an attached ring on top. The grandmother said that the menorah belonged to the family of her childhood friend Jeanette. One day during her childhood when she went to play with Jeanette, she saw Jeanette and her family being led away by the police. She ran back home to tell her mother and asked where Jeanette was going. The mother assured the little girl that her friend would be back soon.

On returning to the scene she found the villagers looting Jeanette's home. She picked up the menorah, thrown away by the looters in the street, and remembered that the family used to light it during the Christmas season. In her mind the eight-year-old girl decided that she would keep it until they returned. Jeanette and her family never returned.

She had kept it hidden for over fifty years from every one including her own family. She told her husband about it later on. She didn't know why she hung on to it for so long. Perhaps she wanted to return it to someone who could put it in perspective and appreciate its significance. With a strange twist of fate her granddaughter's illness had brought another Jew into their lives and now she could return the symbol to a person who could carry on the tradition.

Overwhelmed by significance of the symbol, the weight of history and extraordinary circumstances under which it had come to him, Dr. Grubb wept. The brass menorah had in a strange and personal way made him feel the enormity of holocaust.

As he bade farewell to his hosts that evening the lady, who would die two months later of breast cancer, remarked that the menorah should once again see the light.

Last Hanukkah it did.

PLACES

View from the Khyber Pass
May 3, 2003

Khyber Pass, Pakistan - The recent war in Iraq has pushed other hot spots in the world to the sidelines. Even here in the tribal areas that straddle Pakistan and Afghanistan, and where there are still some glowing embers found here and there from the war against the Taliban and Al Qaeda, Iraq dominates the conversations in the bazaars. The airways and broadsheets all over Pakistan are awash with the news of the fall of Baghdad and the end of Saddam Hussein's regime.

Viewed from this vantage point the tone and scope of coverage has been decidedly different than what the American public has seen or heard.

The eventual success of the American and British campaign in Iraq was never in doubt. It was the way the U.S. broadcast media - CNN, NBC, ABC, Fox, and CBS - and the print media reported the events that was at variance with reports by independent journalists who were on the scene. Objectivity appears to have been the main casualty of the conflict.

Most of the embedded journalists ended up reporting for "their side" just as Saddam's information ministry did for his regime.

In contrast, some of the British reporters stood out through their insightful objective reporting.

All wars are ugly and indiscriminate. To sterilize the reporting to suit one side or the other is to betray a sacred trust.

Another area where the coverage by American media and that of some of the Europeans differed was the interpretation of the Geneva Conventions. When American prisoners were shown on European and Asian TV, Defense Secretary Donald Rumsfeld said it was a gross violation of the conventions.

It took foreign correspondents and commentators to draw a parallel between the treatment meted out to the Taliban and al-Qaeda prisoners at the hands of the American Army in Afghanistan and the treatment of American prisoners of war at the hands of Iraqis. Secretary Rumsfeld's disingenuous designation of the Taliban and al-Qaeda prisoners as enemy combatants and therefore outside the bounds of the conventions does not cut mustard outside the U.S.

Those who are familiar with international law would grant those prisoners the same status as other prisoners of war. It was certainly against the Geneva Conventions to pack them in mosquito-infested cargo containers, transport them in chains and shackles with hoods on their heads, and put them in cages after their arrival at Guatanamo Bay. Their treatment, no matter how grievous their crime, was inhumane.

The foreign press also took note of the bombing of a Baghdad hotel that had been the operation center of many journalists and that the U.S. Army was aware of this fact. In that bombing a reporter from the al-Jazeera TV network was killed. While it would be a stretch even for a paranoid person to think this was a deliberate hit to silence an irritating voice, it does show lack of sensitivity and concern on the part of the American brass.

The war in Iraq has come to an end but the conflict in Iraq is not over yet. More tests of the ingenuity and objectivity of the media are ahead. The reconstruction of Iraq, the trials of Iraqi high command, and legitimate concerns of Iraq's neighbors about their own future would require the American media to abandon the cozy and comfortable bed provided by Mr. Rumsfeld and get back to the kind of reporting that made us aware of My Lai, Watergate, and the Pentagon Papers.

Via e-mail, May 3, 2003:

Hope you are enjoying the view from the Khyber Pass, because we sure aren't enjoying your political view over here. Why don't you stay over there? You sure aren't an American. You are bullshit. Stay over there with the rest of the bullshit.

DB

Dear DB:

I appreciate your very candid comments on my today's column. I thought in a civilized society like ours, there is always room to dissent and disagree without being disagreeable.

I hope it is not a disappointment but I did return home (that is Toledo, Ohio) and found that a good number of people agree with my point of view.

Sincerely,

S. Amjad Hussain

Via e-mail, May 5, 2003:

I AM disappointed at your return. Honest dissent is one thing, sir, but dishonest dissent is quite another. Pointing out a problem which needs addressed and providing a solution is one thing. That is honest dissent, and is as American as apple pie. Ignoring the good things and finding fault in everything that is done is DISHONEST dissent and UN-American.

Our wonderful country has just freed an entire country of your people, the second one in less than a year. It is plain as day to even the most stupid fool that we have made an honorable effort and many Iraqis see it and appreciate it.

A good number of people may agree with you, but a good number in this country are stupid fools too.... Your articles are more than pointing out faults, they are discriminatory against Americans. I for one, am insulted by them, which is why I give you insults. So when you truly dissent and disagree without being disagreeable, you can expect the same in return. Otherwise, forget it.

DB

Via e-mail, May 3, 2003:

Dr. Hussain:

I just read your well-reasoned article "View from the Khyber Pass." Your words rang true to me and I applaud your efforts to bring objectivity to the current political crisis. The BBC has excellent coverage without propaganda. I believe the Iraqi people were inhumanely oppressed by Saddam Hussein but I am not convinced that war, with the loss of civilian life, was the answer.

AD

Via e-mail, May 3, 2003:

Dear Doctor Hussain,

Do you seriously think that we will now believe that Baghdad Bob was the same as the USA reporters – your "Independent Reporters" – showed scenes of dead Muslims only to inflame the Arab Street. Millions of Muslims believed Baghdad Bob and were horrified that he had been lying to them. In Pakistan, Muslims called for a million-man protest, but only 10% of them showed up. That tells us what the Arab Street thought.

We know that our journalists are not always objective and that some of them get paid off and lie (CNN), but most are honest. The insightful objective reporting of the British reporters pointed out that an American tank would have had to shoot around a corner in order to hit that Baghdad hotel.

Why couldn't you write that this was the first war in history that took out a regime and not the population? Why don't you tell your people that Saddam killed more Muslims that any other person in history? Why don't you tell your people that millions of Muslims were able to make a pilgrimage to a holy site that they had not been able to visit in many years? Why don't you tell them about the great picture in your paper today showing thousands of Muslims kneeling in prayer in Baghdad? I think that is great reporting.

Contrast that scene to what it would have looked like on Saddam's birthday if it wasn't for George W. Bush and, Tony Blair…It is amazing that you can criticize our reporters when you tell "stories" about only negatives.

DJ

Via e-mail, May 3, 2003:
Dr. Hussain,
Again, I applaud your fair-minded views of the war in Iraq and the way it has been broadcast to us. I have been disturbed at times by the "gung ho" attitude of some journalists. I even witnessed one of them smiling while reporting a particularly large bombing campaign. It disgusted me and frankly made me sad and a little scared for all of us.

Thank you again for all you do to keep an open mind and comment from your point of view. It comforts me to see that I'm not as alone as I feel at times.
AS

Via e-mail, May 3, 2003:
I am writing to you to thank you as a citizen of an open and just society for presenting facts in a truthful manner. By presenting both sides of all international and regional issues you have shown fairness

and character that has been lacking in a lot of other publications recently.

I am also grateful for publishing works of Dr. Amjad Hussain, Thomas Friedman, Gwynn Dwyer and others who bring forward views that are fair, balanced and insightful.

Keep up the good work.

Regards,

IA, MD

Toledo, Ohio

Our failures in Iraq should not surprise
April 23, 2004

A recent book by the *Washington Post* reporter Bob Woodward is making waves in this country. The book *Plan of Attack* sheds light on the way George W. Bush and his close advisers planned the invasion of Iraq.

It appears that Vice President Dick Cheney and Defense Secretary Donald Rumsfeld sold the plan to a gullible president while keeping the Secretary of State Colin Powell out of the loop. They had decided to invade Iraq even though there was hardly any evidence of weapons of mass destruction and there was no tangible link between Saddam Hussein and Al Qaeda. They were driven by a skewed vision of Pax Americana where America was destined to re-arrange the political map of the world. Their vision was enunciated in a document prepared for the Bush team long before the pregnant chads made their appearance on the controversial ballots in Florida.

The Project for the New American Century (PNAC) is a conservative think tank headed by the archconservative William Kristal. It publishes position papers and documents on domestic and international issues. One particular document titled "Rebuilding America's Defense" is of particular interest. It advocates regime change in Iraq, Syria, Iran and China and stresses American domination and control of space. It calls for the development of biologic weapons "that can target specific genotypes (and) may transform biological warfare from the realm of terror to a politically useful tool."

The document underscores the difficulty of selling such an enormous undertaking to American people but wished for a watershed event to make it all happen. It states: "(Transforming the U.S. into) tomorrow's dominant force is likely to be a long one in the absence of some catastrophic and catalyzing event like a new Pearl Harbor." The terrorist attacks on 9/11 provided the excuse if not the context.

That Afghanistan and Iraq were already in the crosshairs when Team Bush entered the White House is becoming increasingly plausible. Bob Woodward's current book and his previous book *Bush At War* give credence to this notion. So does, even if indirectly, the book by former Bush aids Paul O'Neill and Richard Clarke.

The neo-conservatives who shoved this war down the throats of a reluctant nation were, it seems, oblivious to the complexities of Iraqi society. They had no insight into the ethnic, cultural or religious underpinning of a people they wanted to liberate. The result should not be a surprise. It was predicted by many informed people on both sides of the political divide in this country. Brent Scowcroft, National Security Advisor under Bush Senior, warned in a *New York Times* op-ed piece exactly what we are seeing now. I believe the planners of the war were dazzled by the echoes of their own hollow arguments.

So here we are hopelessly stuck in the Iraqi quagmire one year after the invasion with no end in sight. The cheering crowds that were to welcome the liberators never materialized. The refreshing winds of democracy that were to engulf the entire region are nowhere to be seen. Instead we are being challenged by an organized insurgency that has spread to most of the major population centers in Iraq, exacting a heavy toll on both sides. The coalition of the willing has turned into coalition of the reluctant. Already three coalition partners have announced withdrawal from Iraq.

Somewhere in those policy debates there should have been discussions about the reasons why people the world over, and in some instances that includes our allies as well, do not trust America. To brush aside genuine grievances as jealousy of American liberty and affluence is to ignore the real reasons why they hate us.

Unattended grievances always breed militancy and fanaticism and each slight or insult adds to the layers of resentment in those affected by our policies. The recent shift in American policy in the Middle East by ceding parts of the West Bank to Ariel Sharon and allowing him to realize his dream of a Greater Israel on Arab lands would not win our country any friends in the Arab world. On the contrary even moderates would be propelled towards militancy. A man pushed hard against the wall becomes angry and unpredictable.

Bob Woodward's book should give all of us a pause to contemplate the perils of a superpower gone amuck.

Via e-mail, April 27, 2004:
Dr. Hussain:

Your piece in last Friday's Blade *was right on the money (and, I'll wager, has earned you a few nasty e-mails). Unfortunately, the polls tell us that a majority of Americans still buy the jingoistic "patriotism" of the Bush Gang. With the most critical presidential election since 1860 coming up, it gets harder and harder to be optimistic.*
TB
Bowling Green

Dear TB:
Thank you for your note. I agree with you that somehow our people are not paying attention to the realities. I am afraid we are about to re-learn the Vietnam lesson.
Regards,
Amjad Hussain

Via e-mail, April 24, 2004:
I am very surprised at our failures in Iraq. I believed that the opportunity for self-government in Iraq would lead to a general uprising by freedom seeking Arab populations in the entire region, that they would establish representative governments, and the entire world would almost immediately become a much safer place.
The government in nearly every Arab state is a throw back to Nazi Germany or Fascist Italy and truly a disgrace to all humankind.
I now believe an Arab with any brains has migrated to the west.
RL

Dear RL:
Your assumption that only we in this country know what is good for the rest of the world is naive and perhaps self-righteous. An outside solution to internal domestic problems seldom succeeds. We should use our influence (short of war and occupation) to make that point. America had tremendous clout and I think it ought to be used to influence people.
Regarding your comments about Arabs being stupid does not really need any comment. It speaks volumes about your own mind set rather than the stupidity of Arabs (or lack thereof). I say this as a non-Arab and as one who has been a student of history.
I am grateful that you took the time to write.

S. Amjad Hussain

The genocide by Saddam in Iraq, the rampant execution of women on the notorious soccer field in Afghanistan and the widespread acts of terrorism by Muslims against civilian populations through out the world are intolerable. This is not naive or self-righteous.

I thought the best solution would be self-determination for the people of Iraq; that self-determination would spread like wild fire through the Arab world. and the atrocities against humanity by Arabs would cease. About this, I possibly am naive and self-righteous.

Your current solution, "for the United States to use its considerable political influence," is truly naive and is nothing more than a recipe for the status quo.

So long as terrorism by Arabs is rampant, I stand by my statements and hold the Arab nations responsible.

Regarding my statement reflecting on Arab brain function (which excluded those who have migrated west), maybe "frame of mind" would have been a better choice of words. Anyhow, I would be delighted in being proven wrong!

Would you be happier if the UN were involved in pacifying the Middle East?

RL

Via e-mail, April 24, 2004:

Dear Dr. Hussain:

I read with great interest your article on Iraq and with sadness about Kristal's neoconservative imperialistic think tank. Actually, this "New American Century" of centralizing power had its birth when Lincoln ascended to the Presidency. Whig, turned Republican, Lincoln embraced the old Whig platform of what was called the "American System" and replaced democracy with a British style mercantilism.

The American System also was a dominating plan to usurp power from the states to the federal government, first over the south and then over the Indians. The federal government in turn used taxes to fuel it's own power for its own agenda, using it's favorite corporations for government projects that benefited few but those favorite sons of the incumbents. Of course, Grant followed Lincoln and continued the destruction. It started with this country and then began to grow abroad.

A good book to read is DiLorenzo's "The Real Lincoln." It's well researched and documented. I only suggest this because it will give you a thread of history to understand the beginnings of the centrailzation of power movement from which this nation at its birth attempted to divorce.

We have no business in Iraq, just like the government of the United States had no right to invade southern states, or get involved in The Mexican War, The Spanish-American War and a few other conflicts, including Viet-Nam.

By the way, I love my country and consider myself a loyal patriot. But a patriot doesn't have to agree with the government, especially when it is a corrupt one.

Peace,

MB

Via e-mail, April 24, 2004:

DR. HUSSAIN – YOUR ARTICLES CONTINUE TO AMAZE ME WITH YOUR DEEP HATRED OF AMERICA AND PRESIDENT BUSH. YOU CHOOSE TO BELIEVE ONLY PEOPLE LIKE WOODWARD AND CLARK BECAUSE THEY FURTHER YOUR CAUSE IN THIS ELECTION YEAR. YOU NEVER GIVE ANY CREDITABILITY TO COLIN POWELL OR CONDOLEEZZA RICE WHEN THEY TELL THEIR SIDE OF WHAT HAPPENED. YOU ONLY CHOOSE TO BELIEVE THOSE THAT HAVE BOOKS TO SELL, NOT THE PEOPLE THEMSELVES. SOMEDAY AFGHANISTAN AND IRAQ WILL PRODUCE EDUCATED, INTELLIGENT, CAPABLE WOMEN LIKE DR. RICE, WITH THE HELP AMERICA IS GIVING!

YOU DEMANDED THAT PRESIDENT BUSH FIRE A GENERAL FOR SPEAKING OF HIS RELIGION. HOWEVER, YOU OR ANY OF YOUR MUSLIM LEADERS NEVER SPEAK UP AGAINST YOUR CLERICS THAT CALL FOR THE KILLING OF AMERICAN MARINES, WORKERS AND EVEN IRAQ PEOPLE THAT ARE TRYING TO FREE IRAQ. BY YOUR SILENCE YOU SHOW YOUR APPROVAL. WHAT YOU SEEM TO BE SAYING IS THAT THE WHOLE AREA DOES NOT HAVE A VISION, UNDERSTAND, OR CARE WHAT FREEDOM REALLY MEANS. NOW SOME PEOPLE ARE BEGINNING TO SAY THE WHOLE AREA IS NOT WORTH OUR WORRY, EFFORTS, AND SACRIFICE. SOME BELIEVE WE

SHOULD LET THEM GO BACK TO THEIR DICTATORS, MASS GRAVES, TORTURE CHAMBERS, RESTRICTED EDUCATION AND POOR HOSPITALS.

AS YOU COMPLAIN ABOUT AMERICA YOU SHOULD ASK YOURSELF – WHAT COUNTRY IN THE HISTORY OF THE WORLD HAS EVER GIVEN AS MUCH OF ITSELF TO TRY TO HELP SUFFERING PEOPLE THE WORLD OVER? ACCORDING TO YOU WE HAVE NEVER GIVEN ENOUGH AND IT WAS ALL FOR NOTHING. MAYBE YOU ARE RIGHT – IT SHOULD ALL STOP SINCE IT DOES NO GOOD AND ONLY BRINGS HATRED FROM YOU AND THOSE WE ARE TRYING TO HELP!!

ONE LAST THOUGHT – -IF AMERICA IS SO VERY BAD, WHAT BROUGHT YOU TO AMERICA IN THE FIRST PLACE?

GDB

Sir:

Your blindness to the policies of our government also amazes me. You expect all Americans to file in line to support whatever policies our government makes. If I wanted that I should have migrated to China or North Korea. (Perhaps you should consider doing that.)

I love this country as much as you do and perhaps more. But I also know that it is my right to disagree with my government. You do not seem to differentiate between a country and its government. Perhaps next time when you start fuming you ought to understand the difference between the two.

I do not think I can carry on a CIVIL conversation with you. In future, sir, I would suggest you direct your comments to the attention of the editor for possible publication in the *Readers' Forum*.

Sincerely,

S. Amjad Hussain

Israel would redraw map of Middle East
July 31, 2006

For the past two weeks Israel has wreaked havoc on Lebanon by indiscriminately bombing not only Hezbollah's stronghold in the south but civilian targets in the north of the country as well. The abduction and capture of two Israeli soldiers by Hezbollah, the stated reason for this onslaught, appears to have happened inside Lebanon.

After two weeks of relentless ground, sea, and air assault, the success is far from certain.

It is a replay of what Israel has done many times. In 1982 Israel invaded Lebanon to kick the Palestinians out of the country. It was accomplished at the cost of 18-thousand Palestinian and Lebanese lives and the destruction of much of Beirut. The present invasion has already killed more than 400 Lebanese men, women, and children and has left more than 600-thousand homeless.

Hezbollah was born during Israel's 18-year occupation of southern Lebanon and it was Hezbollah that eventually forced Israel to quit Lebanon in 2000. It is a grass-roots organization that enjoys widespread public support in Lebanon and across the Arab world. The current operation might cripple it to some extent but will not be enough to eliminate it completely. In fact Moshe Arens, former Israeli foreign minister, thinks Hezbollah could emerge from the conflict unscathed.

It is ironic that Israel refuses to negotiate with Hezbollah for the release of captured soldiers even though Israel has done so in the past and has exchanged prisoners. The negotiations will eventually take place, but much more damage to Lebanon will have been done by then.

It is bound to further inflame the Arab and Muslim world against Israel and its main supporter and benefactor, the United States. These events will push more young Arab men and women into the arms of militants and terrorists.

The irony is that the kidnapping of soldiers and civilians has been a common occurrence in the Middle East. The issue has always been resolved by direct or indirect negotiations and the exchange of prisoners. Israel has been kidnapping Lebanese and Palestinians citizens at will. There are an estimated 9,000 Palestinians in Israeli jails, including members of the Palestinian parliament and some Hamas ministers. There are also a small number of Lebanese in Israeli captivity. These captured men, women, and children have no recourse. Why did Israel respond so ferociously?

Hezbollah has been a constant source of worry and irritation for Israel because of its military prowess, its links with Iran and Syria, and its influence and power in Lebanese politics. According to a recent report by Mathew Kalman in the *San Francisco Chronicle*, Israel started planning for the current operation soon after its withdrawal from Lebanon in 2000. The plan, shared with the United States and other key allies, spelled out the current three-week operation in great detail.

Israel had expected worldwide condemnation of its exaggerated and out of proportion response to Hezbollah's provocation. It is, as it has always been, oblivious to and dismissive of world opinion. Thanks to the awesome influence of the Jewish lobby in America, Israel can get away with anything. The Bush Administration's callous attitude to the carnage in Lebanon and a lopsided 410-8 vote in the House of Representatives cheering Israel for its actions speaks volumes about the impotence of the United States.

Israel wishes to redraw the map of the Middle East at the expense of Arabs and Palestinians. On her recent visit to the region, Secretary of State Condoleezza Rice justified the widespread destruction caused by Israel as the birth pangs of a new Middle East. Unless the world finds an equitable and honorable solution to the 58-year-old conflict, this is going to be a long, protracted, and fruitless labor.

In the Toledo Blade Readers' Forum, *August 7, 2006:*
"Columnist in denial of the basic facts"
Dr. S. Amjad Hussain's July 31 column was most disappointing. In the past I have enjoyed his thoughtful contributions to the Toledo community but his closed-minded method of attacking Israel has revealed him as a man in denial of basic facts.

Applying passion, not reason, to a discussion of the conflict between Hezbollah and Israel, Dr. Hussain failed to mention, even once, the hundreds of Hezbollah rocket attacks intended to harm and kill as many Jews as possible. Is this not a fact worth mentioning when discussing the conflict?

A million Israelis are in bomb shelters, according to this newspaper. I am not saying that Israel is faultless in its bombing;

indeed no one in the world is without blame in this ever-enlarging conflict. But total denial of critical evidence, the lethal rockets, suggests that Dr. Hussain is so biased he cannot hold the relevant facts in his mind.

Israel did not murder hundreds of our Marines sleeping in their barracks in Lebanon on a true peacekeeping mission. How long ago that was, but some of us do not forget such an atrocity. Can Dr. Hussain, in praising Hezbollah, justify Hezbollah's suicide murders of U.S. Marines? Perhaps in his passion he has lost all capacity to deal with facts?

DN
Broadway Street

In the Toledo Blade Readers' Forum, *August 7, 2006:*
"Israel has every right to defend itself"
Israel has a right to defend itself. Hezbollah in 1983 attacked our embassy in Beirut, killing 17 American citizens. Later that year they killed 241 U.S. military persons stationed in Beirut. Again in 1984 they killed two more Americans at our embassy annex, and later that year they killed 18 U.S. servicemen in Torrejon, Spain. In 1985 Hezbollah hijacked TWA Flight 847 and killed a U.S. Navy diver.

On July 12 Hezbollah, unprovoked and with premeditation, attacked Israel by way of long tunnels and, using Katyusha rockets, killed and kidnapped Israeli soldiers.

How would the U.S. respond to a similar assault if many hundreds of rockets were launched against us, with civilians and military killed and property destroyed?

It would do what Israel is doing. After the tragic attack of Sept. 11, the US attacked Afghanistan, conquered the Taliban and al-Qaeda, and is still occupying the country.

If it is OK for the United States to defend itself from attack, then it sure ought to be OK for Israel to do the same.

PDG
Corey Road

In the Toledo Blade Readers' Forum, *August 7, 2006:*
"Israel doesn't want to change the map"

The anti-Israeli diatribe by Amjad Hussain left out vital information. Dr. Hussain falsely charges that Israel wants to change the map of the area.

He feigns shock that Israel won't "negotiate" with groups whose entire existence is based upon their determination to wipe Israel from the fact of the earth!

Talk about your map change!

Dr. Hussain fantasizes that Hezbollah force Israel out of southern Lebanon. The great "mistake" Israel made was believing the United States and the United Nationals would prevent Hezbollah attacks from Lebanon against Israel.

"Trade land for peace," Israel was told. So trade Israel did! Where's the promised peace?

Did Dr. Hussain demand that Hezbollah respect Israel's pullout and not attack Israel?

Are Jewish lives of such little value?

Are members of Hezbollah and Hamas to be pitied? After all, if they cannot live in Israel, where can they live?

Don't let facts changed preconceived notions! First, hundreds of thousands of Palestinians have lived and worked in Israel since it became independent in 1948.

Second, the total size of Israel is less than 8,000 square miles. Lebanon has more than 10,000 square miles. Jordan has more than 34,000 square miles. Syria has more than 71,000 square miles. Egypt has more than 385,000 square miles!

And those are just the majority Muslim states that border Israel! Why aren't Hezbollah and Hamas welcome to live there? Why isn't a total of more than a half million square miles enough land?

The ravings of Hamas and Hezbollah leaders sound a lot like Hitler to me: Jews are in the way...kill them all!

Muslim hegemony over this region by engulfing Israel sounds a lot like "lebensraum" did 70 years ago.

DP

Sylvania

In the Toledo Blade Readers' Forum, *August 7, 2006:*
"Why is Israel always the scapegoat?"

Why does this small Democratic country of Israel become the scapegoat of the Middle East every time there is a provocation in that area of the world?

What is so different between the Muslims, the Jews, and the Christians of that region of the world?

It appears to me that the answer is political. The brainwashed and deprived general population of the region around Israel is exploited by the ruling class, sheiks, dictators, and so-called presidents.

There is no question that the Islamic extremists have a goal of total world control.

Iran, Syria, and many other sympathetic factions in the Middle East want nothing more than to control the world and convert it to their form of Islamic rule (if not rule, then their form of world domination).

How can such a small country, Israel, be so intimidating to so many large countries that greatly outnumber it?

Maybe the rules of the region are afraid of the possible beneficial change that would more than likely happen with peace in the region.

Israel has become a major agricultural are, a flower-growing center, a major medical center, a diamond-cutting center, and highly industrialized country, which the rest of the area could possibly learn from.

BL

Lewis Avenue

Via e-mail, July 31, 2006:

Dr. Hussain,

I am saddened by today's column re: Israel. You have often vented your views through the pages of the Toledo Blade. *While I often disagree, I remember the wonderful thing about America, our ability to have freedom of speech and of the press. Differing views is one of the rights that make this a great country. Israel is also a democratic country. Freedom of speech is also allowed there. Even today, in the heat of battle, public debate is allowed as to future courses of action.*

Why did your article today prompt a written response from me? The anger within? The attack on Israel? No, it was your careless use of promoting and inciting anger and ill will on the Jewish people, the American Jewish people of which I am a proud member. Perhaps you were encouraged by Mel Gibson's ramblings this past weekend against

*Jews? Perhaps it was the attack on the Seattle Jewish community?
Don't you think you could have chosen a different way to word this?
Perhaps "the Israeli lobby?" Do you think that conservative Christ-
ians aren't also lobbying congress on behalf of Israel?*

*In light of what is happening, there is heightened security at all
local Jewish institutions. I am now wondering what kind of security I
will need at my son's bar mitzvah. Did I mention he is autistic? Will
you show anger next to the special needs community? You know, in
anti-Semitic Germany, the special needs community was also
exterminated!!*

*Why don't you condemn Hezbollah or Hamas for digging tunnels,
shooting rockets, unprovoked!! Or kidnapping? Why don't your run a
column about how Israel had pulled out of Gaza?? Wasn't that a good
thing?*

*Anger incites! What should I expect in Toledo? Should I explain to
my children the risks of being together??*

Fred

Dear Fred:

I am grateful for your comments. You have raised some very interesting points in your e-mail. Incidentally, Mel Gibson's despicable
tirade against the Jews had nothing to do with me writing this column. I
do not think any sensible person with two functioning brain cells would
agree with him.

You said I should have used the phrase Israeli lobby rather than
saying Jewish lobby. I do not see any difference between these two
phrases.

Your assertion is very true that Christian conservatives also support
Israel. But they support Israel for a different reason. According to their
3-act play Palestine would be given to Jews in the first act. In the
second there will be the second coming of the messiah. In the 3rd act
everyone who does not accept Christianity will be eliminated. I am at a
loss to understand why would some Jews accept the help of Christian
evangelists when their ultimate aim is to eliminate the Jews?

I am also at a loss to understand the connection between your son's
Bar Mitzvah and what happened to special needs community in Germany. I can however assure you that if there ever is a need it will be an
honor to protect the Jewish (and Christian and other) places of worship

against the deplorable actions of some crazies. You might be surprised to know that as a Muslim it is incumbent upon me to protect the places of worship of other faiths.

I do have a question though. Why is it that the Jewish community in the U.S., with very rare exceptions, never ever criticizes Israel for some of its brutal policies towards Palestinians? I said with rare exceptions because there is a full-page ad in the *New York Times* today that is very poignant and compelling. It is signed by a number of Jews, Christians and Muslims. I wish the parties concerned – Israel, Arabs, the U.S. and the Europeans – would act upon this outline and prevent any further bloodshed in the Middle East.

I am really grateful that you took the time to write.

Cordially,

Amjad

Many a hunter hears call of the wild on a crisp fall day
December 8, 2002

Camden, Mich. - A full moon shines in a star-studded black velvet sky as I make my way into the thick brush of the Michigan forest near Lake Diane. It is 6:30 in the morning and I am in these woods indulging in my favorite annual pastime of deer hunting. At this time of the year some of us who still have the primordial urge to hunt hear the clarion call and head for the wilderness. This urge is as old as the history of mankind.

It is still dark and quiet. But in this quiet I hear the sounds of nature. A heavy frost has left a thin silver coating on leaves, masquerading as finely sprinkled snow dust. The leaves, some crisp and dry, others wet and soggy, make crunching muffled sounds under my boots. The drip-drip-drip of dew falling from tree branches adds muffled sounds to the symphony of nature.

I find a suitable spot in the brush that has a wide view of the sloping hill and the ravine beyond. In the breaking dawn I can hardly make out the silhouettes of the trees at the farther edge of the ravine. For all I know, there may be a deer or even a herd bedded down in the thicket. I pour myself a cup of coffee from my Thermos, sip the precious brew, and take in the fresh crisp air. It just cannot get any better.

After some effort, one can think and look at the same time. Eyes become periscopes, scanning the woods in a 180-degree arc for any unusual movement; movement of tiny horizontal line - a fragment of a deer's silhouette - against the vertical topography of woods. While eyes scan the surroundings, the mind wanders free and unhampered.

Deer are elusive animals. Over hundreds and thousands of years they have learned to avoid arrows, flintlock guns, and modern firearms. A whiff of human scent, an unnatural sound, or unexpected movement sends them into hiding. This past year I saw plenty of deer in these woods, but now they are nowhere to be seen or heard.

A thin blanket of fog rolls down the treetops and shrouds everything in sight. This surreal scene could be a perfect backdrop for a Shakespearean play. I could half expect to see Marcellus Bernardo and Horatio awaiting the ghost of Hamlet's father somewhere under the shadow of nearby tree. I strain to hear their imaginary voices, but all I hear is the drip-drip-drip of the falling dewdrops. I can barely see 10 feet through the mist. I guess the gods have decided to favor the deer on this morning.

Gods have a way with deer. Native Americans consider them sacred. The New Mexico Pueblo Indians have special deer dance and some tribes in Arizona and Mexico mime the hunting of deer in their rituals. After all, the deer had provided them with food, clothing, and instruments of survival.

Though traditions, concepts, and beliefs have changed over eternity, hunting remains deeply embedded in the hidden recesses of our brains. Come hunting season, many of us hear the call of the wild. We stop at the neighborhood hardware store to buy a permit, don our orange coats and hats, and head for the woods to play the ancient game of hide and seek.

Why do people hunt? The answer to this simple question defies a two-plus-two-makes-four answer. It is a frame of mind. It is a vestige of a primordial instinct we inherited from our hunter-gatherer ancestors of a remote past. Or perhaps it is a deep-rooted desire to be with nature and all its beauty, mystique, and enchantment. As Charles Dickens said in *Oliver Twist*, "There is a passion for hunting, something deeply implanted in the human breast."

Maybe there is no logical explanation other than to be with oneself in an inspiring setting.

As the sun peeks through the veil of fog, the ground glass cover begins to dissipate. Shafts of light filter through the trees and in a playful display create an eerie surreal scene. I tiptoe around the trees to spot the illusive horizontal lines of a deer. But not today.

The ancient game of hide and seek will have to wait for another day.

Via e-mail, December 9, 2002:
Gentlemen,
Thank you for the insightful treatment on hunting that you have provided in The Blade *during the '02 deer season. It's refreshing to read rational and sensitive columns on the topic.*
I've just returned from the Noble Co. farm that I have hunted for over 20 years. Wandering the hills and hollows, reading nature's signs, and being away from the modern world is a personal renewal. Hours

spent on the stand are hours of introspection and reflection about life, and is probably as close to meditation as I'll ever get.

I do my own processing, and find a unique satisfaction in completing the path from forest to freezer, sans butcher and shrink wrap. Perhaps it's the bond that the Native Americans felt with the game that gave them life. In that spirit, I try to care for my kills with honor and respect.

SP, Outdoors Writer),

I've always wanted to tell you how much I enjoyed your column "Bang for Buck Most Impresses Hunters." I believe it was from 1996. The tattered copy is still in my desk drawer, and is often reread.

Again, thank you both for putting a positive note on an activity, or should I say "passion," that is increasingly misunderstood.

BH

Napoleon, OH

Via e-mail, December 10, 2002:

Dr. Amjad Hussain;

I just want to tell you that I enjoyed your column in The Blade's *Dec.8 edition. Your description of the location of the hunter was so impressionable. .absolutely beautiful. Love of nature and one's being aware of being in the midst of it is truly heartwarming. Thank you for giving your readers those moments to relive your description.*

HA

Fremont, OH

British whites, minorities still far apart
July 30, 2007

London – The recent spate of attempted car bombings in London and Scotland have added another layer of suspicion and distrust of minorities in this country. Though it is not apparent in everyday life, there is definitely a gulf separating ethnic minorities and the mainstream white population.

The complicated race relations in this island nation have had a checkered past. The small trickle in the early 1950s of immigrants from the Indo-Pakistan Subcontinent and other British Commonwealth countries increased sizably in subsequent decades. Over time the changing demographics have transformed the city of London and many other large cities into clusters of ethnic ghettos.

Muslims now constitute a large minority in Britain. They number close to 2.5 million out of a total population of 58 million. There are more Muslims in Britain than the Jews, Hindus and Sikhs combined. Their average age is lower than the native Brits and they tend to have bigger families.

This has led to some demographic disparities in the population. School age children constitute over 30% of Muslims in Britain compared to 13% in the white population. A relative isolation of Muslims from the mainstream and a rather high unemployment has led many to conclude that militancy and terrorism are the result of poor education and lack of economic opportunities. Most of British bombers however were educated and the most recent ones were doctors. There is no clear-cut answer except that somehow these young men were susceptible to recruitment by the terrorists.

In the backdrop of this complex tapestry where people live in parallel socio-religious universes it is not difficult at all to become judgmental. I fell myself into that trap while traveling on the London underground during rush hour last week.

A bearded young man got onto the train with a backpack. I could tell he was an orthodox Muslim from his shaved moustache and a calloused forehead from repeatedly touching the ground during prayers. He put his backpack between his feet and immediately started reading and sending text messages on his cell phone. Was he sending a text message before detonating his backpack or was he merely conducting his business on cell phone like others on the train? When I got off at my destination he was still working his cell phone.

This racial and ethnic divide was brought into sharp relief by two other encounters I had in Britain.

At a London hotel I came across a meticulously dressed Pakistani employee.

The extremely polite and highly polished young man was an immigrant who had put himself through university and had obtained double masters in a short span of three years. He had decided to go back to Pakistan and face an uncertain future there instead of subjecting himself to ongoing ethnic and religious discrimination. He could not fathom living under suspicion for the rest of his life. A deeply religious man he had nothing but contempt for the terrorists who use his religion to perpetrate their crimes.

On the train to the picturesque English countryside called the Cotswolds, I met a white university student from Nottingham. An intense and engaging young man he had just returned from a hitchhiking trip to Morocco. He said there was fear of terrorism in the big cities but not in the countryside. He linked the war in Iraq, which an overwhelming majority of his countrymen oppose, to the rise of militancy and terrorism. On the question of integration and or assimilation of minorities in the mainstream he was not very optimistic. To him it might happen in few generations but not in the near future.

One avenue of integration is to participate in political process. There are at this time Muslims elected to local councils (municipalities) and British Parliament. There is even a Pakistani Muslim in the House of Lords. This representation however is much less than their numbers. These leaders have started to talk openly about religion and terrorism and are trying to find ways and means to insulate Muslim youth from the influence of jihadi recruiters.

They have also called for a ban on the importation of imams (religious leaders) from Arab and Muslim countries that cannot speak English and have little or no insight in western religions and cultures and thus inadvertently end up alienating the youth from the society they live in.

Via e-mail, August 5, 2007:

Amjad,

Thanks for including me with copies of your Blade *articles. Your voice of reason and moderation is certainly needed during these troubled times, and no where more so than here in the United States as we become more religiously and politically polarized on the far right and far left. You would not believe some of the bigoted emails I receive from people who now openly denigrate Muslims and advocate such things as placing the Christian cross in all public places.*

Oh, for the "good old days" of past centuries when religions and cultures were insulated from each other by geography and confined within cultural boundaries. The Catholics and Protestants may have fought each other in open warfare during the 30 years war, but reached a treaty and agreed to draw a line though the center of Europe with Catholics confined to one side and Protestants the other. The Ottoman Empire boundaries supplied insulation for many Muslim countries from Christian for centuries, and British Empire boundaries did the same.

No more. Now all religions are intermixed without insulation or barriers. Internet messages flow instantly between virtually all countries of the world, and multi-national companies are everywhere. We have not yet learned how to live in a global culture where competing religions and cultures are intermixed with no buffer zones. It takes more religious tolerance, understanding, and cultural discipline than we possess. The entrenched religious cultures from times past now in today's climate are clearly bigoted and create great conflict.

So far, except for 9/11 in New York City, most of the open conflict has been overseas, but we will see that conflict move onshore in the future. When will a "dirty" suitcase atomic bomb or a gas attack wipe out a population in Washington DC or some major city? What will be our domestic reaction then?

When I was in Toledo a couple years ago at your invitation, I attended a session of their Interfaith Organization at which a couple dozen local churches met to seek common ground and how to live in harmony with each other, even though they had differing religious faiths. It was a marvelous experience, and I wondered why such a thing could not happen elsewhere. Perhaps it has, but I am not aware of it. The people in the United States (and perhaps elsewhere) seem to

*be growing more religiously and politically polarized, and the silent
majority in the middle ground seem to be shrinking.*

Too bad.

*Amjad, it is important for people such as you to continue to assist
others to seek a middle ground of religious and cultural tolerance and
understanding.*

Incidentally, I found a box with a couple more copies of Riding the
Fence Lines, *so could send you a couple copies if you still want any.
As I reread that book written pre-9/11, I find it still provides about the
right religious message. Maybe we should revise, edit, and reissue?*

Regards,
Bernie

Thank you, Bernie, for your encouraging words.

Yes, the world is getting very polarized and scary. I do intend to
keep writing.

Recently my name was recommended to the governor for appointment to the UT Board of Trustees. The governor's chief of staff called
to chat and brought up the issue of my writing op-ed pieces. He
wondered if I would consider stop writing if appointed...I said I would
not write about the university or higher education but I will not trade
my writing for appointment to the university board...

I would very much like to have those extra copies.

Warmest regards,

Amjad

Via e-mail, August 5, 2007:
Hello,

*I agree with a lot of the sentiments in the well thought out message
below and I agree with the message that we should never forget the
pain of human suffering. History is a good lesson that we should
always remember and not commit the same mistakes. USA does not
seem to do that!*

*We are entitled to our views and opinions without abusing anybody.
Rather than pat everybody at the back I think we should face difficult
issues where we disagree.. I agree that the present conflicts are
regional and not religious and based upon personal interest and greed
as rightly pointed out.*

With regard to god with a small g or a capital G and the religious orientation, I have to say this: My Muslim parents went to Hajj before I was born. At the age of 12, I had read Qur'an in Arabic, parrot fashion, without understanding it, and believed in the fundamentals of Islam without questions.

In adulthood and during my educational research in engineering I was told to question every belief. We were not allowed to question any fundamental beliefs in Islam. I read Qur'an in Urdu translation and English translation by a Muslim-Arab scholar from Cairo. This is just my personal opinion; I found the text full of threats and full of repetitions.

Like every young man I prayed (not 5 times a day), and none of these prayers were answered in my favor…We are told that god is with us 24 hours a day not only observing but knowing our intimate thoughts.

I don't believe a word of it now.

Regards,

MA

Israel is faced with a difficult choice
January 29, 2007

The debacle in Iraq has brought into sharp focus the festering Israeli-Arab issue that has been totally neglected for the past six years, thanks to George W. Bush. A recent book by former president Jimmy Carter, *Palestine: Peace not Apartheid*, is an attempt to bring the issue back into public consciousness. Mr. Carter has known the Middle East conflict firsthand and was the first U.S. president to have successfully brokered a peace agreement between Israel and Egypt. The book reveals for the first time the horrible oppression and persecution of the Palestinian people.

The response of the Jewish lobby and its friends in this country has been predictable. Mr. Carter has been called anti-Semitic and an enemy of Israel. He has also been labeled a bigot, a liar, and a plagiarist. Jimmy Carter has the honesty, integrity, and compassion (both for Jews and Palestinians) to be anything but those. This says more about the intellectual bankruptcy of his detractors than the honesty and integrity of the former president.

Mr. Carter used the word "apartheid" in describing Israeli occupation of the Palestinian lands. Naturally the word invokes the image of the white supremacist regime in South Africa. And there are parallels.

It is apartheid when an occupying power deliberately isolates the native population by fencing them in, passes discriminatory legislation against them, controls their movement in and out of their homes, institutes a dual education system, uses disproportionately different scales to fund Jewish settlers and Palestinians, controls water and food distribution, and empowers Jewish settlers to deal with Palestinians any way they wish.

This view was further strengthened when Israeli Prime Minister Ehud Olmert brought the Yisrael Beitenu Party into his coalition government and appointed Avigdor Lieberman as deputy prime minister and minister for strategic threats. Mr. Lieberman advocates forceful expulsion of all Palestinians from occupied territories and Israel.

Mr. Lieberman is not alone in his views. Gamla, an Israeli organization founded by Jewish settlers and former Israeli military officers, has published detailed plans for the "complete elimination of the Arab demographic threat to Israel."

This, according to the plan, would translate into forcibly expelling all Palestinians, whether they are living in occupied territories or in the state of Israel, within a period of three to five years. For this plan to succeed it needs "only a modicum of support from its closest ally, the United States."

Considering that the Bush Administration has always capitulated to the dictates of Jewish organizations, including the powerful American Israel Public Affairs Committee, this scenario is not farfetched.

Unlike in Israel, where a healthy and robust public debate on the Palestinian issue has been the norm, no such public discourse has been possible here in the United States. In a knee jerk response, Jewish leaders in this country are always ready and willing to curb and suppress any dissenting voices by using the all-too-convenient label of anti-Semitism. The treatment meted out to Mr. Carter has been dished out to all others who have advocated an even-handed policy in resolving the Palestinian issue.

In an interview on National Public Radio recently, Mr. Carter claimed considerable Jewish support for his views on Palestine. Unfortunately, that support has not been out in the public domain. That the policies of Israel in occupied territories are discriminatory and inhuman are known to Jewish communities. Yet there have been very few voices from these communities raised in public against these policies.

Except for discussion and deliberation in some moderate-to-liberal Jewish publications, there is hardly any discussion or debate at the community level. So it is left to the likes of Abe Foxman of the Anti-Discrimination League and Alan Dershowitz of Harvard Law School to set the tenor and tone of this one-sided debate and to decide what is kosher and what is not.

The resolution of the Palestinian issue is the sine qua non for a peaceful Iraq. A just resolution will placate Syria, Iran, and Saudi Arabia and in turn their warring proxies in Iraq. Efforts to de-link the Palestinian issue from Iraq are bound to fail. The road to peace in Iraq, as indicated by Jim Baker's Iraq Study Group, would have to pass through Jerusalem.

Israel has a choice, albeit a difficult one. It could continue the apartheid in occupied lands and in return accept an ongoing low-level violence by Palestinians against its citizens, or it could start treating Palestinians as human and give them their land back.

Via e-mail, February 2, 2007:
Dr. Hussain:
Congratulations on penning the insightful Op-Ed column of January 29th ("Israel is faced with a difficult choice"). These days when President Carter and his truthfulness and boldness are being maligned by the ever-strong American-Jewish lobby, your powerful defense is a welcome sign. It was very heart-warming. I wish more Muslims would rather raise their pens than arms to stand up for what is right.
May Allah bless you.
Wassalam,
A-MA, Ph.D.
The University of Toledo

Thank you for your kind note.

The Arabs and Muslims only know the language of confrontation and are rather ignorant of language of reconciliation and persuasion. I have been deeply disappointed with their apparent lack of interest in their own issues. They are good at wringing their hands in private but will not, with notable exceptions, come out in the open and say what they complain about in private. They are in my view missing out on a great opportunity to become full partners in this important debate.

I have over the years become very contemptuous of our local Muslim leaders. They are good at hiding behind the language of religion (Inshallah, Masha Allah, Alhamado Lillah etc. etc.) but in practical terms they are hopeless. They still believe they can change events by prostrating in prayer.

I think we are on the same page on many of these issues.

Regards,
Amjad Hussain

In the Toledo Blade Readers' Forum, February 1, 2007:
"Israel is faced with implacable hatred"
S. Amjad Hussain's sweeping resolution to all the difficulties of the Middle East raised exceedingly difficult questions. Dr. Hussain states

that the "resolution of the Palestinian issue is the sine qua non for a peaceful Iraq." Does he mean that Shiites will cease killing Sunnis? Can he possibly believe that Sunnis will cease bombing Shiite mosques? Will the slaughter of innocents in Baghdad suddenly come to an end? Will the heartless suicide bombers who so pitilessly detonate in open markets of the poorest ordinary citizens immediately convert themselves into merciful Salvation Army bell ringers?

Dr. Hussain stated that peace in Jerusalem will placate Syria, Iran, and Saudi Arabia. Does that mean that the Saudis who teach an export the extremist Wahabi version of Islam that produced Osama bin Laden will modify their curriculum to teach the brotherhood of humanity? Does he expect us to accept that Syria, which gives aid and refuge to terrorists, will convert itself into a model nation that eschews brutality? Can he seriously believe that Iran, which openly supports the terrorist groups such as Hezbollah, will turn its back on unbridled violence? Has he forgotten that Iran's president has called for the extermination of Israel?

Tragically, on the same day that Dr. Hussain's simplistic placebo of a solution was published, a terrorist suicide bomber killed three ordinary human beings, worked in a bakery in Israel. A masked Palestinian spokesman in Gaza bragged about killing Jews.

The headline on Dr. Hussain's column tells us that "Israel is faced with a difficult choice." It is true. In the face of implacable hatred, Israel is faced with a most difficult choice. It must choose between obliteration or survival.

Rabbi AS
Pine Ridge Road

In the Toledo Blade Readers' Forum, *February 1, 2007:*
"Israel has no choice but to defend itself"
Words have specific meanings and when one is loose with those meanings, one is also loose with the truth. Such is the case with S. Amjad Hussain and President Carter in their use of the word "apartheid," and its application to Israel and the Palestinians. Apartheid, as created and formerly practiced in South Africa, was racial discrimination against the non-white citizens of that country. Palestinians are not citizens of Israel. Just as non-citizens in the United States do not have all the rights of citizens, so it is with the

Palestinians.   In addition, they are a hostile population, which has freely elected a governing body sworn to the destruction of Israel, and which advocates the destruction routinely in its schools, mosques, and media.

It is the Palestinians who have a choice to make.   They can accept Israel's existence and live peacefully beside it, or they can continue on their self-destructive path toward anarchy and ruin.   Until they choose the former, Israel has no choice but to defend its citizens to its maximum ability.

JG

Plymouth, MN

In the Toledo Blade Readers' Forum, *February 1, 2007:*

"It is the Palestinians who must choose"

S. Amjad Hussain's recent column, "Israel is faced with a difficult choice," was so full of innuendo and biased portrayal of facts it hardly deserves a response. He claims that dissenting voices like his are suppressed even as his column is prominently published and sent around the world in the Blade's *online edition.*

He latches onto widely rejected views of a tiny minority in Israel, the Middle East's only true democracy, and falsely suggests that those views reflect the mainstream. He naively suggests that somehow the civil war in Iraq between Shiites and Sunnis will come to a halt if Israel would just give in to the Palestinians.

Dr. Hussain's column appeared on the day on which a terrorist blew himself up and killed three individuals in the previously peaceful Israeli city of Eilat. Islamic Jihad bizarrely justified the suicide bombing as an attempt to halt Palestinian factions fighting each other in the Gaza Strip.

It is the Palestinians who have a choice to make. Israel stands ready to negotiate a two-state solution – a peace that will create a Palestinian state next to the Jewish state of Israel. Prime Minister Ehud Olmert has taken a number of steps in recent weeks to attempt to reopen negotiations with the Palestinians.

However, Hamas, the governing party chosen by the Palestinians, rejects Israel's right to exist at all. Israel's legendary statesman Abba Eban once said: "The Palestinians never miss an opportunity to miss an opportunity." It is time for Palestinians to place the blame where it belongs: on their own leaders who refuse to create a decent life for the average Palestinian. It is time for Palestinians to seize an opportunity for peace.

HMF
Jewish Community Relations Council
Sylvania

In the Toledo Blade Readers' Forum, *February 1, 2007:*
"Palestinians must come to their senses"
Columnist S. Amjad Hussain and President Carter are both honorable men and certainly not anti-Semitic. Unfortunately they share another characteristic: bad timing. The last time Dr. Hussain wrote in favor of the long-suffering Palestinians, The Blade *happened to report that rockets from Gaza maimed and killed young people in Israel who were simply walking down their street.*

Then I read Dr. Hussain joining President Carter in criticizing Israel, and I also read that a deranged Palestinian blew himself up in order to kill three Jewish bakers who were simply making their daily bread.

Like many Americans, I used to sympathize with all the down-trodden Palestinians. And I still care about their children, their innocents, and their refugees. But I stopped sympathizing with most adult Palestinians when I read that the majority favor suicide bombing and rocket terror. Those who think that it is just fine to strap explosives around the bodies of their children in the hope that Jewish children will be blown to bits are far beyond sympathy.

How do you deal with those who favor suicide bombings and rocket attacks deliberately aimed at civilians?

How do you deal with those who will do anything to destroy you? Building a wall to protect your children and bakers and setting up checkpoints are mild responses. Apartheid was something else entirely.

I do not know what will bring the Palestinians to their senses, for the sakes of their lives and the lives of their children, but certainly the misdirected criticism by Dr. Hussain and President Carter will not. One does not tell the members of a suicide cult that their behaviors are understandable under the circumstances.

DLN

Broadway Street

In the Toledo Blade Readers' Forum, *February 11, 2007:*
"Balancing debate on Middle East"
Amjad Hussain's column on the Israeli-Palestinian issue was enlightening, as was Jimmy Carter's book, Palestine: Peace not Apartheid. *Both authors provide some balance in an argument that is heavily weighted by the media in favor of Israel.*

The near apoplectic reaction by many American Jews to President Carter's views, a politician who as "fallen out of line," is curious. To castigate the only President who made real progress in establishing peace in the region with the Camp David Accords and to accuse him of supporting violence represents a defensiveness that clearly indicates a desire to obfuscate the full truth about Israeli actions.

Bottom line: The Palestinians accepted the 2002 Quartet's Roadmap in full, while Israel with its 14 caveats basically refused it. The idea of returning all occupied land, previously approved by Israel in U.N. Resolution 242, has been thoroughly undermined by the Israeli settlements.

As Ariel Sharon once said, "Everybody has to move, run, and grab as many hilltops as they can to enlarge the settlements because everything we take now will stay ours . . ."

To date, that is more than 150 settlements in the West Bank involving more than 255-thousand Jews. Some 150 countries agree that this is illegal according to international law, including the Fourth Geneva Convention, "which forbids an occupying power from transferring any parts of its civilian population into territories seized by military force."

The Iraq Study Group concluded "The United States will not be able to achieve its goals in the Middle East unless the United States deals directly with the Arab-Israeli conflict," the keystone of which is the Israeli-Palestinian issue. The Bush Administration has finally put a two-state solution at the top of its agenda and hopefully it can mediate a compromise, a long shot given its diplomatic ineptitude to date.

PA
Perrysburg

In the Toledo Blade Readers' Forum, *February 11, 2007:*

"A sound defense of Carter's latest book"

I would like to compliment S. Amjad Hussain's Jan. 29 column for defending the honesty and integrity of Jimmy Carter and giving an open view of the Israeli-Arab issue.

I have read Jimmy Carter's Palestine: Peace not Apartheid *and do not find it anti-Semitic. I have recommended it to family and friends.*

AS

Bowling Green

Via e-mail, January 29, 2007:

Actually, Jimmy Carter is ignorant, morally bankrupt and senile. I'm ashamed that I voted for him in 1976 and proud that I didn't in 1980. I have written to Dr. Hussain before about his columns - he is apparently impervious to reality, truth and justice. Propaganda like this makes me want to make aliyah immediately and live in the West Bank, which is my right.

HR

Via e-mail, February 4, 2007:

Mr. Hussain,

In most cases I just blow off you usual anti Israel banter as that of another confused and bigoted Muslim. The last article I referenced was more than even I could take.

It seems appropriate that you would back the likes of Jimmy Carter. He is by far one of the most spineless and ineffective presidents we have had. I do not see him as so much of an anti-Semite as I do a pro Palestinian. The Palestinian leaders have been corrupt and completely ineffective in developing an atmosphere of trust and respect, so Israel is within their rights to protect their people and existence by ignoring calls by the likes of Jimmy Carter and every other Palestinian apologist to give, give, and give.

As for you, your pathetic attempts at chastising the Muslim nations for both their outward and hidden support of terrorism are not even worth the paper they are written on. They are all just feeble attempts to show you are even handed so that you can go back to your anti Israel rhetoric.

Please tell me there is some local hospital that can use your services during your retirement instead of filling up the editorial section with your one sided views.

SW

Dear SW,

Thank you for your comments.

It is difficult to carry on a civil conversation when insults become part of the vocabulary.

Nevertheless I am grateful that you took the time to write.

Regards,

Amjad Hussain

Mr. Hussain

In retrospect, my words did come across as insulting, and for that I apologize. I struggle constantly to control my anger toward The Blade *and their leftist editorials, which has provided the platform for you and your opinions. However, if my email to you is used only to express my anger instead of providing MY opinion in opposition to yours, then my actions achieve nothing.*

Thank you for your reply. I expect that you will hear from me in the future, although hopefully in a more civil manner.

SW

Via e-mail, January 29, 2007:

Dear Dr. Hussain,

I admire your courage in writing your 1/29/07 Blade *article. I think you are entirely correct. I also have a great deal of respect for Jimmy Carter. He does not deserve the criticism that he is receiving over his book. In my opinion, his ideas are part of the solution, but he is being treated (by some) as part of the problem. It is very regrettable.*

RJ

Toledo, OH

Time for vigorous debate on the Middle East
February 12, 2007

My last column on former president Jimmy Carter's book *Palestine: Peace not Apartheid*, elicited the usual responses from familiar circles. The questions raised by the book were left unanswered by them. Instead the letters to the editor and those sent to me directly repeated the oft-repeated litany of what has now become a familiar pattern of response; just blame the victims for their misfortunes.

The arguments put forward are circuitous and ingenious. Some of them talked about Israel being the only democracy in the region and that it is such a tiny, small country. It is true but this line of reasoning somehow absolves Israel from following international laws and the United Nations Resolutions.

Israel and its supporters have also blamed Palestinians for becoming refugees. They contend that they were told by the Arab leaders to leave their homes and all of them did that voluntarily. It is true that some well-to-do Palestinians left on their own accord, but the bulk of the one million refugees were forced out of their homes by militant Jewish groups under a well-planned program.

A recent book based on declassified Israeli government documents (*The Ethnic Cleansing of Palestinians* by Ilan Peppe) puts that myth to rest. Mr. Peppe, a senior lecturer at Haifa University and other Jewish historians like Simha Flapan, Tom Segev, Avi Schlaim, and Benny Morris have written on the subject to the discomfort and embarrassment of right wing Jewish historians.

The recent inclusion of Yisrael Beitenu Party into Israeli government and the appointment of Avigdor Lieberman, an avowed supporter of Palestinian ethnic cleansing, as deputy prime minister should be of concern to everyone, including the moderate Jews.

Another argument put forward by the proponents of Israel is that Israel has no partner to talk peace with. Yes, the Palestinian Authority is in shambles. A good many of its leaders and legislators are in Israeli jails and because of a total economic and financial boycott there is widespread unrest. A systematic destruction and dismantling of the infrastructure of the Palestinian Authority by Israel is responsible for the current conditions. Hamas rose to power in that vacuum.

Hamas was supported and nurtured by Israel as a counterbalance to the intransigent Yassar Arafat. According to Zeev Sternell, a historian at the Hebrew University of Jerusalem, "Israel thought that it was a smart ploy to push the Islamists against the Palestinian Liberation Organization (PLO)". There have been a lot of unintended consequences of that policy.

I also said that while there is a vigorous and forceful debate about the Palestinian issue in Israel, no such public debate has been possible in this country. The majority of Jews in this country will not speak against the policies of Israel. Any departure from the straight and narrow earns them the wrath of organized Jewry. Recently Joel Benin, a professor at Stanford, found himself dis-invited by Harbor School in San Jose where he was scheduled to talk to the students about the Middle East Policy. He blamed his fellow Jews in silencing his voice.

And while many Jews and Gentiles are trying to talk openly about the Palestinian issue in this country one wonders about the almost total absence of Arab voices at the community level. If the Arabs have a compelling story to tell, and I think they do, why are the Arab professionals and the businessmen dead on arrival? Can the wringing of hands in private conversations replace the robust public discourse? Is it that they would rather have others do their bidding while they stay on the sidelines under the radar? Is it the fear of economic consequences that are at times inevitable part of a public debate? Perhaps all of these are true at some level.

And where are the self-appointed and self-anointed custodians of the Islamic faith who, while good at preaching to the choir and brow beating others to their restrictive religious viewpoints, are less than honest in their public discourse?

Ours is a pluralistic society where everyone has the right (dare I say, a duty) to pick up the bullhorn and take part in public debate on important issues. The fiasco in Iraq and the ongoing conflict in Palestine are of interest to the people in our country. It is time Arabs and Muslims wake up and take their rightful place in the public square. And while they shuffle their way there, they should be grateful to courageous Jews and Gentiles who have been speaking on their behalf.

In the Toledo Blade Readers' Forum, *February 27, 2007:*
"No justice in taking land and freedom"

It was unfortunate to read the criticisms of Amjad Hussain for his column a few weeks ago supporting former president Jimmy Carter and his book, Palestine: Peace, not Apartheid. *I'm sure more critics will be at work following Dr. Hussain's second report regarding the Palestinian/Jewish problem.*

To those who scoff at President Carter's book, I suggest they also read the book The Lemon Tree *by Sandy Tolan. This is a true account of the Israelis forcing the Palestinians from their homes and land in 1948, without providing restitution for any of it. Prior to this time, the Jews and Arabs had lived in peace together until the influx of many Jewish refugees from Europe following World War II.*

Although I am very sympathetic to the plight of the Jewish people, I can see no justice in their taking away the land and freedom of another group of people. I am very disappointed in our government's role in this. For too many years we have provided the Israelis with a blank check and have failed to speak up or intervene when they commit injustices against the Palestinians. Why wouldn't the Palestinians react with anger after being treated as second class citizens with 60 years of Israeli domination of their lives?

The Middle East is in chaos today thanks to our President and his unnecessary war, as was predicted by his father in 1991. As we struggle in Iraq, it just gives the present administration another excuse to turn a blind eye and let the Israelis continue to oppress the Palestinians. All people deserve justice, not just the ones who think they're right.

JB
Archbold

In the Toledo Blade Readers' Forum, *February 27, 2007:*
"Columnist distorts Middle East realities"

Yet again Blade *readers were subjected to characteristic distortions and generalities from Dr. Amjad Hussain.*

Dr. Hussain calls on Israel to adhere to UN resolutions but refrains from quoting precise references. By now everybody recognizes the farcical nature of those resolutions: Israel's single vote against the

*overwhelming votes of 56 Arab and Islamic petroleum-rich countries –
plus most countries that depend on Arab petrol.*

*Another often repeated lie is that Israel's actions in 1948 created
the Arab refugee problem. To prove his point, Dr. Hussain relies on
the dubious writings of the like of Ilan Pappe, which is similar to
relying on the writings of Holocaust deniers. The fact that Mr. Pappe
is allowed to write and teach in Israel is in itself proof of Israel's
vibrant democracy.*

*Suppose that Israel forced the Arabs out. Why are they still
"refugees" 60 years later? Why have the rich Arab states resettled
them just as Israel absorbed 800,000 Jewish refugees expelled by Arab
countries?*

*Dr. Hussain claims that Avigdor Lieberman's party, Yisrael
Beitenu, advocates "ethnic cleansing" of Israel's Arab population.
What Mr. Lieberman actually says is different: If a Palestinian state
materializes, and if Jews are evicted from it as from Gaza, Arabs who
live in Israel should also move to their newly established country.*

*Israel has no interlocutor not because the convicted "partners" sit
in Israeli jails, but because the terrorist organization Hamas, voted-in
overwhelmingly by the Arab-Palestinians, refuses to recognize Israel.*

*Dr. Hussain protests that the "Palestinian compelling narrative" is
not being heard enough in the media. The opposite is true. With one
exception, Palestinian propaganda blankets the media all over the
petrol-thirsty world.*

*Finally, Dr. Hussain keeps referring to "Palestine." Evidently, the
maps he uses are as reliable as his writings.*

YZ
Maumee

Nature's display puts world into perspective
August 13, 2007

Last Thursday, my deadline for this column, started out routine enough. I was going to write either on Pope Benedict or on General Pervez Musharraf of Pakistan. The Pope had asserted that only his flock, the Catholics, had any chance of salvation and the rest, a big chunk of humanity living in the world, were flawed and injured and thus doomed. The shock waves from that sweeping holier-than-though generalization are still being felt.

In Pakistan General Pervez Musharraf was poised to impose a state of emergency when a strong public condemnation at home and a not-too-subtle nudge from Washington stopped him in his tracks. Caught between the hard rock of terrorism and the deep blue cauldron of adverse public opinion he is hanging on to power by a thread.

The sedate tranquility of my morning however was overshadowed by a gathering summer storm that somehow made all other topics less important. I watched with wonder as the subdued early morning light gave way to twilight-darkness. I could feel and see the stirring of a big storm coming my way.

Then the electricity went out and plunged the house in darkness. With it the computer screen went blank, music vanished and all the appliances went silent.

While listening to the howling wind and the falling rain on the awning I realized that the loss of electricity had instantaneously connected me to billions of people around the world who have no electricity and are always privy to the sounds, spectacle and at times fury of nature. The array of my now-useless appliances – stove, refrigerator, coffee maker, electric clocks, stereo, computer, fax machine, air conditioner and what not – had leveled the playing fields. At least a villager somewhere in the world could make a cup of tea on his hearth or kerosene stove to savor the moment.

So by the flickering light of a candle I took out my pen and paper and started writing what I saw and what I felt. The exercise was comforting and also liberating.

A summer storm is nature's way making us understand that there are powerful forces that cannot be controlled at the flick of a switch or push of a button. It is also nature's way to bring relief and hope when high temperatures and humidity make us miserable and vulnerable. The downpour of life-sustaining rain not only refreshes the air, it lifts the spirits as well. When the first drops of a long-awaited rain fall on the parched earth, the aroma and fragrance is intoxicating. The drooping plants and sad trees sway in exhilaration and nod their approval as the torrents of water quenched their thirst.

As the wind picked up last Thursday morning it started to rain. Unlike the soft drizzle of a spring shower, the raindrops of a summer storm are big and heavy and they announce their arrival with a bang. They fell on the metal awning outside my study producing at first a slow rhythm of a xylophone in the beginning of a performance. Then the tempo picked up, the wind added to the crescendo and in no time a symphony of the sounds of nature was in full swing.

Then the lightening came, adding visual effects to the music of wind and rain. Branching arcs of lightening pierced the charcoal gray sky illuminating in dazzling white everything underneath the sky, including inside of the house, if only for a fleeting moment.

The heavens stayed open for what appeared to be a long time. A passing storm is in reality a passing show that must move on to dazzle, mesmerize and at times scare people in its path. So after about an hour or so the storm passed and the rumble of thunder became distant. The torrent of rain diminished and turned into a light shower making the raindrops on the awning into a slow decrescendo tempo. It was as if the galloping herd of wild horses was now cantering to an eventual stop.

The power was restored after four hours enabling me to finish this piece on the computer and file it electronically. Otherwise I would have had to hand-deliver my hand-written column to my editor at the *Blade*. Nature has a way of turning the clock back on us once in a while.

PASSAGES

Time doesn't stand still for homes or for people
January 16, 1996

Peshawar, Pakistan – It is a nondescript small house tucked in the middle of a narrow street. The glitter of the merchandise in small shops in the street – embroidered clothes, bangles, jewelry – and the accompanying hustle and bustle prevents the passersby from lifting their gaze to notice the fading white arches and the bamboo stick curtains covering the windows.

Dwellings, like people, also get old with age. My recent visit to our ancestral home was like visiting a dying kin. I had always imagined that place staying young and vibrant but time and elements had caught up with it.

I knocked at the heavy front door. Someone released the door latch by pulling the rope from upstairs. A familiar musty smell greeted me as I entered the dark foyer.

I pushed open a door into a small room. This oversized closet was my domain when I was in college. A small light bulb dangling from the ceiling spread a faint light. A familiar shaft of sunlight with millions of dancing dust particles illuminated a spot on the cement floor. A cot, few chairs and a rickety small table were still there. From this small and restricted space I would peer out through the window and observe the daily rhythm and rhyme of the neighborhood. I was surprised to see a Sylvester Stallone poster on the wall, perhaps left there by a recent resident. Monosyllable grunts were not part of the cultural landscape in my days. It was here that I discovered the joys of written words and kept company with the Bard, Longfellow, Kipling and the likes.

The real shock awaited me upstairs on the main floor. The brick courtyard had sagged precariously at one end. Peeled off plaster from the walls littered the floors of the unused rooms around the small courtyard.

There were memories scattered all over those ruins. In another time this was an enchanting place. A large extended family made this place full and exciting. My aunts and my mother kept the place neat and clean, cooked and cared for the family and the ever present guests. There on a wooden platform in the courtyard neighborhood children sat cross-legged chanting the Koran. From the confusing scramble of all those voices and noises mother's attentive ear would pick up a mispronounced word and she would correct it while still cooking on the hearth in the courtyard.

I walked to the room at one end of the courtyard. Five of us children shared this twelve by fourteen feet space with our widowed mother. Two beds, a dressing table and a wall cupboard were all the furniture we had. Clothes were kept in metal trunks under the beds. Jumping from one bed to the other across three feet of space, at the time as big as a huge canyon, was a favorite bedtime activity. So was sitting on the floor of that canyon and listening to my mother spinning enchanting yarns of benevolent kings and beautiful princesses.

Time does seem to stand still, at least for a fleeting moment, and help relive the past. But it is also a painful reminder of lost innocence, an era long passed and people long gone. It is difficult to see that enchanting place in its present crumbling and dilapidated state. Like watching an aged parent at the end of life. The last reluctant rays of a fading sun.

I plan not to be there when the place is torn down later this year to make room for a shopping arcade.

Soul mate touched many with her grace
December 18, 2006

It is not often that I use this space to talk about people close to me. I beg your indulgence as I pay tribute to my dear friend and soul mate Dottie, who was also my wife of 38 years.

It was 42 years ago that our paths – that of a student nurse from Chelsea, Michigan and that of a surgery resident from Peshawar, Pakistan – crossed at Maumee Valley Hospital in Toledo.

It wasn't the proverbial love at first sight. On the contrary it was the battle of the minds and principles that defined our friendship. She was an idealistic young nurse who placed her profession and its integrity ahead of all other considerations. And I was an impatient young man incapable of distinguishing between ideal patient care and insubordination. In my Pakistani mind, doctors gave orders and nurses carried them out. For that irrepressible girl, things were not that cut and dried. A few years later the man from Mars and the girl from Venus decided to tie the knot.

There could not have been two more incompatible people. In due course, however, religious and cultural differences gave way to mutual love, respect, and admiration. That was the mainstay of our life together, and in that milieu we would raise a daughter and two sons.

It was with considerable apprehension that she moved back to Pakistan with me in 1970. After all, when the news of our marriage reached Peshawar, the family had mourned and friends and neighbors had come to offer their condolences. But it took no time at all for the family to welcome and accept the new bride into the clan. For her part, Dottie lived the traditions, and established bonds with the family that endured the rest of her life. Knowing my deep emotional attachment to Peshawar, she spent the rest of her life nurturing my yearning for that place and helped me with a score of educational and literary projects for the city.

She joined me on many of my foreign trips, and when she would not or could not travel she took care of the home and hearth and waited for my return. At times she was apprehensive when I took our boys on expeditions, but she never wavered in her support of what I wanted to do.

It was not, however, the big or glamorous stuff that highlighted our life journey. The mundane everyday little things defined her life and accented our marriage: soccer games, piano recitals, school plays, parent-teacher conferences, daily pick up of our granddaughter Hannah from school, and, above all, the gathering of the family around the table at dinner time.

Nursing was her passion and she excelled at it. So it was startling when in 1996, at the age of 52, she decided to call it a day. She had made an error in calculating the dose of a medication but had caught herself in time. That misstep affected her deeply, and she decided to bow out while she was still on top. In her mind there was no room for acts of omission or commission. No persuasion on my part could make her change her mind. She was an idealist and also very stubborn.

As the relentless march of ovarian cancer took its toll, she wished to visit Peshawar just one more time to say farewell to our family. But it was too late. In the end she accepted death with the same quiet dignity that she had embraced life.

On her passing there was a flow of family friends, relatives, and even strangers to our ancestral home in Peshawar. This time they came to pay respects to the American girl who was able to narrow the East-West gap. She had lived seamlessly in two disparate worlds and in the process touched many people with her grace. As Ezra Pound said, "The quality of affection, in the end, is in the trace it leaves in the mind." There was plenty of it in Peshawar and Toledo these past two weeks.

Throughout history the prophets, sages, and wise men have tried to unravel the mysteries of life and death, mostly in vain, and fell short of explaining the stubborn "why?"

One could rely on science to understand the cannibalistic orgy of cancer consuming the body or playing havoc with the delicate bio-chemical symphony that makes the music we call life. But there is really no good explanation. Prayers cannot alter what God wills.

"I have no more words," said Rumi, the great 13th-century Turkish poet, "let the soul speak with the silent articulation of face."

Thank you for listening.

Via e-mail, December 18, 2006:
Dear Dr. Hussain,

It was with deep sorrow I read of your loss.

You have provided many of us with a positive and encouraging view of our troubled world. You have had the fortitude to say what many would not like to, but needed to hear. That applies to both sides of this cultural canyon.

Reading your tribute to Dottie was a very moving moment; again you speak with the passion that could only come from love. Thank you for sharing it with us; it was a privilege.

I have never responded to an article before but felt moved to do so this time. God gives us so few people who are selfless and kind. We knew o you and now we know of Dottie, I am sure that God's blessing to her was you.

Thank you for trying, with all your heart, to bring some peace to this world. You will be in my prayers, asking that you will again have the opportunity to experience your soul mate and the peace a good man deserves.

With sincere condolences,
VM

Via e-mail, December 18, 2006:
I should have cc'd you on the original. This is the letter I sent to the Blade *just now. It is attached. Ann*
Editors:

We have a tendency to remember only the good qualities of our deceased friends, but in the remarkable essay about Dottie Hussain, her husband Dr. Amjad Hussain, seems to have captured her personality, her values, and her essence perfectly.

I was blessed to have been a close friend and colleague of Dottie Hussain. She was a strong woman who exerted her influence always in gentle ways. Although she was a bright and articulate person who was recognized as a superb nurse, although she traveled the world and entertained cultural and political leaders, she maintained that her proudest achievement was her loving relationship with her husband, her children and her grandchildren.

She was a devoted friend, and she knew who her friends were. She taught us that one gets credit in life for what they do for others today, not what they wish to do at some point in the future. Although it sounds cliché, this is how Dottie humbly lived her life - not wasting her days cursing her diagnosis and treatment, but living her best life in spite of it.

She was, simply, the best.

I thank Dr. Hussain for this moving tribute of his wife, his soul mate, our friend.

AB

Medical University of Ohio/ University of Toledo

Via e-mail, December 18, 2006:

Dear Amjad,

I expect that you have received responses to today's column. It is a fabulous piece of writing and very moving; it reveals so much about you, Dottie, and the lives you shared while bridging two worlds. The sadness of her loss can be relieved when you consider that it is possible for you to write such a description of your four-decade life with her. You serve as a role model for many people, who can only imagine such happiness.

John (Robinson Block, publisher, Toledo Blade*)*

Via e-mail, December 22, 2006,

Dear Amjad:

This is a beautiful column. I was particularly struck by your comment about "the battle of the minds and principles that defined our friendship," and how two incompatible people's "religious and cultural differences gave way to mutual love, respect, and admiration."

You, Dottie, and your children seem to live a very full and satisfying life. I'm sure Dottie will be sorely missed, but what she left behind will sustain you. Do let me know if I can do anything – however small.

With warm regards,

EM

Via e-mail, March 29, 2007:

Dr. Hussain:

I have kept the Toledo Blade *of Dec. 18th in a pile of "for further consideration" and am just now writing. I read your column when it appears and felt so moved when I read, "Soul mate touched many with her grace." I don't know you and I didn't know Dottie but through that*

article felt such a sense of sadness for her death.   Thank you for sharing your sorrow so publicly . . . it may cause some of us to realize how precious every day is instead of taking each new morn for granted.
   Very sincerely,
   DS
   Perrysburg

People of hospice provide graceful passage
January 1, 2007

Death is the inevitable part of life, and still we feel lost and adrift when we are confronted with end-of-life issues. Our dazzling accomplishments in the field of medicine have assured us a long and healthy life, but have also added increasing numbers of people who suffer from chronic and debilitating illnesses in the twilight and, on occasion, the full prime of their lives. This incapacitating period between good health and eventual passage from this world may last days, weeks, and even months. It is in that uncharted course that the patient and the family feel helpless, hopeless, and vulnerable.

Before the advent of modern hospitals, people died at home and families took care of them. As the traditional caregivers - women of the family - started entering the work force, hospitals became the only choice for end-of-life care.

The line between curative care and palliative care is often indistinct. A moral and ethical dilemma confronts us when we contemplate letting go of a family member and allowing only comfort care. To escape this feeling of guilt some families end up requesting, and sometimes forcing, physicians to do everything possible regardless of the cost or benefit, even though they see life fading away in front of their eyes. Very few people leave clear instructions about their end-of-life care.

Six weeks ago my three grown children and I were faced with a similar dilemma during the terminal illness of my wife Dottie. Should she continue to be poked and probed and infused with medicines and potions that were becoming increasingly redundant? Amidst this hopelessness there was always a glimmer of hope, imagined by our irrational loving minds, that there must be something else that could be done to make a difference, even the slightest difference. How do we wade through a minefield of doubts and false hopes and accept the inevitable and salvage the dignity of a dying person? There is something to be said about dying in peace and dying in dignity.

The desire for a dignified exit from this world is not new. The concept has been with us through antiquity. Asoka, the great Indian ruler, is believed to be the first to build hospices in 225 B.C. for pilgrims who died while visiting the Ganges River. The Augustine monks built the Hospice of Saint Bernard in the Swiss Alps, still functioning, in 962 A.D. In the Middle East there were 40 such facilities built by Muslims in 1160 A.D. where spiritual and physical needs of the dying were provided for and their transition from this life made comfortable.

The Hospice of Northwest Ohio is a unique organization and a valuable community resource. In the past 25 years this organization has been providing end-of-life care to our town and surrounding areas. From a humble start in 1981, with a staff of three and five home-care patients, the organization now has a staff of 390 and cares for more than 300 patients every day. In 1995 an inpatient facility was constructed in Perrysburg on a 20-acre parcel donated by the Knight family. Since then another facility has been built in South Toledo at the corner of South Detroit and Arlington avenues. Both these facilities are affiliated with the College of Medicine of the University of Toledo for teaching medical students about death and dying.

The shiny buildings and manicured lawns, however, tell but part of the story. The real assets are the people who work for hospice and make it what it is: a network of dedicated, compassionate, competent, and extremely professional men and women who ease the suffering not only of the patient but also of the family in the most difficult time in their lives. Whether the patient is at home or in one of the facilities, the care is the same. And no one has ever been turned away because of inability to pay.

In our case, the hospice rose to the occasion and our two days together at home were filled with sadness, elation, and contentment. The familiarity and comfort of one's own bed and surroundings and the easing of unrelenting pain played a pivotal part in a dignified and graceful passage.

For that I owe a debt of gratitude to the angels of mercy from hospice.

In the Toledo Blade Readers' Forum, *January 11, 2007:*
"Column on hospice care enlightening"
I enjoyed S. Amjad Hussain's Jan. 1 column on hospice. I have worked for and with hospices across the country over the last ten years, and his column got at the heart of what makes hospice care special:

*being able to support an individual with a life-limiting illness and their
family during a very difficult time.*

*As they say in hospice care, "It's not about adding days to your life,
but life to your days."*

*Sharing his family's experience with hospice during his wife's
terminal illness was very enlightening, and I hope it allows others to
see the benefits of hospice care. Community-based hospices are the
backbone of palliative care in our country and local residents are lucky
to have one of the best in the country, Hospice of Northwest Ohio, right
in our backyard.*

PDL
Sylvania

Via e-mail, January 4, 2007:
Dear Dr. Hussain,
*Some time ago you spoke to an adult education class at Christ
Presbyterian Church where my husband serves as pastor. Your wife
Dottie accompanied you that day and I remember staying after class
and talking with her, along with Tim and Jodi Schmidt.*

*I am writing to thank you for the eloquent words you shared with
the Toledo-area community in your last* Blade *column. I currently
work part-time as one of the chaplains with Hospice of NW Ohio and I
consider my work here to be a blessing. I am grateful that your family
felt the care and support of our staff during the final days of your wife's
illness. The staff, patients, and families who are a part of hospice
continue to teach me what it means to "come alongside" and to
accompany those who are making their way from this life to what lies
beyond it. I am continually privileged to witness glimmers of a kind of
healing that transcends physical cure.*

*My thoughts and prayers will continue to be with you and your
family as you mourn Dottie's passing, and I give thanks for the gift of
her life.*

With Regard,
CN

Via e-mail, January 4, 2007:
Dr. Hussain, hello,

I wanted to thank you for the beautiful editorial in Monday's Toledo Blade *about Hospice. I am sorry for the loss of your wife, but was comforted to read of your wonderful experience with Hospice of Northwest Ohio. I had the honor to serve on their board and serve as their President of the Board of Trustees.*

I was continually amazed and impressed with the compassion and professionalism that Hospice employees provide for our community. We are truly blessed to have this wonderful facility in NW Ohio. And I can tell you that your experience was not unique. We received comments such as yours on a regular basis.

But to have them come from a physician/surgeon is an extra honor. Education of the public about their mission was a key strategy of Hospice, and this article truly helps in that endeavor.

Thank you for taking the time to do so, and again my sincere sympathy at your loss.

With kindest regards,

DJ

Hospice of Northwest Ohio

Putting together the pieces of a broken life
July 16, 2007

It was seven months ago that I entered a new phase in my life when Dottie, my wife and friend of 38 years, passed away. According to conventional wisdom, with each passing day the pain and the longing becomes less and that in due course – does any one really knows what that means? – the sadness and lament would slowly but surely recede in the background and will be replaced, bit by slow bit, with happy and cheerful memories of a life spent together and spent well. I am still waiting to turn that elusive corner.

Hidden from the discerning eyes of the world there has been a scary and unexplainable turmoil and helplessness that has raged below the apparent tranquility of my everyday life. Only family and close friends could see beyond the exterior façade. This led me to join a support group of eight men at the Hospice of Northwest Ohio. Like me, they were also trying to pick up the pieces and cobble together a new life from the shards of a shattered dream. We met weekly and through streams of tears ("tears from the depth of some divine despair," as Lord Tennyson so aptly said) and choked voices we shared our stories with each other. To our surprise we all had a common or similar narrative.

All of us, men from different walks of life and most in the autumn of our lives, were trying to negotiate our unsteady steps through the seemingly unending minefields of sorrow, doubt, lament, anger, betrayal, guilt and unfulfilled promises. We could not see the light at the end of the long and dark tunnel in which we were thrown by fate. Wrapped up in our own pain and misery we often forget that there are others who are also experiencing the same uncertainties. Intensity and severity of pain may vary but an open and bleeding wound is just as hard to take.

We all felt utterly lost without our spouses. The feeling of helplessness and hopelessness was overwhelming; the inability to write checks and balance the checkbook, to take care of the house, to entertain, to cook a meal, to iron a shirt or to run the vacuum. Or to deal with the callous and greedy monopoly-driven world of grave markers and cemetery rules.

We also talked about the ongoing onslaught of unsolicited mail and telemarketers. In my case, despite requests on the contrary, I still receive unsolicited mail in her name and unsolicited phone calls for her. They do not believe me when I tell them she has passed away. I don't think anyone would engineer the death of a spouse to get these pests off their backs. Of late, however, I have been telling them that she has moved away and then give them her new address at the cemetery.

We learned that some friends and acquaintances could be unpredictable and at times unkind and insulting while expressing their condolences. One extended an open invitation to come to his home for dinner and then went on to lecture on how to get on with my life. In his exuberant naivety he compared my loss to his contentious and ugly divorce. Yes, he has moved on since but still harbors a deep contempt of his ex. One man wrote to compare my loss to his when his wife left him for another man. Another invited me to Florida where there are thousands of extremely wealthy widows just waiting for a person like me. And to top it off one man said he knew exactly how I felt because he had lost his dog recently.

We all bear our own crosses and who is to tell which ones are easy and which ones are not? It is difficult to feel some one else's pain unless you have experienced it yourself. Nevertheless, I remain grateful and indebted to friends and strangers alike for what William Wordsworth called their "nameless, unencumbered acts of kindness and love."

All of us in the support group were adrift on the vast and stormy ocean of grief. Though our individual destinations are different we have, for a while, huddled together to see the storm through. Experts and those who have been through this tell me that such storms almost always pass and there is usually a comforting sunrise at the end of a dark and scary night. I look forward to that dawn.

Via e-mail, August 3, 2007:
Dear Amjad,
I wanted to write to tell you how much I appreciated your July 16th column on grief and grieving. I admire your courage in sharing such a personal process.
I wish you well.
Take care.
JFM

Thank you for your kind words. It has been difficult but then such milestones are anything but simple.

We, my children and I, remain indebted to you for your kindness and your help in the last few days of Dottie's life. It meant so much to us.

As always,

Amjad

Via e-mail, July 17, 2007:

A friend gave me the Monday Blade *with your article. My wife passed away in April; we were married for 34 years. The Hospice people were very helpful, but I resisted their "social work" during the last days. You made it sound like it could help.*

Thanks,

MG

Via e-mail, July 17, 2007:

Dear Dr. Hussain,

I am sorry that your journey through grief has been so hard but I am glad that you have found some help through our men's support group. Our society does not prepare us well for how to deal with all of the feelings during the bereavement period and certainly many individuals end up saying the wrong thing.

I always think that those who love the most grieve the hardest and imagine that you and your wife had a wonderful marriage. She must have been a great person.

I forwarded your column to Dr. Erel who is in Turkey. I know she will love reading it, even if it is about the hard work of grief.

Anyway, take care and let me know if there is anything else we can do for you or your family.

With deep sympathy,

JS

Hospice of Northwest Ohio

Via e-mail, July 17, 2007:

Dear Dr. Hussain,

I read your column in the Blade *this week. You are so brave to share this personal grief with your readers. I knew Dottie as a lovely lady devoted to her family but also as a superb nurse. My heart goes out to you during this most difficult time in your life. I have many memories of you at St. Charles and the patient care that you gave. I will never forget the Sunday morning that you reinserted a Quinton catheter on an African-American lady. We talked about faith and how all of us in the room worship differently but still believe in a Supreme Being or God. I never forgot that conversation and it enlightened my view not only of God but how important it is to respect others.*

The daughters of the patient were singing AMEN. You touched my heart that day.

Peace to you, my friend.

CH, St. Charles Emergency

Via e-mail, July 17, 2007:

Dear Dr. Hussain,

I want to thank you for your kind spiritual sharing in the article entitled "Putting Together The Pieces." I read your article on line in Alameda, CA. I was born and raised in Toledo, and taught at the University for seven years before leaving in 1967....

At the time of this writing my wife is bedridden trying to recover from five surgeries associated with abdominal cancer. Now I am also bedridden with a back injury. Our son, 47, died unexpectedly of a heart attack a year and a half ago.

It is not important to share the details of our suffering. What IS important is expressing my gratitude that you were able to put into words many of the seeds of sorrow that we have experienced both within our hearts and from less wise friends (as well as consolations from what seem to be the few blessed with the gift of compassion who understand the mystery of suffering).

Thank you for your words that captured so well the experience of grief so many feel but are unable to adequately express. Through your personal sharing you have made the burden more bearable for many of us.

I will hold your continued life journey in prayer.

Sincerely,

ALD

Via e-mail, July 18, 2007:

Dear Dr. Hussain:

When I worked at St. Charles Hospital, back in the 80s, I always marveled at your command of the English language. Your recent essay in The Blade, *"Putting together the pieces of a broken life," is a wonderful example of your literary skill. While your essay serves as a lesson in etiquette for some, and was, perhaps, a cathartic exercise for you, I see it as meaningful prose, complete with classic literary references and metaphors.*

Now that I am teaching again, I would like your permission to make copies of your article to share with my students. I have many examples of poor writing, but very few examples of a well-constructed essay such as yours. I would be copying your essay, just as it appeared in The Blade *to distribute to my students. Please let me know via the e-mail address below if you are okay with this.*

It was sad to read about your loss, but was good to learn that your support group is helping with this difficult transition. I hope your "dark and stormy night" becomes, at the very least, a calm and hopeful dawn for you soon.

Sincerely,
DJ
St. Charles Hospital Librarian

Thank you for your very kind note. I remember with fondness our interactions at St. Charles. You were always helpful and always with a ready smile.

I am flattered that you wish to share my essay with your students. Kindly feel free to do so.

Regards,
Amjad Hussain

Via e-mail, July 17, 2007:
Dear Doctor,
I read your column in the Monday, July 16 issue of The Blade. *I express my empathy in your writings. I can relate to everything you wrote about. I have been there and we all have our own ways of dealing with loss. No one is the same. No one has a scale to say this will happen and then you will feel this, etc.*

I have learned over the many years I have been alone that you never really get over it, you just learn to adjust to a different way of life and eventually learn to live with it.

Nothing anyone tells you is the answer until you yourself learn to sort it all out. I have learned and have forced myself to go places and do things alone because sometimes when I do go with a friend, it just reminds me how alone I am and that I am still going home alone.

Yes, support groups can help to an extent, because they make you realize you are not the only one in this situation, but beyond that, you must work it out by yourself. The big thing missing is the sounding board, that one person who meant the world to you, the support of that someone to tell you, you are not going crazy! Doctor, you will learn to live with it at your own pace! Hang in there, God Bless!

LS

Via e-mail, October 18, 2007:

Dr. Hussain,

I was just looking over some articles in the Blade *archives and saw your article on the loss of your spouse. It really hit home. I lost my husband Nov. 13, 2005 three days after his 50th birthday. He had a sudden heart attack at the end of the evening of his birthday party, which we now call his "going away party." I truly understand how callous some people can be. I actually had friend of mine who is going through a very ugly divorce tell how lucky I was to have my husband died because this way I got it all, and didn't have to fight over property. I also had someone else ask why I still wear my rings, and I have to remind them that I did not have a divorce or end my relationship by choice but that it was thrust upon me. My advice to you is to just smile say thanks for your advice and then quietly pray that they will one day see the foolishness of their comments.*

Hang in there. It doesn't get easier, but you become stronger and the more stupid comments or suggestions you hear the more you will learn to laugh them off. I was happily married for 28½ years and I hope that what I took from my marriage was strength – strength to go on and know that he is still by my side and laughing with me at those stupid comments.

God Bless and I will say a prayer for you and your wife.

OP

Peshawar's traditions a balm on the soul
January 15, 2007

Peshawar, Pakistan - I have lived away from Peshawar, the place of my birth, for more than 40 years and still in so many ways it feels as if I never left. It is not the awful traffic, pollution, clogged sewers, deafening street noises, or the shrill call for prayers broadcast over the ever-powerful and amply amplified speakers that give me the reassureance of continuity. It is the peaceful and tranquil slice of the old city that still connects me with my early life and which can still be found, but only at odd hours of the day. For that one has to venture into the maze of brick-lined narrow alleys of the old city. While the haphazard urban sprawl has swept away the ancient city wall and the 16 gates, for some of us diehards the city of yore remains even if for a few fleeting moments.

There is a tiny mosque located about 100 yards from our house where I can attend the first prayer of the day an hour before sunrise. A short flight of stairs leads to a tiny courtyard at the end of which there are two large carpeted rooms that serve as the prayer area. On a recent morning there were about 15 worshippers from the neighborhood who, wrapped in wool blankets to ward off bone-chilling cold, came for congregational prayers just as their fathers and their fathers' fathers had done before them.

I am always amazed and envious of their devotion to faith and family that surpasses mine in so many ways. An elderly worshipper was praying fervently for his family, his city, and the world beyond through a steady stream of tears flowing down his grey beard. He was repeating the ancient prayers that have, because of mere repetition, lost their real meaning for many of us.

People in other parts of the city also respond to the call for prayers and show a humility that is becoming a rare commodity in this violence-prone world. As opposed to the grenade-tossing, machine gun-toting fanatics who kill and maim in the name of this very religion, these simple people from every walk of life are the real believers. It is a privilege to be in their company.

On my way to the mosque there is the neighborhood baker's shop. Every day before dawn the owner fires up the large underground clay oven. The aroma of freshly baked bread wafts through the neighborhood. On the way back from the mosque I greet him and his early customers and ask him if he would bake me a thin flat bread called lavash. As a special favor he bakes one for me. By the time I reach our home, half of the bread is gone. No one has heard of Dr. Atkins and his diet in these parts. A breakfast of freshly baked bread and sweetened cream called malai is enough to gladden any heart in this town, including that of a hopelessly romantic native son from America.

Another thing that has not changed is the way people come to offer condolences. Unlike in the West and for that matter the rest of this country, long-time city residents come whenever they can to visit. Our family went through that process when the news of my wife's death reached here. Upon my arrival a few weeks later the process started again. Some of them bring an offering of food as a token of their affection. A poor woman, a distant acquaintance, brought a handful of spinach leaves that she most likely gathered in the fields in the outskirts of the city. It is the equivalent of neighbors bringing a cake or food for the bereaved family. They raise their hands, bow their heads, and utter the familiar verse from the Qur'an, "To God we belong and to Him shall we return."

It is comforting and reassuring to find a few old traditions that are still in vogue here even though the city I knew and loved has ceased to exist, except of course only in the minds and hearts of some of us.

On a personal note, I am most grateful to my readers who wrote in such numbers after the publication of my column about my wife Dottie. Thank you for your kindness.

Journey difficult after loved one's death
December 3, 2007

Death anniversaries, especially the first one, are always difficult. If it were not for the resilience of human spirit and the support of family and friends the dark clouds of despair would push many of us mortals into the throes of deep depression. It is through these tenable bonds that we face calamities and overcome obstacles.

This is the third column I am writing on the loss of my wife who passed away a year ago yesterday. At this time of introspection most of the world happenings, exciting and intriguing as they may be, appear remote and distant. I beg your indulgence as I look back at the roller coaster ride my family and I have endured this past year.

It has been a difficult and at times painful journey of adjustment and understanding. It was made easy and bearable because many of you wrote and shared your stories. Your individual circumstances were different but your narratives of loss and lament and hope were strikingly similar. You helped me see more clearly through the frightening fog of uncertainty and disbelief.

All of you mentioned the void, a big hole as some of you put it that has become part of your being. Not as an outside garment that covers the exterior but as what Lord Tennyson called "the captive void of noble rage." Passage of time does take away some of the sharp edges but the void remains.

Nine months ago when I joined a support group at the Hospice of Northwest Ohio the counselors cautioned us to brace ourselves for an uneven ride on the terrain of our remaining life. They told us that while in time surface wounds do heal, lurking under the surface, barely a tiny scratch away, are memories both painful and pleasant. The sudden appearance of a trigger – a flash of a favorite color, whiff of a familiar perfume, aroma of freshly baked bread or a melody inextricably linked with a long-past romance – opens the floodgates of uncertain emotions. A million reminders, big and small, force one to return to the sad realization that what once was and now is not.

In some ways it has also been an interesting journey. In the deepest of the blue moods – where one is engulfed with uncertainties – there appears, from nowhere it seems, a ray of hope for a better tomorrow. In those moments in the mind's eye one sees and feels the presence up close but still separated by a mysterious and unknowable abyss.

I can, a year since, look back and realize that death and dying is an awkward situation for most people. We try to camouflage the stark reality with euphemisms and clichés. "She is in a better place," goes one worn-out statement. I am expected to nod my agreement. Instead, to the bewilderment of the consoling person, I say there was nothing wrong with the place she was. I am sure, given the choice, she would not have opted to go to that better place.

"It must be God's will," goes another oft-repeated feel-good cliché. Being a person of faith, I cannot question that without treading on thin theological ice. In the past year, however, there have been moments, however transitory, when faith and reason have clashed. Some consider faith as a convenient crutch, but for others it is indispensable. Lord Tennyson in his timeless elegy *In Memoriam* said it eloquently: "By faith and faith alone, embrace/Believing where we cannot prove."

The passage of time and a persistent longing for a departed spouse makes most of us see the person through the prism of emotions and perceive her to be perfect and the union with her more so. Realities of life, however, tell us otherwise but we celebrate, just as generations before us, ordinary lives in extraordinary ways. So I mourn and celebrate the life of a woman who considered herself very ordinary but to me, my family and friends who was, in the words of William Wordsworth, "A perfect woman, nobly planned" and "Fair as a star when only one/Is shining in the sky."

When I wrote about Dottie a year ago, I concluded the column by thanking my readers for listening. Now, a year later, I close by thanking you for sharing your stories and helping me understand mine.

I am grateful.

Via e-mail, December 3, 2007:
Dear Dr. Hussain,
I have enjoyed your various writings for the Blade *throughout these last several years, and my heart went out to you when you shared the news of your wife's death. After reading your tribute to her and the process of grieving her loss, I felt compelled to write to you.*

You brought a tear to my eye as you shared the roller coaster ride of emotions and experiences over the last year. I remember, and still experience those moments myself. My husband and I lost our oldest daughter, Claire, seven years ago. On the heels of this great tragedy my older sister, Karen, died nearly four years ago. We miss them both dearly, and like you, remember them well, and celebrate their lives and memory often. We've created an event in Claire's memory, Claire's Day, which is held at the Maumee library every third Saturday in May. It's proven to be a very healthy and good way to focus our grief energy on. For more information on this special family book festival, visit clairesday.org.

More so than the wonderful joy that we bring to families in the community in Claire's memory and honor, I'm most proud of how we've continued to celebrate life with our two other children, and each other. As we attended bereavement support groups in the earliest, darkest days after her death, we saw too many families that not only lost a child, but lost their relationships with each other as well. I would not stand for that, and neither would Claire.

I really appreciated your comment about the clichéd statement, "She's in a better place," as I replied pretty much the same as you; Claire was in a pretty good place here with us as it was. The other comment made at the funeral home (I filed this one in the dumb and stupid things people say, when they truly only mean well) was that "God must have wanted her more!" He must have wanted her pretty bad, too, as she was loved very much here on this earth.

Thank you for sharing your grief and your pain. My loss is different than yours, and some might say greater, although losing Brad would be devastating, and selfishly I secretly pray that we both die together to spare each other the loss of the other.

You reflected on this very difficult year, and so very accurately described the pain, and yes, even the joy that comes with the territory.

Thanks for sharing.

Sincerely,

JKR

Via e-mail, December 6, 2007:

Wow. God bless you and thank you for having the courage to share your journey. I lost my brother to suicide six months ago and I can

*definitely call it a journey. You are right that it is so difficult to talk
about death in our society and much harder when it is suicide. Then
mix it with militant Islamic fanatics who questioned us burying our
brother in an Islamic tradition.*

*Thank you, again, for sharing and may all of the prayers give you a
greater understanding of life and its complexities and to feel great joy
in the moment of such great grief.*

Sincerely,

MS

Thank you for sharing your story. It is most unfortunate that we still
have to face ignorant religious bigots in the most trying times of our
lives. They are the people who have never heard of the healing process
after the death of a dear one and are totally oblivious to the physical
and mental illnesses that induce us to take our own life. Compassion for
them is an abstract concept.

Please do know that there are people in our tradition who are sick
and tired of these so-called custodians of out faith.

Warmest regards,

Amjad Hussain

Via e-mail, December 7, 2007:

Dr. Hussain:

I had the opportunity to read your article in the Blade *on Monday
morning. With 3 little children, I don't have much time these days...but
I was so grateful that I had a moment to stop and read your article. I
have to admit, I'm very behind the times . . .I wasn't aware of your
wife's passing last year. I just wanted to let you know that I was very
sorry to hear that, and you will continue to be in my thoughts and
prayers. I did have the opportunity to meet Dottie, while we were
working together, and for the brief times we met, I remember what a
warm, kind person she was.*

*She always made me feel so comfortable when I stopped by the
house once or twice to drop off some things. I'm glad that I had the
opportunity to meet her.*

*This time of year is always difficult, especially when you lose some-
one close to you. After 17 years, I still miss my dad. Sometimes I think
I miss him more, now that I have children. I so wish that he could be*

here to see them. However, I do find comfort in knowing that he has a great view from where he is...and I also know his spirit lives in my children. It amazes me when they will say or do something that reminds me of him.

I just wanted to let you know that I'll be thinking of you this holiday season and through the New Year.

And I hope we have the opportunity to cross paths again.

My best wishes to you,

JK

Via e-mail, December 5, 2007:

Assalamualaykum

Dear Dr. Amjad,

Thanks for sharing you feelings with us.

My mother just passed away on Nov 29. I am obviously in the early stages of my grief. She was a very graceful and the most pleasant person that I had ever met, like almost all women of that generation. She was a companion to my father for almost 61 years. My father is very distressed. I had never seen him grieve like this except when his younger brother was killed.

What I'd like to ask you is what as a child can I do to help him through this time, especially since I live in the U.S. and he is in Pakistan?

Thanks,

RH

Thank you for your kind note.

In our culture we do not verbalize our feelings to our loved ones. Somehow it is understood but never enunciated. I would suggest you make it a point to call your father often enough and tell him you think about him all the time and that you wished you were with him in this difficult time. And if you can, go and spend some time with him in Pakistan. These are the things that will soothe his pain and give him hope.

Regards,

Amjad Hussain

Via e-mail, December 6, 2007:

Amjad,

I just finished reading your thoughts on the day of Dottie's death anniversary. Your faith is much stronger than mine since mine did not survive after August 1, 1985 when I buried my 23-year-old daughter Aniqa in Lahore; she had died on July 29, 1985 in Pakistan....

I no longer believe in divine justice nor restitution. In my new faith, we the human beings created the Heavens and God in our mind to hide behind the intoxicating thoughts that this was his will and this separation is temporary to meet in a better place. We never think twice about crushing to death the ants under our feet without realizing what we have done, although these creatures for their size are as much intelligent, sentimental and family oriented as we are yet we don't think of God raising them and restoring them in the heaven as we pretend he (Why not She?) will restore us.

Although in due course the pain gets dulled or attenuated by the analgesia and amnesia provided by time and other business of the world around us, this relief is a very thin veneer that gets rubbed off every morning when I wake up or when I suddenly wake up in the middle of the night....

What I am trying to say is that this pain is eternal. One may not utter a word but inside the hurt of the loss is forever. My Father was married to a lady for over 10 years when she died of tuberculosis in 1930. He married my mother in 1934. Many years later I overheard a conversation between my Father and mother. Mother - who will you ask for if in the next world God wanted you to choose an eternal partner? My father's immediate response was I will ask for TWO.

He must have loved his first wife very much and must never have gotten over the grief of his loss to spontaneously come up with that answer.

I am sharing these few thoughts that are buried deep in my soul since the shared grief may lessen the eternal pain, albeit momentarily.

AT

Via e-mail, December 7, 2007:

Asalam Alaikum Uncle,

I just wanted to post a comment on how deeply touched and how greatly inspired I was after reading your beautiful column. I still can't believe a year has gone by. I do agree that it is a tremendous help with all the support our close friends and close community members give to us. I know that whenever I go to visit my papa, I always say a prayer for Aunty Dottie too. She truly was one of my favorites in the community. I looked forward to seeing her in our community gatherings. She is and always will be greatly missed. May Allah continue to bestow his blessings upon you and your family (Ameen). Take care, Uncle.

Shanza Khan

Search of ancient city unearths 'magic lamp'
November 26, 2000

Peshawar, Pakistan – There are many important issues that could be the topic for this column. The ongoing conflict in neighboring Afghanistan forcing thousands of Afghans to take refuge across the border in Pakistan. And of course, the great "cliffhanger," the American presidential election, that has now turned into a cliff dweller.

I wish to write about a quest that led me all over this ancient city in search of some special mementos. It was like looking for a needle in a proverbial haystack. I was looking for small fragments of a demolished house in warehouses that recycle materials salvaged from torn down houses. I was born 62 years ago in a ramshackle old house in this walled city that had been our homestead since 1870. In this 10-room brick and white-plaster ordinary house with wood-beams roofs, cement floors and dirt-covered roof terraces, a large family of nine brothers and sisters, three aunts and a few orphaned cousins lived. It was here that new additions to the family were born and raised and it was from this house that we bade farewell to the aged and some times not too aged members of the family in death. Together we celebrated weddings, family reunions and religious holidays.

When I left home for America in 1963, I took nothing but a few snap shots and a rich album of memories. Those memories sustained me in the initial difficult times that are part of an immigrant experience. And whenever I returned, just as my elders, I came back to the house to reaffirm myself.

Dwellings, like people, also succumb to the ravages of time. It was an abandoned dying place when I last visited it a few years ago. Like an aged parent, it was at the end of its life; a setting sun radiating its pale reluctant rays for the last time. Recently it was sold to new owners who had planned to build a shopping arcade in its place. Before leaving for Pakistan I asked if they would wait a week before tearing it down. I wanted to visit the place just one more time to say good bye, whisper a prayer and shed a tear in memory of a life long past. But commerce triumphed over sentimentality and my request for the stay of execution was ignored.

A five-member crew armed with crowbars, hammers and axes brought the noble structure down and hauled away every thing that they could. Left behind was the empty void of a tiny piece of naked land that had been stripped of its modesty.

Hence my visit to the dark and damp world of warehouses where they recycle salvaged material from old houses. Scattered in these gigantic flea markets are forgotten memories of unknown people; faded doors, old almirahs and vintage windows that had been witness to countless loves, many quarrels and a few intrigues that are part of any household. Ours was no exception.

I finally found them: familiar doors and windows leaning against the wall, totally out of place. I asked the shopkeeper if I could take an old rusted latch-chain from one of the doors. Not comprehending my sentimental attachment, the kind man offered to give me a brand new one for free.

In the story of Aladdin and the Magic Lamp, a crafty lamp-seller goes around the streets offering to exchange old lamps with new ones hoping to get his hands on the old magic lamp. Why would I want a new lamp? At my insistence, he pried loose the latch from the door and gave it to me. Now I have my old magic lamp or at least a tiny bit of it.

Via e-mail, November 28, 2000:

Dear Amjad,

JoAnne read your "magic lamp" column first and pointed it out to me. We both enjoyed it immensely. It is a fine piece of writing, obviously from the heart. We could feel your intake of breath when you found the pieces of your old house; what a moment that must have been for you.

Thanks for providing a fine few minutes of reading.

Peace and regards,

MT

Via e-mail, November 26, 2000:

I'm a Sunday Blade *reader. Thanks for your recent "magic lamp" column, and for your many other past columns. Each has offered to me and other readers a unique, welcome perspective on various topics - which often then attain/recall relevance to our own lives!*

Thanks again.
WB,
Findlay OH.

INDEX

Our list of current titles

OUR CURRENT LIST OF TITLES

Abdullah, Morag Mary, *My Khyber Marriage* - Morag Murray departed on a lifetime of adventure when she met and fell in love with Sirdar Ikbal Ali Shah, the son of an Afghan warlord. Leaving the comforts of her middle-class home in Scotland, Morag followed her husband into a Central Asia still largely unchanged since the 19th century.

Abernathy, Miles, *Ride the Wind* – the amazing true story of the little Abernathy Boys, who made a series of astonishing journeys in the United States, starting in 1909 when they were aged five and nine!

Atkinson, John, *Afghan Expedition* – The author travelled to Afghanistan in 1838. He had been designated the Superintending Surgeon of a massive British invasion force resolved to place a sympathetic ruler on the Afghan throne. Soon after Atkinson was released from duty, and thus escaped the catastrophe which awaited his comrades. The British political agent was beheaded and an estimated 16,000 British soldiers and their dependents were slaughtered in a week by the vengeful Afghans. This book is a must for anybody interested in Afghanistan – then and now.

Beard, John, *Saddles East* – John Beard determined as a child that he wanted to see the Wild West from the back of a horse after a visit to Cody's legendary Wild West show. Yet it was only in 1948 – more than sixty years after seeing the flamboyant American showman – that Beard and his wife Lulu finally set off to follow their dreams.

Beker, Ana, *The Courage to Ride* – Determined to out-do Tschiffely, Beker made a 17,000 mile mounted odyssey across the Americas in the late 1940s that would fix her place in the annals of equestrian travel history.

Bird, Isabella, *Among the Tibetans* – A rousing 1889 adventure, an enchanting travelogue, a forgotten peek at a mountain kingdom swept away by the waves of time.

Bird, Isabella, *On Horseback* in *Hawaii* – The Victorian explorer's first horseback journey, in which she learns to ride astride, in early 1873.

Bird, Isabella, *Journeys in Persia and Kurdistan, Volumes 1 and 2* – The intrepid Englishwoman undertakes another gruelling journey in 1890.

Bird, Isabella, *A Lady's Life in the Rocky Mountains* – The story of Isabella Bird's adventures during the winter of 1873 when she explored the magnificent unspoiled wilderness of Colorado. Truly a classic.

Bird, Isabella, *Unbeaten Tracks in Japan, Volumes One and Two* – A 600-mile solo ride through Japan undertaken by the intrepid British traveller in 1878.

Blackmore, Charles, *In the Footsteps of Lawrence of Arabia* - In February 1985 Captain Charles Blackmore and three others of the Royal Green Jackets Regiment set out to retrace Lawrence's exploits in the Arab Revolt during the First World War. They spent twenty-nine days with meagre supplies and under extreme conditions, riding and walking to the source of the Lawrence legend.

Boniface, Lieutenant Jonathan, *The Cavalry Horse and his Pack* – Quite simply the most important book ever written in the English language by a military man on the subject of equestrian travel.

Bosanquet, Mary, *Saddlebags for Suitcases* – In 1939 Bosanquet set out to ride from Vancouver, Canada, to New York. Along the way she was wooed by love-struck cowboys, chased by a grizzly bear and even suspected of being a Nazi spy, scouting out Canada in preparation for a German invasion. A truly delightful book.

de Bourboulon, Catherine, *Shanghai à Moscou (French)* – the story of how a young Scottish woman and her aristocratic French husband travelled overland from Shanghai to Moscow in the late 19th Century.

Brown, Donald; Journey from the Arctic – *A truly remarkable account of how Brown, his Danish companion and their two trusty horses attempt the impossible, to cross the silent Arctic plateaus, thread their way through the giant Swedish forests, and finally discover a passage around the treacherous Norwegian marshes.*

Our list of current titles

Bruce, Clarence Dalrymple, *In the Hoofprints of Marco Polo* – The author made a dangerous journey from Srinagar to Peking in 1905, mounted on a trusty 13-hand Kashmiri pony, then wrote this wonderful book.

Burnaby, Frederick; *A Ride to Khiva* – Burnaby fills every page with a memorable cast of characters, including hard-riding Cossacks, nomadic Tartars, vodka-guzzling sleigh-drivers and a legion of peasant ruffians.

Burnaby, Frederick, *On Horseback through Asia Minor* – Armed with a rifle, a small stock of medicines, and a single faithful servant, the equestrian traveler rode through a hotbed of intrigue and high adventure in wild inhospitable country, encountering Kurds, Circassians, Armenians, and Persian pashas.

Carter, General William, *Horses, Saddles and Bridles* – This book covers a wide range of topics including basic training of the horse and care of its equipment. It also provides a fascinating look back into equestrian travel history.

Cayley, George, *Bridle Roads of Spain* – Truly one of the greatest equestrian travel accounts of the 19th Century.

Chase, J. Smeaton, *California Coast Trails* – This classic book describes the author's journey from Mexico to Oregon along the coast of California in the 1890s.

Chase, J. Smeaton, *California Desert Trails* – Famous British naturalist J. Smeaton Chase mounted up and rode into the Mojave Desert to undertake the longest equestrian study of its kind in modern history.

Chitty, Susan, and Hinde, Thomas, *The Great Donkey Walk* - When biographer Susan Chitty and her novelist husband, Thomas Hinde, decided it was time to embark on a family adventure, they did it in style. In Santiago they bought two donkeys whom they named Hannibal and Hamilcar. Their two small daughters, Miranda (7) and Jessica (3) were to ride Hamilcar. Hannibal, meanwhile, carried the baggage. The walk they planned to undertake was nothing short of the breadth of southern Europe.

Christian, Glynn, *Fragile Paradise: The discovery of Fletcher Christian, "Bounty" Mutineer* – the great-great-great-great-grandson of the *Bounty* mutineer brings to life a fascinating and complex character history has portrayed as both hero and villain, and the real story behind a mutiny that continues to divide opinion more than 200 years later.

Clark, Leonard, *Marching Wind, The* – The panoramic story of a mounted exploration in the remote and savage heart of Asia, a place where adventure, danger, and intrigue were the daily backdrop to wild tribesman and equestrian exploits.

Clark, Leonard, *A Wanderer Till I Die* – In a world with lax passport control, no airlines, and few rules, this young man floats effortlessly from one adventure to the next. When he's not drinking whisky at the Raffles Hotel or listening to the "St. Louis Blues" on the phonograph in the jungle, he's searching for Malaysian treasure, being captured by Toradja head-hunters, interrogated by Japanese intelligence officers and lured into shady deals by European gun-runners.

Cobbett, William, *Rural Rides, Volumes 1 and 2* – In the early 1820s Cobbett set out on horseback to make a series of personal tours through the English countryside. These books contain what many believe to be the best accounts of rural England ever written, and remain enduring classics.

Codman, John, *Winter Sketches from the Saddle* – This classic book was first published in 1888. It recommends riding for your health and describes the septuagenarian author's many equestrian journeys through New England during the winter of 1887 on his faithful mare, Fanny.

Cunninghame Graham, Jean, *Gaucho Laird* – A superbly readable biography of the author's famous great-uncle, Robert "Don Roberto" Cunninghame Graham.

Cunninghame Graham, Robert, *Horses of the Conquest* – The author uncovered manuscripts which had lain forgotten for centuries, and wrote this book, as he said, out of gratitude to the horses of Columbus and the Conquistadors who shaped history.

Cunninghame Graham, Robert, *Magreb-el-Acksa* – The thrilling tale of how "Don Roberto" was kidnapped in Morocco!

Cunninghame Graham, Robert, *Rodeo* – An omnibus of the finest work of the man they called "the uncrowned King of Scotland," edited by his friend Aimé Tschiffely.

Our list of current titles

Cunninghame Graham, Robert, *Tales of Horsemen* – Ten of the most beautifully-written equestrian stories ever set to paper.

Cunninghame Graham, Robert, *Vanished Arcadia* – This haunting story about the Jesuit missions in South America from 1550 to 1767 was the inspiration behind the best-selling film *The Mission*.

Daly, H.W., *Manual of Pack Transportation* – This book is the author's masterpiece. It contains a wealth of information on various pack saddles, ropes and equipment, how to secure every type of load imaginable and instructions on how to organize a pack train.

Dixie, Lady Florence, *Riding Across Patagonia* – When asked in 1879 why she wanted to travel to such an outlandish place as Patagonia, the author replied without hesitation that she was taking to the saddle in order to flee from the strict confines of polite Victorian society. This is the story of how the aristocrat successfully traded the perils of a London parlour for the wind-borne freedom of a wild Patagonian bronco.

Dodwell, Christina, *Beyond Siberia* – The intrepid author goes to Russia's Far East to join the reindeer-herding people in winter.

Dodwell, Christina, *An Explorer's Handbook* – The author tells you everything you want to know about travelling: how to find suitable pack animals, how to feed and shelter yourself. She also has sensible and entertaining advice about dealing with unwanted visitors and the inevitable bureaucrats.

Dodwell, Christina, *Madagascar Travels* – Christina explores the hidden corners of this amazing island and, as usual, makes friends with its people.

Dodwell, Christina, *A Traveller in China* – The author sets off alone across China, starting with a horse and then transferring to an inflatable canoe.

Dodwell, Christina, *A Traveller on Horseback* – Christina Dodwell rides through Eastern Turkey and Iran in the late 1980s. The Sunday Telegraph wrote of the author's "courage and insatiable wanderlust," and in this book she demonstrates her gift for communicating her zest for adventure.

Dodwell, Christina, *Travels in Papua New Guinea* – Christina Dodwell spends two years exploring an island little known to the outside world. She travelled by foot, horse and dugout canoe among the Stone-Age tribes.

Dodwell, Christina, *Travels with Fortune* – the truly amazing account of the courageous author's first journey – a three-year odyssey around Africa by Landrover, bus, lorry, horse, camel, and dugout canoe!

Dodwell, Christina, *Travels with Pegasus* – This time Christina takes to the air! This is the story of her unconventional journey across North Africa in a micro-light!

Duncan, John, *Travels in Western Africa in 1845 and 1846* – The author, a Lifeguardsman from Scotland, tells the hair-raising tale of his two journeys to what is now Benin. Sadly, Duncan has been forgotten until today, and we are proud to get this book back into print.

Ehlers, Otto, *Im Sattel durch die Fürstenhöfe Indiens* – In June 1890 the young German adventurer, Ehlers, lay very ill. His doctor gave him a choice: either go home to Germany or travel to Kashmir. So of course the Long Rider chose the latter. This is a thrilling yet humorous book about the author's adventures.

Farson, Negley, *Caucasian Journey* – A thrilling account of a dangerous equestrian journey made in 1929, this is an amply illustrated adventure classic.

Fox, Ernest, *Travels in Afghanistan* – The thrilling tale of a 1937 journey through the mountains, valleys, and deserts of this forbidden realm, including visits to such fabled places as the medieval city of Heart, the towering Hindu Kush mountains, and the legendary Khyber Pass.

Gall, Sandy, *Afghanistan – Agony of a Nation* - Sandy Gall has made three trips to Afghanistan to report the war there: in 1982, 1984 and again in 1986. This book is an account of his last journey and what he found. He chose to revisit the man he believes is the outstanding commander in Afghanistan: Ahmed Shah Masud, a dashing Tajik who is trying to organise resistance to the Russians on a regional, and eventually national scale.

Gall, Sandy, *Behind Russian Lines* – In the summer of 1982, Sandy Gall set off for Afghanistan on what turned out to be the hardest assignment of his life. During his career as a reporter he had covered plenty of wars and revolutions before, but this was the first time he had been required to walk all the way to an assignment and all the way back again, dodging Russian bombs *en route*.

Gallard, Babette, *Riding the Milky Way* – An essential guide to anyone planning to ride the ancient pilgrimage route to Santiago di Compostella, and a highly readable story for armchair travellers.

Galton, Francis, *The Art of Travel* – Originally published in 1855, this book became an instant classic and was used by a host of now-famous explorers, including Sir Richard Francis Burton of Mecca fame. Readers can learn how to ride horses, handle elephants, avoid cobras, pull teeth, find water in a desert, and construct a sleeping bag out of fur.

Glazier, Willard, *Ocean to Ocean on Horseback* – This book about the author's journey from New York to the Pacific in 1875 contains every kind of mounted adventure imaginable. Amply illustrated with pen and ink drawings of the time, this remains a timeless equestrian adventure classic.

Goodwin, Joseph, *Through Mexico on Horseback* – The author and his companion, Robert Horiguichi, the sophisticated, multi-lingual son of an imperial Japanese diplomat, set out in 1931 to cross Mexico. They were totally unprepared for the deserts, quicksand and brigands they were to encounter during their adventure.

Grant, David, *Spirit of the Vikings: A Journey in the Kayak Bahá'í Viking From Arkosund, Sweden, to Odessa, Ukraine* – David Grant takes his kayak on an adventure-filled and spiritual journey from Sweden to Odessa on the Black Sea.

Grant, David, *The Wagon Travel Handbook* - David Grant is the legendary Scottish wagon-master who journeyed around the world with his family in a horse-drawn wagon. Grant has filled *The Wagon Travel Handbook* with all the practical information a first time-wagon traveller will need before setting out.

Gray, David and Lukas Novotny, *Mounted Archery in the Americas* – This fascinating and amply illustrated book charts the history of mounted archery from its ancient roots on the steppes of Eurasia thousands of years ago to its current resurgence in popularity in the Americas. It also provides the reader with up-to-the-minute practical information gleaned from a unique team of the world's leading experts.

Hanbury-Tenison, Marika, *For Better, For Worse* – The author, an excellent story-teller, writes about her adventures visiting and living among the Indians of Central Brazil.

Hanbury-Tenison, Marika, *A Slice of Spice* – The fresh and vivid account of the author's hazardous journey to the Indonesian Islands with her husband, Robin.

Hanbury-Tenison, Robin, *Chinese Adventure* – The story of a unique journey in which the explorer Robin Hanbury-Tenison and his wife Louella rode on horseback alongside the Great Wall of China in 1986.

Hanbury-Tenison, Robin, *Fragile Eden* – The wonderful story of Robin and Louella Hanbury-Tenison's exploration of New Zealand on horseback in 1988. They rode alone together through what they describe as 'some of the most dramatic and exciting country we have ever seen.'

Hanbury-Tenison, Robin, *Mulu: The Rainforest* – This was the first popular book to bring to the world's attention the significance of the rain forests to our fragile ecosystem. It is a timely reminder of our need to preserve them for the future.

Hanbury-Tenison, Robin, *A Pattern of Peoples* – The author and his wife, Marika, spent three months travelling through Indonesia's outer islands and writes with his usual flair and sensitivity about the tribes he found there.

Hanbury-Tenison, Robin, *A Question of Survival* – This superb book played a hugely significant role in bringing the plight of Brazil's Indians to the world's attention.

Hanbury-Tenison, Robin, *The Rough and the Smooth* – The incredible story of two journeys in South America. Neither had been attempted before, and both were considered impossible!

Hanbury-Tenison, Robin, *Spanish Pilgrimage* – Robin and Louella Hanbury-Tenison went to Santiago de Compostela in a traditional way – riding on white horses over long-forgotten tracks. In the process they discovered more about the people and the country than any conventional traveller would learn. Their adventures are vividly and entertainingly recounted in this delightful and highly readable book.

Our list of current titles

Hanbury-Tenison, Robin, *White Horses over France* – This enchanting book tells the story of a magical journey and how, in fulfilment of a personal dream, the first Camargue horses set foot on British soil in the late summer of 1984.

Hanbury-Tenison, Robin, *Worlds Apart – an Explorer's Life* – The author's battle to preserve the quality of life under threat from developers and machines infuses this autobiography with a passion and conviction which makes it impossible to put down.

Hanbury-Tenison, Robin, *Worlds Within – Reflections in the Sand* – This book is full of the adventure you would expect from a man of action like Robin Hanbury-Tenison. However, it is also filled with the type of rare knowledge that was revealed to other desert travellers like Lawrence, Doughty and Thesiger.

Haslund, Henning, *Mongolian Adventure* – An epic tale inhabited by a cast of characters no longer present in this lackluster world, shamans who set themselves on fire, rebel leaders who sacked towns, and wild horsemen whose ancestors conquered the world.

Hassanein, A. M., *The Lost Oases* - At the dawning of the 20th century the vast desert of Libya remained one of last unexplored places on Earth. Sir Hassanein Bey befriended the Muslim leaders of the elusive Senussi Brotherhood who controlled the deserts further on, and became aware of rumours of a "lost oasis" which lay even deeper in the desert. In 1923 the explorer led a small caravan on a remarkable seven month journey across the centre of Libya.

Heath, Frank, *Forty Million Hoofbeats* – Heath set out in 1925 to follow his dream of riding to all 48 of the Continental United States. The journey lasted more than two years, during which time Heath and his mare, Gypsy Queen, became inseparable companions.

Hinde, Thomas, *The Great Donkey Walk* – Biographer Susan Chitty and her novelist husband, Thomas Hinde, travelled from Spain's Santiago to Salonica in faraway Greece. Their two small daughters, Miranda (7) and Jessica (3) were rode one donkey, while the other donkey carried the baggage. Reading this delightful book is leisurely and continuing pleasure.

Holt, William, *Ride a White Horse* – After rescuing a cart horse, Trigger, from slaughter and nursing him back to health, the 67-year-old Holt and his horse set out in 1964 on an incredible 9,000 mile, non-stop journey through western Europe.

Hope, Thomas, *Anastasius* – Here is the book that took the world by storm, and then was forgotten. Hope's hero Anastasius was fearless, curious, cunning, ruthless, brave, and above all, sexy. He journeyed deep into the vast and dangerous Ottoman Empire. During the 35 years described in the book (1762-1798) the swashbuckling hero infiltrated the deadly Wahhabis in Arabia, rode to war with the Mamelukes in Egypt and sailed the Mediterranean with the Turks. This remarkable new edition features all three volumes together for the first time.

Hopkins, Frank T., *Hidalgo and Other Stories* – For the first time in history, here are the collected writings of Frank T. Hopkins, the counterfeit cowboy whose endurance racing claims and Old West fantasies have polarized the equestrian world.

Jacobs, Ross, *Old Men and Horses – A Gift of Horsemanship* - Ross Jacobs is an extraordinary and experienced Australian horseman, trainer and writer. In *Old Men and Horses* he has created three fictional characters whose role in the history of equestrian training will never be forgotten.

James, Jeremy, *Saddletramp* – The classic story of Jeremy James' journey from Turkey to Wales, on an unplanned route with an inaccurate compass, unreadable map and the unfailing aid of villagers who seemed to have as little sense of direction as he had.

James, Jeremy, *Vagabond* – The wonderful tale of the author's journey from Bulgaria to Berlin offers a refreshing, witty and often surprising view of Eastern Europe and the collapse of communism.

Jebb, Louisa, *By Desert Ways to Baghdad and Damascus* – From the pen of a gifted writer and intrepid traveller, this is one of the greatest equestrian travel books of all time.

Kluckhohn, Clyde, *To the Foot of the Rainbow* – This is not just a exciting true tale of equestrian adventure. It is a moving account of a young man's search for physical perfection in a desert world still untouched by the recently-born twentieth century.

Lambie, Thomas, *Boots and Saddles in Africa* – Lambie's story of his equestrian journeys is told with the grit and realism that marks a true classic.

Our list of current titles

Landor, Henry Savage, *In the Forbidden Land* – Illustrated with hundreds of photographs and drawings, this blood-chilling account of equestrian adventure makes for page-turning excitement.

Langlet, Valdemar, *Till Häst Genom Ryssland (Swedish)* – Denna reseskildring rymmer många ögonblicksbilder av möten med människor, från morgonbad med Lev Tolstoi till samtal med Tartarer och fotografering av fagra skördeflickor. Rikt illustrerad med foto och teckningar.

Leigh, Margaret, *My Kingdom for a Horse* – In the autumn of 1939 the author rode from Cornwall to Scotland, resulting in one of the most delightful equestrian journeys of the early twentieth century. This book is full of keen observations of a rural England that no longer exists.

Lester, Mary, *A Lady's Ride across Spanish Honduras in 1881* – This is a gem of a book, with a very entertaining account of Mary's vivid, day-to-day life in the saddle.

MacDermot, Brian, *Cult of the Sacred Spear* – here is that rarest of travel books, an exploration not only of a distant land but of a man's own heart. A confederation of pastoral people located in Southern Sudan and western Ethiopia, the Nuer warriors were famous for staging cattle raids against larger tribes and successfully resisted European colonization. Brian MacDermot, London stockbroker, entered into Nuer society as a stranger and emerged as Rial Nyang, an adopted member of the tribe. This book recounts this extraordinary emotional journey

Maillart, Ella, *Turkestan Solo* – A vivid account of a 1930s journey through this wonderful, mysterious and dangerous portion of the world, complete with its Kirghiz eagle hunters, lurking Soviet secret police, and the timeless nomads that still inhabited the desolate steppes of Central Asia.

Marcy, Randolph, *The Prairie Traveler* – There were a lot of things you packed into your saddlebags or the wagon before setting off to cross the North American wilderness in the 1850s. A gun and an axe were obvious necessities. Yet many pioneers were just as adamant about placing a copy of Captain Randolph Marcy's classic book close at hand.

Marsden, Kate, *Riding through Siberia: A Mounted Medical Mission in 1891* – This immensely readable book is a mixture of adventure, extreme hardship and compassion as the author travels the Great Siberian Post Road.

Marsh, Hippisley Cunliffe, *A Ride Through Islam* – A British officer rides through Persia and Afghanistan to India in 1873. Full of adventures, and with observant remarks on the local Turkoman equestrian traditions.

MacCann, William, *Viaje a Caballo* – Spanish-language edition of the British author's equestrian journey around Argentina in 1848.

Meline, James, *Two Thousand Miles on Horseback: Kansas to Santa Fé in 1866* – A beautifully written, eye witness account of a United States that is no more.

Moates, Tom, *A Horse's Thought* – This is a collection of the author's popular writings exploring his personal exploits with horses as he sincerely attempts to improve his horsemanship skills. This book combines an abundance of new, previously unpublished material regarding this ongoing odyssey.

Muir Watson, Sharon, *The Colour of Courage* – The remarkable true story of the epic horse trip made by the first people to travel Australia's then-unmarked Bicentennial National Trail. There are enough adventures here to satisfy even the most jaded reader.

Naysmith, Gordon, *The Will to Win* – This book recounts the only equestrian journey of its kind undertaken during the 20th century - a mounted trip stretching across 16 countries. Gordon Naysmith, a Scottish pentathlete and former military man, set out in 1970 to ride from the tip of the African continent to the 1972 Olympic Games in distant Germany.

Ondaatje, Christopher, *Leopard in the Afternoon* – The captivating story of a journey through some of Africa's most spectacular haunts. It is also touched with poignancy and regret for a vanishing wilderness – a world threatened with extinction.

Ondaatje, Christopher, *The Man-Eater of Pununai* – a fascinating story of a past rediscovered through a remarkable journey to one of the most exotic countries in the world — Sri Lanka. Full of drama and history, it not only relives the incredible story of a man-eating leopard that terrorized the tiny village of Punanai in the early part of the century, but also allows the author to come to terms with the ghost of his charismatic but tyrannical father.

Our list of current titles

Ondaatje, Christopher, *Sindh Revisited* – This is the extraordinarily sensitive account of the author's quest to uncover the secrets of the seven years Richard Burton spent in India in the army of the East India Company from 1842 to 1849. "If I wanted to fill the gap in my understanding of Richard Burton, I would have to do something that had never been done before: follow in his footsteps in India..." The journey covered thousands of miles—trekking across deserts where ancient tribes meet modern civilization in the valley of the mighty Indus River.

O'Connor, Derek, *The King's Stranger* – a superb biography of the forgotten Scottish explorer, John Duncan.

O'Reilly, Basha, *Count Pompeii – Stallion of the Steppes* – the story of Basha's journey from Russia with her stallion, Count Pompeii, told for children. This is the first book in the *Little Long Rider* series.

O'Reilly, CuChullaine, (Editor) *The Horse Travel Handbook* – this accumulated knowledge of a million miles in the saddle tells you everything you need to know about travelling with your horse!

O'Reilly, CuChullaine, (Editor) *The Horse Travel Journal* – a unique book to take on your ride and record your experiences. Includes the world's first equestrian travel "pictionary" to help you in foreign countries.

O'Reilly, CuChullaine, *Khyber Knights* – Told with grit and realism by one of the world's foremost equestrian explorers, "Khyber Knights" has been penned the way lives are lived, not how books are written.

O'Reilly, CuChullaine, (Editor) *The Long Riders, Volume One* – The first of five unforgettable volumes of exhilarating travel tales.

Östrup, J, (*Swedish), Växlande Horisont* – The thrilling account of the author's journey to Central Asia from 1891 to 1893.

Patterson, George, *Gods and Guerrillas* – The true and gripping story of how the author went secretly into Tibet to film the Chinese invaders of his adopted country. Will make your heart pound with excitement!

Patterson, George, *Journey with Loshay: A Tibetan Odyssey* – This is an amazing book written by a truly remarkable man! Relying both on his companionship with God and on his own strength, he undertook a life few can have known, and a journey of emergency across the wildest parts of Tibet.

Patterson, George, *Patterson of Tibet* – Patterson was a Scottish medical missionary who went to Tibet shortly after the second World War. There he became Tibetan in all but name, adapting to the culture and learning the language fluently. This intense autobiography reveals how Patterson crossed swords with India's Prime Minister Nehru, helped with the rescue of the Dalai Lama and befriended a host of unique world figures ranging from Yehudi Menhuin to Eric Clapton. This is a vividly-written account of a life of high adventure and spiritual odyssey.

Pocock, Roger, *Following the Frontier* – Pocock was one of the nineteenth century's most influential equestrian travelers. Within the covers of this book is the detailed account of Pocock's horse ride along the infamous Outlaw Trail, a 3,000 mile solo journey that took the adventurer from Canada to Mexico City.

Pocock, Roger, *Horses* – Pocock set out to document the wisdom of the late 19th and early 20th Centuries into a book unique for its time. His concerns for attempting to preserve equestrian knowledge were based on cruel reality. More than 300,000 horses had been destroyed during the recent Boer War. Though Pocock enjoyed a reputation for dangerous living, his observations on horses were praised by the leading thinkers of his day.

Post, Charles Johnson, *Horse Packing* – Originally published in 1914, this book was an instant success, incorporating as it did the very essence of the science of packing horses and mules. It makes fascinating reading for students of the horse or history.

Ray, G. W., *Through Five Republics on Horseback* – In 1889 a British explorer – part-time missionary and full-time adventure junky – set out to find a lost tribe of sun-worshipping natives in the unexplored forests of Paraguay. The journey was so brutal that it defies belief.

Rink, Bjarke, *The Centaur Legacy* – This immensely entertaining and historically important book provides the first ever in-depth study into how man's partnership with his equine companion changed the course of history and accelerated human development.

Our list of current titles

Ross, Julian, *Travels in an Unknown Country* – A delightful book about modern horseback travel in an enchanting country, which once marked the eastern borders of the Roman Empire – Romania.

Ross, Martin and Somerville, E, *Beggars on Horseback* – The hilarious adventures of two aristocratic Irish cousins on an 1894 riding tour of Wales.

Ruxton, George, *Adventures in Mexico* – The story of a young British army officer who rode from Vera Cruz to Santa Fe, Mexico in 1847. At times the author exhibits a fearlessness which borders on insanity. He ignores dire warnings, rides through deadly deserts, and dares murderers to attack him. It is a delightful and invigorating tale of a time and place now long gone.

von Salzman, Erich, *Im Sattel durch Zentralasien* – The astonishing tale of the author's journey through China, Turkistan and back to his home in Germany – 6000 kilometres in 176 days!

Schwarz, Hans *(German)*, *Vier Pferde, Ein Hund und Drei Soldaten* – In the early 1930s the author and his two companions rode through Liechtenstein, Austria, Romania, Albania, Yugoslavia, to Turkey, then rode back again!

Schwarz, Otto *(German)*, *Reisen mit dem Pferd* – the Swiss Long Rider with more miles in the saddle than anyone else tells his wonderful story, and a long appendix tells the reader how to follow in his footsteps.

Scott, Robert, *Scott's Last Expedition* – Many people are unaware that Scott recruited Yakut ponies from Siberia for his doomed expedition to the South Pole in 1909. Here is the remarkable story of men and horses who all paid the ultimate sacrifice.

Shackleton, Ernest, *Aurora Australis* - The members of the British Antarctic Expedition of 1907-1908 wrote this delightful and surprisingly funny book. It was printed on the spot "at the sign of the Penguin"!

Skrede, Wilfred, *Across the Roof of the World* – This epic equestrian travel tale of a wartime journey across Russia, China, Turkestan and India is laced with unforgettable excitement.

The South Pole Ponies, *Theodore Mason* – The touching and totally forgotten story of the little horses who gave their all to both Scott and Shackleton in their attempts to reach the South Pole.

Stevens, Thomas, *Through Russia on a Mustang* – Mounted on his faithful horse, Texas, Stevens crossed the Steppes in search of adventure. Cantering across the pages of this classic tale is a cast of nineteenth century Russian misfits, peasants, aristocrats—and even famed Cossack Long Rider Dmitri Peshkov.

Stevenson, Robert L., *Travels with a Donkey* – In 1878, the author set out to explore the remote Cevennes mountains of France. He travelled alone, unless you count his stubborn and manipulative pack-donkey, Modestine. This book is a true classic.

Strong, Anna Louise, *Road to the Grey Pamir* – With Stalin's encouragement, Strong rode into the seldom-seen Pamir mountains of faraway Tadjikistan. The political renegade turned equestrian explorer soon discovered more adventure than she had anticipated.

Sykes, Ella, *Through Persia on a Sidesaddle* – Ella Sykes rode side-saddle 2,000 miles across Persia, a country few European woman had ever visited. Mind you, she traveled in style, accompanied by her Swiss maid and 50 camels loaded with china, crystal, linens and fine wine.

Trinkler, Emile, *Through the Heart of Afghanistan* – In the early 1920s the author made a legendary trip across a country now recalled only in legends.

Tschiffely, Aimé, *Bohemia Junction* – "Forty years of adventurous living condensed into one book."

Tschiffely, Aimé, *Bridle Paths* – a final poetic look at a now-vanished Britain.

Tschiffely, Aimé, *Coricancha*: A fascinating and balanced account of the conquest of the Inca Empire.

Tschiffely, Aimé, Don Roberto – *A biography of Tschiffely's friend and mentor, Robert Cunninghame Graham.*

Tschiffely, Aimé, *Little Princess Turtle Dove* – An enchanting fairy story set in South America and displaying Aimé Tschiffely's love, not only for children and animals, but also for South America.

Tschiffely, Aimé, *Mancha y Gato Cuentan sus Aventuras* – The Spanish-language version of *The Tale of Two Horses* – the story of the author's famous journey as told by the horses.

Our list of current titles

Tschiffely, Aimé, *Ming and Ping:* An adventure book for older children. The title characters go exploring South America together. They meet many tribes of Indians and learn about their way of life. Exhilarating and effortlessly instructive.

Tschiffely, Aimé, *Round and About Spain:* Tschiffely sets off to explore Spain, but this time his steed is a motorbike, not a horse! With wit, wisdom and a sharp eye for the absurd, he travels to all four corners of this fascinating country and makes many friends along the way. So much has changed since the Second World War that that this book is a unique snapshot of Spain as she was in 1950.

Tschiffely, Aimé, *The Tale of Two Horses* – The story of Tschiffely's famous journey from Buenos Aires to Washington, DC, narrated by his two equine heroes, Mancha and Gato. Their unique point of view is guaranteed to delight children and adults alike.

Tschiffely, Aimé, *This Way Southward* – the most famous equestrian explorer of the twentieth century decides to make a perilous journey across the U-boat infested Atlantic.

Tschiffely, Aimé, *Tschiffely's Ride* – The true story of the most famous equestrian journey of the twentieth century – 10,000 miles with two Criollo geldings from Argentina to Washington, DC. A new edition is coming soon with a Foreword by his literary heir!

Tschiffely, Aimé, *Tschiffely's Ritt* – The German-language translation of *Tschiffely's Ride* – the most famous equestrian journey of its day.

Ure, John, *Cucumber Sandwiches in the Andes* – No-one who wasn't mad as a hatter would try to take a horse across the Andes by one of the highest passes between Chile and the Argentine. That was what John Ure was told on his way to the British Embassy in Santiago – so he set out to find a few certifiable kindred spirits. Fans of equestrian travel and of Latin America will be enchanted by this delightful book.

Warner, Charles Dudley, *On Horseback in Virginia* – A prolific author, and a great friend of Mark Twain, Warner made witty and perceptive contributions to the world of nineteenth century American literature. This book about the author's equestrian adventures is full of fascinating descriptions of nineteenth century America.

Weale, Magdalene, *Through the Highlands of Shropshire* – It was 1933 and Magdalene Weale was faced with a dilemma: how to best explore her beloved English countryside? By horse, of course! This enchanting book invokes a gentle, softer world inhabited by gracious country lairds, wise farmers, and jolly inn keepers.

Weeks, Edwin Lord, *Artist Explorer* – A young American artist and superb writer travels through Persia to India in 1892.

Wentworth Day, J., *Wartime Ride* – In 1939 the author decided the time was right for an extended horseback ride through England! While parts of his country were being ravaged by war, Wentworth Day discovered an inland oasis of mellow harvest fields, moated Tudor farmhouses, peaceful country halls, and fishing villages.

Von Westarp, Eberhard, *Unter Halbmond und Sonne* – (German) – Im Sattel durch die asiatische Türkei und Persien.

Wilkins, Messanie, *Last of the Saddle Tramps* – Told she had little time left to live, the author decided to ride from her native Maine to the Pacific. Accompanied by her faithful horse, Tarzan, Wilkins suffered through any number of obstacles, including blistering deserts and freezing snow storms – and defied the doctors by living for another 20 years!

Wilson, Andrew, *The Abode of Snow* – One of the best accounts of overland equestrian travel ever written about the wild lands that lie between Tibet and Afghanistan.

de Windt, Harry, *A Ride to India* – Part science, all adventure, this book takes the reader for a thrilling canter across the Persian Empire of the 1890s.

Winthrop, Theodore, *Saddle and Canoe* – This book paints a vibrant picture of 1850s life in the Pacific Northwest and covers the author's travels along the Straits of Juan De Fuca, on Vancouver Island, across the Naches Pass, and on to The Dalles, in Oregon Territory. This is truly an historic travel account.

Woolf, Leonard, *Stories of the East* – Three short stories which are of vital importance in understanding the author's mistrust of and dislike for colonialism, which provide disturbing commentaries about the disintegration of the colonial process.

Our list of current titles

Younghusband, George, *Eighteen Hundred Miles on a Burmese Pony* – One of the funniest and most enchanting books about equestrian travel of the nineteenth century, featuring "Joe" the naughty Burmese pony!

We are constantly adding new titles to our collections, so please check our websites:

www.horsetravelbooks.com - www.classictravelbooks.com

The Equestrian Wisdom & History Series: www.lrgaf.org

Printed in the United States
151221LV00002BA/13/P